# CENTERING EDUCATIONAL ADMINISTRATION

## Cultivating Meaning, Community, Responsibility

# Topics in Educational Leadership
*Larry W. Hughes, Series Editor*

**Gaynor** • Analyzing Problems in Schools and School Systems: A Theoretical Approach

**Earle/Kruse** • Organizational Literacy for Educators

**Shapiro/Stefkowitz** • Ethical Leadership and Decision Making in Education: Applying Theoretical Perspectives to Complex Dilemmas

**Bizar/Barr, Eds.** • School Leadership in Times of Urban Reform

**Brouillette** • Charter Schools: Lessons in School Reform

**Fishbaugh/Schroth/Berkeley, Eds.** • Ensuring Safe School Environments: Exploring Issues—Seeking Solutions

**Starratt** • Centering Educational Administration: Cultivating Meaning, Community, **Responsibility**

# CENTERING EDUCATIONAL ADMINISTRATION

## Cultivating Meaning, Community, Responsibility

Robert J. Starratt
*Boston College*

 LAWRENCE ERLBAUM ASSOCIATES, PUBLISHERS
2003   Mahwah, New Jersey                          London

Lawrence Erlbaum Associates, Inc., Publishers
10 Industrial Avenue
Mahwah, New Jersey 07430

Cover design by Kathryn Houghtaling Lacey

**Library of Congress Cataloging-in-Publication Data**

Starratt, Robert J.
  Centering educational administration : cultivating meaning, community, responsibility /
Robert J. Starratt.
    p.   cm.
  Includes bibliographical references and index.
  ISBN 0-8058-4238-1 (cloth : alk. paper) — ISBN 0-8058-4239-X (pbk. : alk. paper)
  1. School management and organization—Study and teaching (Higher).   2. School
administrators—Training of.   I. Title.

  LB2805 .S7438   2003
  371.2'0071'1—dc21                                                                2002192726
                                                                                        CIP

Books published by Lawrence Erlbaum Associates are printed on acid-free paper,
and their bindings are chosen for strength and durability.

Printed in the United States of America
10  9  8  7  6  5  4  3  2  1

# Contents

# Preface

This book has been written out of a conviction that educational administrator preparation programs need to become more responsive to changes and challenges in the complex and dynamic social arena we call education. These changes and challenges are embedded in the local and regional political context of schooling, in new approaches to teaching as a profession, and in the federal and state public policy regarding standards of student achievement. One of the first courses in a graduate program in educational administration is usually a course on fundamentals or foundations of educational administration. This book is an attempt to help beginning administrators, or those seeking state certification to become administrators, get started on the right foot in a program that will build on the perspectives developed in such a beginning course.

A fundamentals course should introduce the beginning administrator to the essentials of administering an individual school or of being a member of an administrative team in an individual school. Those who are moving into district office administration or state education departments can learn more about their responsibilities in courses dealing with district- or state-level administration, although I would hope that those courses also point to the individual school as the place where their efforts will bear fruit (Elmore, 2000).

Even when other fundamentals texts in educational administration concentrate on the individual school site, they tend to provide treatments of discrete functions of administration. Hence, we find chapters dealing with special education, extracurricular programs, testing and counseling programs, parent and community relations, scheduling, resource allocation, communication, decision making, delegating responsibilities, legal and safety concerns, and so on. Again we find a diffusion of focus—a sampling of functions that, although touching on real concerns for school administrators, reveal the trees but provide little sense of the forest. This book asks the large question: What is fundamental to educational administration? What is its center?

In response, we focus attention on three themes that are fundamental to the work of educational administration: cultivating meaning, cultivating community, and cultivating responsibility. These themes necessarily involve perspectives derived from philosophical and sociological scholarship. In some administrative preparation programs, students are encouraged to take philosophy of education or sociology of education courses as a way to develop a broad understanding of the contexts and purposes of schooling—an understanding that will enable them to bring these perspectives to bear on their work of leading schools. Valuable as these courses are, they are rarely taught with the work of school administration in mind, but as more general courses for all students of education. This book attempts to bring philosophical and sociological perspectives to the very work of administration, suggesting that they illuminate the challenges that constitute the *substance* of administrative work in education. With clarity about their responsibilities in these three areas, administrators can provide a focus to their decision making, resource allocation, communication processes, and parent–community relations.

## SCHOOL ADMINISTRATION IN HISTORICAL CONTEXT

There is an even more pressing need, however, for another change in the fundamentals course. Past administration courses have tended to reflect limited and fragmented conceptual frameworks that derive from earlier historical and theoretical developments in the fields of education and educational administration. Murphy and Beck (1993) provided a historical overview of the metaphorical themes that shaped understandings of principalship during the past 70 years in the United States. Their study indicates how the ways of understanding the principalship were influenced by historical events such as the Great Depression, World War II, and the success of the Soviet space program. The political and academic worlds influenced different periods of school administration in the United States with various concerns, such as social homogenization of disparate communities of immigrants, scientific management, and accountability for measurable student learning.

Whereas Beck and Murphy pointed to the fluctuations of thought about school administration, the critiques of Greenfield (1991), Foster (1986),

Bates (1984), Carr and Kemmis (1986), among others, challenge the grounding of administrative theory and practice in rational decision making and scientistic rationalism. This book stands firmly with their contentions that much of what has been considered mainstream educational administration literature makes unsupportable assumptions that (a) truly professional administrators make rational decisions based on facts derived from scientific research; (b) educational administrators work within (or can create) rational organizational systems; and (c) they can control the school as an organization (and, indeed, have the responsibility and right to do so) by applying scientifically grounded knowledge to make the school work according to rationally derived goals. We take up that criticism in the early chapters of the book.

## EDUCATIONAL ADMINISTRATION AND CRITICS
## OF THE SCHOOLS

For the past quarter century, schools have come under relentless criticism from both the right and the left. The criticism from the right, fueled by a resentment toward "The 1960s," when schools and universities were perceived by critics as foundering in a directionless sea of permissiveness, has focused on the supposed abandonment of "the three Rs"—the pandering to fads such as nurturing self-esteem (disconnected, they assumed, from the achievement of rigorous standards), multiculturalism (which was equated with disparagement of patriotism as well as the Eurocentric cannons of literature and history), and creativity (equated with a standardless aesthetic and anti-intellectual bias). The criticism from the left focused on the school as an instrument of the sociopolitical reproduction of inequality through its systems of curriculum tracking; the dead end of special education programming; the ambivalence of bilingual programs toward foreign cultures; the predominance of male perspectives in pedagogy, learning theory, and curriculum programming; and the perpetuation of academic failure through bureaucratic labeling of *at-risk* student populations and the serious lack of early resourcing of remedial programs in the early grades. In other words, the left argued, schools have not responded to the "war on poverty" and the racial desegregation of public life, nor to the emerging promise of feminists perspectives in schools. Instead, schools have continued to pour the new wine of progressive public policy into the old wineskins of institutional status-quo arrangements.

From either perspective, the primary villains were the mindless, ineffective educators who appeared rudderless—without a policy compass or the leadership to articulate a clear direction for the school. Indeed, the critics were right in this regard: The educational community seemed to lack the

voices that could articulate a mission sufficiently broad and deep enough to
blunt the criticism of the right and the left by absorbing their concerns into
a larger synthesis of what kind of education was needed at this particular
historical era. Educational administrators, by and large, tutored in university preparation programs to manage the daily operations of the schools ef-
ficiently (according to orthodox management and organizational theory),
while attempting to negotiate the local political climate (read: "Respond to
the centers of power in the community"), were apparently incapable of ris-
ing above the withering attacks of either side. Not energized by a large and
compelling vision of schooling, they continually found themselves in a reac-
tive stance, attempting to placate now one side, now another.

Gradually, the voices from the right have gained ascendancy in the formation of public policy on education at both the state and federal levels.
The so-called *education lobby* representing teacher unions and school administrators either fought a rear-guard action of damage control or were not,
for all intents and purposes, heard at all in the public and political gather-
ings when "school reform" policy was being developed. The university community of educational administration scholars, by and large, did not participate in that policy formation, although individual scholars such as Joseph
Murphy, Alan Odden, Brian Caldwell, Michael Fullan, Richard Elmore,
and others stand out as educational administration academics with an articulate and broad view of schooling who actively participated in the policy
conversation. What appears, by hindsight, however, is that most university
preparation programs in educational administration have not attempted a
consistent, programmatic effort to assist administrators or administrators-
to-be with a deeply grounded educational platform about schooling that
would enable them to speak out in public fora in response to the critics and
local policymakers and powerful interest groups.

## CRITICISM AN OPPORTUNITY FOR DIALOGUE

By hindsight, we can appreciate that the criticism of both right and left, although often exaggerated, one dimensional, and cruel in singling out educators for exclusive blame for situations over which they have limited control, offered potential opportunities to engage in productive dialogue. To
toot my own horn, I cite an example from an occasion when, as a newly arrived principal, I was conducting a discussion at a schoolwide evening with
parents. After citing the school's progress in various improvements, and after some polite comments from the parents, a voice from the back of the audience asked in an accusatory tone, "Yes, but what are you doing to improve
discipline at the school?" The question brought several approving nods
from the audience, and they leaned forward with new interest in what I

might say. Instead of defending our discipline policies, I turned the question around and asked about discipline in the home. I cited several examples of what I considered parental failure to teach their children responsibility for following family rules and expectations—simple things like cleaning up after themselves, sharing their toys with their brothers and sisters, settling the inevitable sibling rivalries in nonviolent ways, and helping with the daily and weekly household chores. I concluded by asking the parents to consider the difficulty of expecting youngsters to follow simple rules in schools when parents allowed their children free reign at home. The point was not for us to blame one another for perceived failures in the area of discipline, but to seek common ground in this area. The exchange led to follow-up conversations about how the school and the home might cooperate in supporting each other's efforts in promoting a greater sense of responsibility in *our* youngsters.

Three things stand out in that example. One, I refused to take the whole blame for what was a problem shared by the home and school. Second, I suggested that the school and home might consider how our collective action could benefit our youngsters' development. Third, the subsequent conversations began to place the issue of discipline in a learning context—namely, how to encourage responsibility through a variety of proactively and mutually planned, repeated learning experiences, rather than focusing on a reactionary emphasis on punishment. Both sides of the discussion were able to recast the problem into a broader discussion of teaching values.

The lesson of the past quarter century is that we have to move beyond defensive, reactionary, and sometimes disparaging responses to the critics of the school. We need to invite them to participate in conversations about schooling that take their concerns seriously and bring those concerns to a broader and deeper conversation about the large human issues involved in schooling. As Marty (1997) suggested, that conversation needs to begin with stories that exemplify concerns. Through the exchange of stories, rather than through arguments over abstract principles, conflicting groups can develop an empathy toward the other position.

## EMERGING UNDERSTANDINGS

In looking for emerging understandings of the principalship, Beck and Murphy (1993) summarized the sizable recent literature that indicates a shift of major proportions in understanding the context, process, and purpose of schooling. This shift, in turn, implies new ways to understand the principalship. Principals—and by implication other school-based administrators—are coming to be seen as leaders, servants, organizational architects, social architects, educators, moral agents, and persons in a community. This book is in sympathy with this literature in its (a) espousal of a more collegial style of relationships among educators in a variety of roles who regard themselves as professionals, (b) appreciation of the need for teacher leadership and full participation by teachers in renewal of the school, and (c) focus on the human development of persons.

The recent insistence that schools nurture the success of all students rather than sort the more able from the less able by means of standardized test results finds support in our themes of cultivating meaning, community, and responsibility. The emerging understanding of knowledge as a social construct—as something that develops in social interaction focused on problems seen in specific contexts rather than knowledge as an external entity existing independently of the historically situated human subject—influences the development of the central themes in the book. The book also supports the concern that professionalism go beyond a distorted scientism of facts divorced from values to a recognition of the educational professional's profound value commitments to the human growth of children in a free and open community. Besides these emerging concerns and understandings highlighted by Beck and Murphy, there are other emerging influences within the larger culture that affect the way we think about education and educational administration.

## EDUCATIONAL ADMINISTRATION FACES CULTURAL CHALLENGES

In addition to being grounded in much of the changed perceptions about schooling and administering schools, the book is also grounded in a judgment that the schools cannot continue to ignore the major sociocultural challenges facing American society. If the mission of the school is to prepare future members of American society who will live in the 21st century, the school must interpret and respond to major challenges facing that society in the present and foreseeable future. Those challenges appear to be threefold: (a) a loss, trivialization, or distortion of the deeper meanings that undergird human life; (b) excessive if not exclusive emphasis on the isolated individual as the primary social unit to the detriment of serious consideration of the public community and its common good (at the local, national, and international levels); and (c) as a consequence of the first and second challenge, the goal of excellence in education is superficial, one dimensional, fundamentally accepting of a tacit Social Darwinism (the economic and political survival of those who win in the economic and political struggle at the expense of and in disregard of the losers), and separated from broader and deeper considerations of what constitutes civic and moral responsibility in a whole society or community of human beings. In framing a treatment of fundamentals of educational administration, therefore, it appears that we have to explore how the school will respond to the challenge of (a) dealing with meanings that undergird human life in the 21st century; (b) building a concern for and an understanding of the demands of community in public life; and (c) promoting a broad commitment to civic and moral responsibility—in the private and public lives of young people.

By hindsight, it becomes clearer now that if educational administrators are going to exercise educational leadership, they have to be grounded in an articulate and compelling vision of schooling. That vision should illustrate where schools should be going and what large purposes they should be serving. That vision has to be understandable within familiar themes in the culture of their society—themes that speak to the fundamental values of that culture, yet also relate to the interface of those values with challenges and opportunities that the historical context offers.

This book represents an effort to call educational leaders, whether teachers or administrators, to that conversation about the large human issues in schooling. Although it does not offer recipes for schedules, budgets, and faculty meetings, the book attempts to place the leading of schools within broad historical and cultural frameworks with which to interpret and respond to the local stories. From within those frameworks, these future leaders of schools may begin or continue their efforts to develop an educational platform capable of appealing to and uniting many of the stakeholders in the schooling enterprise.

## OVERVIEW OF THE BOOK

The book is organized into two parts. The first part introduces a perspective on the core work of administrative leadership in schools and goes on to develop three crucial and interdependent themes around which administrators may build a compelling vision of what schools need to become. Those interdependent themes comprise the work of leading schools: cultivating meaning through the dynamic of teaching and learning; cultivating community as an everyday work of the entire school; and cultivating a commitment to responsibility within the entire institutional life of the school. The treatment of these themes is initially situated in the national conversation taking place among scholars in the field of educational administration concerning the core knowledge base that university preparation programs should emphasize as they seek to engage prospective school administrators in a compelling view of their leadership of schools. Besides the present context of leaders in the field of educational administration seeking to refocus the core work educational leadership, there is a larger historical context to these themes that involves the struggles of late modernity to correct or balance the naivete of early modernity. Because schools largely enact many of the naive understandings of early modernity, the articulation and cultivation of a vision of schooling for late modernity needs to take up the necessary transitions from these naive understandings toward a more reflexive and critical synthesis of a mature modern worldview. Part One of the book, then, attempts a generous understanding of these three themes within their historical context in order to suggest a fresh and reasonably argued vision for schooling.

Part Two of the book attempts to place the working out of these themes within the organizational and institutional life of the school. The three themes that characterize the core work of schooling should penetrate all layers of the school organization. Thus, the organization of the school as a learning community requires policies and programs and operational strategies that are consistent with and support the learnings implied in the three themes. In turn, those learnings suggest broad teaching and learning protocols expressed in the design of specific courses or subject matter curricula by grade level, the design of the scope and sequence of whole curricular programs for a cluster of grades, and the design of institutional resources and procedures. The design work of administration is related to the development of internal accountability and an enabling culture of efficacy. The work of administrative leadership is enacted through organic management: the continuous shaping and reshaping of the organization to support the core work of the school—learning.

Part Two concludes with a consideration of administration as autobiography. The work of school administrators there takes on a personal meaning and challenge, suggesting the heroic dimensions of the work, but also acknowledging the unavoidable limitations every human challenge imposes.

At the end of each chapter, I suggest a variety of site-based, action research activities. The material in each chapter presents a way to look at and think about what is going on in schools. The suggested activities are meant to develop an understanding of these frameworks and ideas as they are expressed by students, teachers, and parents or as they are exemplified in the practices and structures of the readers' school. I expect that the action research of these assignments will teach much more than the textual material of each chapter. To only read the chapter and not engage in probing that material in the workplace would be to miss the major learnings of the course. The book is intended to frame the learning that participants can achieve after reading the chapter—through the activities suggested for their own workplace and in the sharing of findings and ideas with the others taking the course or unit.

A central tenet of this book is that administrative leadership is intellectual work. That is, administrators need to know what they are doing to understand the relationship between the work of the school and the challenges facing contemporary society. This book attempts to develop an understanding of historical, philosophical, and sociological frameworks that enable educators to interpret what the school is promoting and not promoting. I believe that the work of administrative leaders needs to be grounded in these understandings. To grasp what is implied in these historical, philosophical, and sociological frameworks is hard work. It requires focused reading; reflective, probing conversations with peers; and a willingness to challenge long-held personal assumptions. The purpose of this work is not to turn participants into professors, but to enable them to bring a large view of what should be happening in schools to their work. More than one study of schools in the recent past has concluded that they are mindless institutions. That conclusion does not say much about the administrators in those schools. Presently, there is a groundswell for school renewal. That renewal requires, beyond an understanding of the dynamics of change, a leadership of ideas.

Another central tenet of the book is that students are the producers of knowledge, not the teacher or the textbook. What participants take away from this book and the course in which it is used are the knowledge and understanding they collectively produce through active engagement with the text and through learning activities suggested by the text and the teacher. The book is intended to get participants to ask themselves challenging questions and to stimulate them to construct practical and workable responses to the questions. Differences of opinion and different conclusions and solutions are to be expected in a class on school administration. No one person—not even the professor—has the perfect answer or, indeed, even understands the question fully. Every class discussion and class project needs the participation of everyone because each person has something to offer. We need the perspectives of others to enrich our own learning. The full participation of everyone in the class will teach us the most important lesson of all about educational administration—that fundamentally it is about our collective cultivation of meaning, community, and moral responsibility.

## REFERENCES

Bates, R. (1984). Toward a critical practice of educational administration. In T. J. Sergiovanni & J. B. Corbally (Eds.), *Leadership and organizational culture: New perspectives on administrative theory and practice* (pp. 260–274). Urbana, IL: University of Illinois Press.

Beck, L. G., & Murphy, J. (1993). *Understanding the principalship: Metaphorical themes, 1920s–1990.* New York: Teachers College Press.

Blumburg, A. (1984). The craft of school administration and some other rambling thoughts. *Educational Administration Quarterly, 20*(4), 24–40.

Carr, W., & Kemmis, S. (1986). *Becoming critical: Education, knowledge, and action research.* London: Falmer.

Elmore, R. (2000). *Building a new structure for school leadership.* Washington, DC: The Albert Shanker Institute.

Foster, W. (1986). *Paradigms and promises: New approaches to educational administration.* Buffalo, NY: Prometheus.

Greenfield, T. B. (1991). *Re-forming and re-valuing educational administration: Whence cometh the Phoenix?* A paper presented at the annual meeting of the American Educational Research Association, Chicago.

Marty, M. (1997). *The one and the many: America's struggle for the common good.* Cambridge, MA: Harvard University Press.

# ELEMENTS OF THE LEADER'S VISION

# Chapter 1

# The Challenging World
# of Educational Leadership

In this chapter, we look at what makes educational administration unique among types of administration. We also consider the present historical context of schooling in America in order to underscore the crucial importance of school administration in the schools of today and tomorrow. The chapter concludes with some questions for self-reflection for those who plan to assume the responsibilities and challenges of school administration.

## FORMER VIEWS OF EDUCATIONAL ADMINISTRATION

For the past 40 years or more, educational administration has been assumed to be one of several types of a generalized, uniform activity labeled *administration*. This label was thought to encompass relatively similar characteristics. That is, if a person were a good administrator in one setting, presumably he or she would be a good administrator in another setting. Sometimes a more idealized form of administration was considered to be found in a specific type of administration, such as military or business administration. Indeed, it has been suggested in the United States and other countries that school administrators should imitate business administrators or, further, that schools be run by people with training and experience in business administration.

This kind of thinking is often based on the assumption that there is a kind of science of administration that, through empirical research extending over decades, has established certain universal principles and management techniques that can be applied in diverse administrative and organizational settings. This belief was well expressed in an influential volume edited by Sergiovanni and Carver (1969):

> Research to date has revealed that human behavior, as a result of organizational life, manifests remarkable similarities as one moves from hospital, to school, to retail store, to welfare agency, and to military unit. Thus, while the school administrator is particularly concerned with one kind of formal organization, his vision may very well be improved by studying organizations in general. (p. ix)

Early in the 20th century, Taylor (1911) sought to create a science of management based on his time and motion studies of a manufacturing process. Cubberly (1916) was an early proponent of the application of scientific principles generated through empirical research in educational administration. Later, the work of Simon (1957) rekindled an interest in administrative theory based on scientific research on the behavior of managers in organizations. His work influenced the administrative theory movement in educational administration. Griffiths (1959) advocated the use of scientific research methods and theories from the social sciences to construct a theory and science of educational administration. He believed that only in this way would educational administration gain the legitimacy and respect accorded to true professionals. Consequently, he stressed the rationality and objectivity that administrators, having been exposed to these studies, would bring to their tasks. Such rationality and objectivity would ensure professional judgment in circumstances of organizational life in the pursuit of rational goals.

Not every scholar, however, endorsed the scientism and rationalism of the mainstream theorists of the 1950s and 1960s. Studies by Lindbloom (1959) and others (Cohen, March, & Olsen, 1972) questioned the assumed rationality and objectivity of administrators in all organizations. Cyert and March (1963) suggested that administrators exercise a bounded rationality: They may make decisions with goals in mind, but they cannot consider all the alternative choices available and then make the best choice among those alternatives according to an independently objective standard. Administrators' understanding of the alternatives is limited by their own experience, training, and imagination, and by the pressure to make timely decisions. Administrators tend to choose a course of action that resolves the immediate situation in some way or another. These decisions, however, may not necessarily be the best decisions for the long run. Lindbloom (1959) also found that administrators tend to make short-term decisions that are not necessarily consistent with earlier short-term decisions, nor with those they make the next day. Their decisions tend to be disjointed and incremental, rather than rationally consistent with long-term, prioritized goals.

Other scholars such as Apple (1982), Bates (1987), and Giroux (1991) reported that, beyond the disjointed and bounded nature of the rationality found in the actions of educational administrators, one finds ideological assumptions and beliefs. These assumptions and beliefs are not subject to empirical proof. More important, they are rarely articulated and indeed consciously attended to, and hence are all the more influential. These criticisms of the *administration as science* perspective are highlighted to caution the well-intentioned administrator to recognize that the job entails more than making decisions based on a rational assessment of the facts. Interpretation, bias, distortion, subjective feelings, beliefs, and assumptions are all at work in determining what one considers as facts, and indeed influence how one goes about gathering facts. Furthermore, administration as science tends to ignore or marginalize the complex moral issues involved in administrative activity.

Administrators need not surrender to the seeming impossibility of acting rationally and simply follow their own private hunches and beliefs. Educational administration requires a constant effort to introduce rationality into decisions. That rationality does not come exclusively from the individual administrator, but comes more from the individuals involved in the decision discussing the merits of alternative choices. Even then, decisions rarely if ever are purely rational; to seek for that kind of rational purity is to chase an unattainable ideal. Rather, what administrators should seek are the most reasonable decisions under the circumstances—decisions for which others can take responsibility because they have been involved in making them.

Besides the assumption of an ever-present rationality, there has been another harmful side effect from the effort to think of educational administration as one form of a general science or theory of administration. That harmful effect has been encouraging school principals to think of themselves primarily as managers rather than educators. Such thinking has led administrators to concentrate on structures, procedures, and the smooth running of the school organization. It has encouraged an emphasis on mechanical control and maintenance through reliance on administrative technique (good public relations, open communications, well-organized meetings, delegation of responsibilities with attendant accountability and reporting structures, etc.).

More recently, that view has come under fire. As Purpel and Shapiro (1985) put it: "Schools are not shops that require clever and ingenious bits of engineering to increase productivity and morale, but major social institutions where wisdom and courage are required to infuse practice with our highest hopes" (p. xvii). Educational administration is coming to be seen by practitioners, policymakers, and scholars as unique among forms of administration and management; it should be shaped and directed by the essential work of learning.

## NEW VIEWS OF EDUCATIONAL ADMINISTRATION

As school renewal policies are legislated and refined in state after state and country after country, we find a much greater emphasis on teachers and principals being held accountable for improved student performances on national and international tests. Under earlier accountability policies, school officials were held responsible for providing multiple opportunities for students to achieve success in school. Now they are held responsible for student outcomes—for actual student success with more rigorous curriculum demands than ever before. Previously, teachers and administrators could claim that they provided the opportunities for students to learn, shifting the blame for poor student performance on lack of student effort and motivation, unsupportive home environments, inadequate educational provisions in earlier grades, and so forth. Now principals can be removed when their students do not show sufficient improvement in test scores over a specified number of years. This kind of pressure has shifted the attention of administrators from general management concerns to more focused educational concerns. Their job is seen more clearly as involving continuous work with teachers to improve the quality of instruction, and to map classroom curriculum to state curriculum standards, the mastery of which state exams are supposed to assess.

Gradually this stress on improved student learning has drawn negative attention to administrators in underperforming school and led to threats of and actual removal from their positions. This attention to ineffective administrators has led to criticisms of the way administrators are selected and prepared for their job. State licensing criteria began to change to reflect this focus on administrative accountability for promoting improved student performance on high-stakes tests. In turn, university preparation programs in educational administration have come under increasing scrutiny by university accrediting associations. Those associations have begun to change their accreditation requirements for graduate departments of school administration, insisting more and more that the graduates of these programs demonstrate in the field that they are acting as instructional leaders involved with improving student success on high-stakes tests. Where these accountability schemes will end is uncertain at present, but professors of educational administration and their deans are feeling the pressure to guarantee the performance of their graduates by pointing to their success at improving student performance. That has already led to a redesign of field/practicum requirements, more performance-based assessments of graduate students, and greater attention to program requirements in curriculum and learning theory.

Two national groups in the late 1980s attempted to draw attention to the unfocused nature of university degree programs in educational administration. The University Council for Educational Administration (UCEA) published a report by the National Commission on Excellence in Educational Administration (1987) calling for more rigorous and selective university programs in educational administration. This led to an effort to by the University Council on Educational Administration (1992) to identify the crucial knowledge base for the preparation of school administrators. In turn, this generated intense debate among scholars in educational administration who resisted the epistemology and the theory perspectives behind the UCEA proposal (Donmoyer, Imber, & Scheurich, 1995). This ferment of scholarly discussion was fueled by the report of the National Policy Board for Educational Administration (1989). This group, representing the major national associations of educational administrators, urged the reform of university-based educational administrator certification programs in the strongest of terms, urging more rigorous admission requirements, greater depth of academic courses, and more careful attention to field or practicum experiences under the guidance of proved educational leaders in the field. The National Policy Board for Educational Administration recently teamed up with the National Council for the Accreditation of Teacher Education (NCATE) to produce a comprehensive curriculum required of all university programs in educational administration, at least those that seek NCATE accreditation.

During this period of intense discussions about the future of educational administration within the UCEA and the National Policy Board, the Danforth Foundation also decided to get involved. That foundation funded specific efforts to revitalize educational administration programs (Milstein, 1993). Those efforts included a 5-year cycle of conversations among universities seeking to improve their educational administration programs. This national exchange of ideas led to further publications (Mulkeen, Cambron-McCabe, & Anderson, 1994; Murphy, 1992) and many improvements in university programs (Milstein, 1993).

At the end of the 1990s, three influential scholars of educational administration—Kenneth Leithwood, Richard Elmore, and Joseph Murphy—called for a major reorientation of the theory and practice of educational administration. Their work decidedly influenced the positioning of this book in the ongoing dialogue about transforming educational administration.

## KENNETH LEITHWOOD

With his customary scholarly thoroughness, Kenneth Leithwood and two colleagues, Doris Jentzi and Rosanne Steinbach, explicitly embraced the ambitious theme of *transformational leadership* as the necessary (not simply an ideal) framework for the future work of educational administration

(Leithwood, Jentzi, & Steinbach, 1999). Based on the earlier work of Burns (1978) and adapted for empirical studies by Bass (1985), this notion of transformational leadership includes components such as charisma, idealized influence, inspirational motivation, intellectual stimulation, and individualized consideration. Leithwood and his colleagues reviewed 20 empirical studies in educational administration that tested the effects of transformational leaders on students, teachers' perceptions, behavior and psychological states of followers, and aspects of organizational life. They went on to identify features of transformational leadership in specific schools. These features are summarized as (a) setting directions, (b) developing people, and (c) redesigning the organization. Leithwood and his colleagues examined the cognitive processes that transformational leaders employ in solving problems, and they explored transformational leadership among teachers.

Although Leithwood, Jentzi, and Steinbach advanced thinking about educational leadership to include the theme of transformation, they focused attention exclusively on the organizational work of the adults in schools. From my perspective, they did not ground their exploration of educational leadership on a close analysis of *what* schools teach and *what* students learn, but more on how adults engage in organizational change. I endorse their claiming the theme of transformation as necessary for educational leadership, as an earlier work of mine witnessed (Starratt, 1993a). I find their analysis of how transformational educational leaders behave illuminating. I believe, however, that their work needs to be complemented by a closer look at the potential of transforming the learning agenda of schools.


## RICHARD ELMORE

Richard Elmore, a scholar at the forefront of thinking about school renewal, has also called for a new structure for school leadership (Elmore, 2000). Elmore proposed that the widespread national and international efforts at standards-based, large-scale instructional change carries with it a wholly different set of demands for school administrators at the system and school levels. Through state-administered exams, the state now has the means to hold individual schools accountable for student achievement in mastering a standards-based curriculum. Hence, local administrators can no longer hide their schools' record of long-term student failure and underachievement. Administrators can no longer function as managers of organizational procedures. They must be knowledgeable about the complexities of teaching and learning. They must work on instructional improvement as their top priority, making all other administrative activity serve that priority.

Elmore's call to the field of educational administration is this: Turn your schools into learning organizations, for only by being involved with the teachers in learning how to bring *all* students up to acceptable achievement of the standards-based curriculum will you and your schools survive. The future of public schools is in the balance. Elmore provided, I believe, a framework for transforming the work of educational administration. Again, I am concerned that his reach does not extend beyond standards-based curriculum and the testing process that drives them. I believe that the transformative work of educational leadership needs to fully explore the *what* of curriculum and *how* it is learned in order to unlock the human side of the learning agenda.

## JOSEPH MURPHY

During these same years, Joseph Murphy composed a challenging analysis of the current state of educational administration programs published by the University Council for Educational Administration (1999). Murphy provided a comprehensive overview of the considerable efforts of the field of educational administration to reform its practice and theory over the past 20 years. Despite these efforts, Murphy asserted, the field remains diffuse and disunited, representing a hodge-podge of interests, functions, and scholarship, not a profession moving forward with a clear purpose. Murphy contended that currently the practice of educational administration as well as the academic field of educational administration has no integrating principle, no "center"—no central focus that integrates the many disparate functions, concerns, activities, or concepts about educational administration. That lack of a center has allowed the profession to drift during the past 20 years despite the efforts of its leading scholars, leaving the profession more or less ineffective in responding to the numerous criticisms leveled against schools, administrators, and educational administration programs.

Murphy (1999) identified three large concerns that seem to surface with increasing repetition within both the scholarship about and the practice of administration—"three powerful synthesizing paradigms" (p. 54) that could provide this center for educational administration. The three themes are: democratic community, social justice, and school improvement.

Murphy argued for accepting the theme of school improvement as the centerpiece for the revitalization and centering of educational administration. He argued that school improvement has a broad appeal for both the academic and practitioner branches of the field of educational administration—two groups that have all too often appeared to be working from different cognitive and value perspectives. Attention to this core focus by both academics and practitioners could lead to an ongoing collaboration where practitioners' efforts to improve student performance would be supported by research on the effectiveness of these efforts and by university preparation programs that now prepare new administrators more clearly focused and enabled to take on these educational leadership roles.

Murphy went on to encourage a complementary role for the other two themes—democratic community and concern for social justice—as integral components of the effort at school renewal. Work on democratic community and social justice would be seen as part of the core work of teaching and learning. Despite Murphy's inclusive posture toward the other two themes, his choice of the school improvement theme as the dominant theme (for both professional, political, and pragmatic reasons) has drawn criticism from those who prefer to see one of the other themes at the center.

It would be an unfortunate mistake for advocates of each of these three positions to compete for dominance of the field because these positions are necessarily and organically related to one another. They should imply each other. The focus on student achievement is a social justice issue; the emphasis here is on success for *all* children, not just for the bright or economically advantaged. Academic achievement in isolation from a societal context is chimerical; learning involves relationships with teachers and other students in some kind of functional community; learning has to be related to responsible participation in various social institutions. Democratic community implies a learning community that engages in discussion and debate about social policy and the common good. Social progress requires reasoned discourse and a continuous assessment of social policy. The critique of structural and cultural injustice in society on behalf of social justice has to be constructed from factual evidence as well as moral argument. All three themes require one another if we wish to create a robust educational program; neither one in isolation from the others can bring about the desired results.

Murphy is correct, I believe, in insisting that educators have to focus on the core work of students—namely, their learning. Educators have to continue to explore with one another and with their students how the learning in the school can become meaningful, deep, lasting, and reflective—whether that learning concerns the elements of rocket technology, computer graphics, group dynamics, poetic expression, conflict resolution, or the difficult balancing of loyalty and justice. By retaining the necessary interpenetration of all three themes, educators will be able to resist the current overemphasis on narrowly academic tests as the sole measure of a school's mission. Because students' mastery of the academic curriculum appears weak—in some communities, more than half of the student body is performing at an unsatisfactory level—this clearly requires vigorous and prolonged attention, but not necessarily the draconian and punitive measures some school systems have adopted. States have imposed stringent demands on schools while offering little or no additional support to achieve those demands—not in professional development funding, not in smaller class sizes, not in better science or library resources, not in more responsive and imaginative remediation programs, to mention a few obvious examples. Instead, the victims of an inadequate system—students, teachers, and administrators—get blamed for all the system's shortcomings.

## ANOTHER PERSPECTIVE

In this book, I offer a perspective on this *center* for educational administration that is somewhat similar to Murphy's position, but takes it deeper. It is similar in that it argues for an interpenetration of three themes as the center while focusing on a common emphasis on learning in all three themes. It is similar in that I too am concerned about school improvement, but a school improvement that includes assessment and accountability issues in a larger perspective. I also want to employ the theme of transformational leadership emphasized by Leithwood, Jantzi, and Steinbach, but I want to emphasize that what needs transforming is the large agenda of student learning and the curriculum and teaching that support that learning. Like Elmore, I believe that the core work of school leaders must be involved with teachers in seeking to promote quality learning for all children, and that all management tasks serve that core work. Unlike Elmore, I want that core work to extend beyond state mandated curriculum standards to a broader curriculum that cultivates meaning, community and responsibility at the same time the school is responding to state standards and testing.

This book's perspective differs from the work of these three scholars, moreover, by looking beyond the present positioning of the argument about a center or focus for educational leadership. This book positions the argument in the larger historical transition from an early, *naive* era of modernity to a later, *reflexive* era of modernity. This enables me to highlight the cognitive and cultural landscape behind the present school reform agenda and thereby reach beyond the glaring shortcomings of that agenda to a deeper and more inclusive vision of what school reform *might* or *should* look like. I also want to recast the vocabulary of the present argument into terminology that I consider more inclusive and interactive—that is, fresher than the more abstract terminology of *higher achievement for all students, school renewal, democratic community*, and *social justice*. I use the phrases *cultivating meaning, cultivating community*, and *cultivating responsibility*.

The agricultural metaphor of *cultivation* suggests the work of the gardener: planting, fertilizing, weeding, watering, pruning (Louis, Toole, & Hargreaves, 1999). That is the work of someone who works with nature, with what nature provides. It involves educators understanding the qualities of soil and terrain, the chemistry of acids and alkaloids, the virtues of sun and shade, and the peculiar energies of winter and spring as metaphors of schooling realities. It is an aesthetic work, as well, appreciating the different colors and hues, variations in blossoming, and harmonies of size, color, and texture in the life one is cultivating. The cultivating work of educators is the work of understanding the native talents and interests of students, their cultural backgrounds, learning styles, and developmental readiness. It is a work of understanding both cognitive and affective development and the psychological logic of certain teaching protocols. It is dialogical work with fellow teachers and students to find out what blocks learning and what facilitates and enables learning to blossom.

Using the phrase *cultivating meaning* in place of Murphy's focus on the core work of teaching and learning enables me to focus on the outcome of teaching and learning, which is the construction of meaning. Within that theme, I can distinguish between *personal* meanings and *public* meanings, between *applied* meanings and *academic* meanings. Each of these differentiations requires different pedagogies, leaning processes, and assessment protocols. The phrase *cultivating community* rather than *democratic community* enables me to bypass what I consider to be a heatedly ideological argument about the meaning of democracy while exploring an education in pluralistic sociality, collaborative civility, and participatory self-governance. The phrase "cultivating responsibility" enables me to speak both to the neglected issues of social justice in the education of poor and minority children, as well as to the education of the young in moral values of justice, care and critique. The rhetoric of responsibility is both more inclusive of conflicting viewpoints and less inflammatory to the ears of a politically complacent public.

By incorporating the three themes into the center of administrators' work, both in theory and in practice, this book advances the basic thrust of Murphy's position. Through the elaboration of the themes we enrich Murphy's initial articulation of the three potential centers. This elaboration, in turn, enables us to develop the implications of these themes in specific curricula—what I have named the curriculum of meaning, the curriculum of community and the curriculum of responsibility. By drawing out the learning implications of these curricula, I can further specify the leadership focus of administrative work with teachers.

## THE CONSCIOUSNESS OF AN EDUCATIONAL ADMINISTRATOR

Educational administration, however intense its focus on teaching and learning, is nevertheless different from classroom teaching. Whereas teachers focus on specific students and specific areas of subject matter, administrators must think of the education of the whole community of youngsters in the school. This requires them to think of the scope and sequence of all the learning activities occurring in the school, not simply as a collection of activities, but as activities that comprise a unity. These activities make up a fitting education for human beings living in this moment of history, in this society, who are preparing for a challenging and demanding future in an increasingly globalized world. A rich grounding in the three foundational themes of cultivating meaning, community, and responsibility provides a focus for a broad consciousness of the desired purposes being served throughout the school.

An educational administrator today, working with the school board and the school district officers, is expected to have a larger sense of what constitutes an educated person and to bring this perspective to the task of coordinating and harmonizing the various separate areas of learning. Although teachers are expected to have a detailed understanding of specific learnings in their curriculum areas, administrators are supposed to bring the work of individual teachers into balance and unity by coordinating the varied activities of the youngsters during the years they spend in school. For example, one might expect that an educated person in 21st-century America would have an understanding of the natural environment and the importance of national and international policies enacted to protect this environment from excessive exploitation and deterioration. Hence, an educational administrator would be concerned that, in various science and social studies courses offered in the school curriculum, such understandings would be nurtured, although he or she might not know at what specific moment in any given course such considerations should be raised.

Similarly, one might expect that educated persons in 21st-century America would have developed an appreciation of the cultural diversity of the region in which they were raised and would have some understanding of the history and culture of communities that are culturally different from their own. That understanding must include a critical awareness of the historical oppression of various racial and ethnic groups by the White community. Thus, an educational administrator would be concerned that, in a variety of classes and extracurricular activities, a proactive multicultural sensitivity would be developed, although the administrator might not know how to bring about such sensitivity in every particular instance.

From the teacher's perspective, we could say that the teacher has a large sense of what youngsters in a particular course are supposed to be learning and a wide variety of learning activities by which the youngsters can arrive at those learnings. One might say that each teacher, after a few years of teaching, carries the course in his or her head. Educational administrators, however, must carry around in their heads the whole school's learning agenda as an integrated unity. One might say that a concert violinist carries the violin score of the symphony in his or her head, but that the conductor must carry the whole symphony in his or her head so that the playing of the various instruments can be integrated. Such an analogy helps explain the difference between the consciousness of the administrator and that of the teacher. The analogy appears to illuminate the difficulty of the administrator's task when we think of the individual musicians not as the teachers, but as the students who are just beginning to learn to play the various instruments. The administrator has to have some sense of how learning musical scales is an appropriate step in learning to play a symphony and, indeed, that both teachers and students need to keep the playing of the symphony in mind as they learn the mechanics of the instrument or the first simple melodies. The administrator also has to recognize that the symphony includes African, Asian, Latin and other motifs and instrumentation, and to allow for both cacophony and invention in the score. It is the vision of what all individual learning activities, linked together and intertwined over the course of several years, are intended to produce that educators must remember. This vision includes the gradual emergence of autonomous, intelligent, caring, and socially responsible human beings who will comprise a community struggling with the wounds of the past, yet full of promise for the future. This is the vision that truly activates transformational leaders of schools.

While keeping in mind the ideal of the *educated person* who understands the tragedies and triumphs of the community and is prepared to participate fully in its public life, the administrator should realize that few youngsters ever achieve the full and harmonious balance of understandings and skills contained in the ideal. Youngsters bring individual talents and liabilities with them to school. They have different interests, abilities, and learning styles. Teachers struggle to bring children to a minimal level of mastery in many areas, yet they find that individual youngsters perform better on some tasks than on others, and their readiness for some tasks differs from their readiness for other tasks. Some youngsters come from homes where English is not spoken, and hence their learning activities may have to be structured to take into account the strengths and diversity of the cultures in which the children were raised. Some youngsters may come from dysfunctional home environments, and thus their educational program may have to be supplemented with other support services.

Educators' ideal of an educated person may reflect class, gender, and racial bias. The ideal of an educated person should always be contextualized by the youngsters being served. In other words, educators have to look at the total condition of the children and respond to it. The symphony may not be Mozart's; for now it might be a symphony in fingerpaint, the symphony of a child learning for the first time how to play with other children, or a symphony of linguistic expression with Latin inflections. In every instance, the educator must work with whatever the youngster brings to the learning situation, but the educator must never stop believing that each child is capable of something wonderful and heroic and that he or she will never exhaust his or her possibilities.

## THE VISION BEHIND ADMINISTRATIVE LEADERSHIP

The prior considerations lead us to consider an all-important quality of administrative leadership—*vision*. I use that term here in two senses. The first refers to a firm commitment to an ideal—the educated person and an ideal educational process for cultivating that person. Educational leaders know full well the difference between the ideal and the realities in schools. Senge (1990) suggested that a tension necessarily exists in corporations between a shared vision and perceived organizational limitations. Senge asserted that this tension can be generative when leaders mobilize the members to use that tension creatively. It is the awareness of the unnecessarily large gap between the ideal and the real that fuels the commitment of educational leaders to close that gap.

Included in the ideal of the educated person is the autonomy of the educated person to choose the direction of his or her life. Hence, that ideal implies a dialogical relationship between the educator and student in which the process of cultivating meaning, community, and responsibility involves both invitation and response—a necessary mutuality in the learning process.

The second sense of vision is the sense of sight: the seeing things clearly, seeing both the foreground and background and being able to situate the foreground within the background. This sense of the educational leader's vision suggests that leaders look into the full reality of what stands before them, see it in its complexity, in its human, existential, and moral dimensions, as well as in its educational and organizational dimensions. This sense of insight refers to *in-sight*—to the grasp of both the deeper and pragmatic dimensions of situations. This sense of vision enables leaders to respond on several levels to the multidimensional quality of situations, to offer short-term responses and accommodate long-term needs. These two senses of vision— the ideal and the talent of insight—are mutually reinforcing. The ideal provides an interpretive lens for seeing into the deeper dimensions of present situations. The talent of insight enables the leader to connect the immediate realities to a larger framework of meaning and value.

This approach to educational leadership enables us to create a model of leadership that illustrates how the leader's vision eventually becomes embodied in the institutional structures and frameworks and policies of the school.[1] There are five basic elements to this leadership:

1. It is grounded in basic meanings about human persons, society, knowledge, human development, the natural world, and schooling.
2. It is energized by a dramatic vision of what education might and should be.
3. It involves the articulation of that vision and the invitation to others to articulate a communal vision of schooling.
4. It seeks to embody the vision in the institutional mission, goals, policies, programs, and organizational structures.
5. It celebrates the vision in ordinary and special activities and seeks a continuous renewal of both the vision and its embodiment.

In succeeding chapters, I lay out a vision of schooling that is grounded in basic meanings about human persons, society, the nature of knowledge, human development, and the natural word. Those chapters challenge the reader to engage those elements of the vision and modify or create their own vision statement. The chapters also suggest ways to engage members of the school staff in discussions about their vision for the school.

The articulation of the vision is crucial. Unless the school community gets its personal visions out on the table for public dialogue, it is difficult for that community to move beyond the customary daily routines into any sense of re-new-ing themselves and their work. Without a communal vision of who they are and where they want to go, the school functions as a shopping mall, with each classroom reflecting the idiosyncratic preferences of each teacher. Inevitably, a vision is imposed from outside. Indeed, state departments of education, pressured by political and corporate leaders whose views of schooling are one dimensional and simplistic, seem quite willing to steep in and impose their view of schooling. A local vision of schooling endorsed by the staff can serve as an interpretive framework for discussing state curriculum mandates.

Often the leader has to take the initiative and put forth a vision statement. That provides the rest of the staff something to consider, but not necessarily to endorse. Individually and in teams, the staff should be encouraged to come up with their own vision—not of where they are now, of how they understand what their work currently consists of, but a vision of who they might become—a vision of new understandings of their work, a vision

---

[1]This material is adapted from my earlier works such as *Leaders with vision: The quest for school renewal.* Thousand Oaks, CA: Corwin Press, 1995, pp. 14–18 and 50–58; and *Supervision: A redefinition* (5th ed.). New York: McGraw-Hill, 1993, pp. 188–198, co-authored with Thomas J. Sergiovanni.

of where they want to go with the students. Because it is not an exercise most staff are comfortable with, some time and space, structure and coaching should be provided. Most university preparation programs do not require its prospective administrators to come up with a vision statement that they are required to defend in some kind of public forum. But that is precisely one of the leadership skills needed by educational administrators (Hargreaves & Fullan, 1998). Neither are these candidates required to work with a group to generate a group vision—again, a key leadership skill needed in the field.

Beyond creating one's own vision statement and collaborating with others on a communal vision statement, administrators need to assess the gap between the communal vision and the institutional processes, structures, policies, and programs that get in the way of the vision ever becoming operationalized. The following diagrams may help visualize this process.

Using what I refer to as the Onion Model of Schools we can visualize a school being made up of layers of intelligible activity (see Fig. 1.1). The outer layer represents the operational level of the school. This is what one sees on walking around the school building on a given day: teachers in front of their classrooms explaining something on the blackboard; students struggling to enact the curriculum; students moving from one classroom to another, banging locker doors, calling out to one another; assistant principals standing in the corridors scowling at the students as they pass by; bulletin boards displaying students' work; bells ringing; announcements coming over the PA system reminding students and teachers about the days events; teachers discussing new textbooks; and so forth. Underneath that layer, one would find a pattern

FIG. 1.1.   Dimensions of school life.

of organization: a class schedule for each day of the week, distribution of subject matter across the class schedule, allocation of 25 students or so to each
classroom, marking of time by bells, allocation of support staff doing their re-
spective jobs, weekly, monthly, and yearly calendar, schedule of meals and
busses, and arrivals and departure arrangements.

Beneath that layer is the deeper layer of schoolwide programs—the various academic disciplines with their scope and sequence for each year, the
guidance program, the discipline program, the health program, the athletic program, and school–parent programs. These programs provide the
substance of the teachers' and students' work.

Under the program layer is the policy layer. This layer guides the execu-
tion of the programs and operations and includes grading and promotion
policies, personnel policies for teachers and staff, pupil personnel policies,
home–school communication policies, crisis management procedures, and
so forth. These are the general rules that govern many of the day-to-day decisions made by everyone in the school community. Beneath the policy
layer is the layer of goals and purposes. This includes the mission statement, perhaps a statement on the core values the school espouses, and
goals referring to students' intellectual, social, and personal development.

Beneath those layers, one finds the level of beliefs and assumptions. Often these are not articulated clearly. Although tacit, they nevertheless exercise an enormous influence over the behavior and routines of people in the
school. When these beliefs and assumptions are made explicit, they comprise the foundation for a vision statement. Sometimes the unarticulated
beliefs and assumptions can be limiting. They might imply an attitude toward students as problems, focused on their limits rather than on their potential, containing subtle forms of bias toward some children and their
communities. The unarticulated beliefs and assumptions may imply a vision
of teaching and learning that focuses on passive learning, rote memorization of textbook materials, and an assessment system designed to reproduce the normal curve of intelligence. By contrast, these beliefs and assumptions might focus on the enormous potential of the children, on the
role of teaching as the highly creative design of exciting learning activities
that motivate students to high-quality learning, as well as focus on the importance of fostering community as the stimulus for individual growth.
When those latter beliefs and assumptions are made public and become co-
alesced into a communal vision, they have enormous potential to energize a
school.

At the core of the onion, often flowing into the unarticulated beliefs and
assumptions, are the myths and meanings by which people make sense out
of their lives. By labeling them *myths*, I do not imply that they are fairy-tale
phantasies fed by infantile fears, desires, and superstitions. Rather, these
myths are stories whose symbolism enable us to define value, judge human

striving, and place ourselves in an identifiable order of things. This core is almost beyond articulation. It includes the myth of heroism, human destiny, and the sacred nature of all life; myth's about society's relationships to nature, about values underlying the nation's identity, about those values considered to comprise the essence of humanity. Those myths—often embodied in story, poetry, highly symbolic literature, sacred texts—shape people's convictions, beliefs, and attitudes about most things. It is in that core of myth, meaning, and belief that leaders find the foundation for their vision of what the school can and should become: the greenhouse for cultivating the educated person.

The leader's work is not completed when the school community has articulated its communal vision. The vision must become embodied in the other layers of the school organization. The onion must be energized by its core. The difficulty experienced by many educators is that they function in schools that, for all intents and purposes, have no center, no articulated vision, mission, or sense of purpose, other than the daily delivery of programs governed by schedules and operating procedures (see Fig. 1.2). In contrast, Fig. 1.3 suggests a school in which the outer layers reflect those core beliefs, values, and meanings. The articulation of a vision enables those school communities to intentionally pursue the vision by means of the programs and structural organization of the school, rather than pursuing the vision by *fighting against* the routines of those outer layers.

A vision statement is not a full-blown philosophy or long-range plan. Much of its power comes from capturing three or four central meanings that are open to multiple applications and representations within the

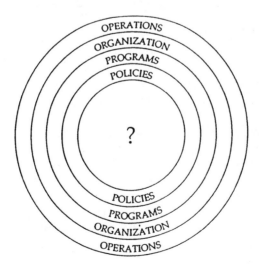

FIG. 1.2.  A school with no vision.

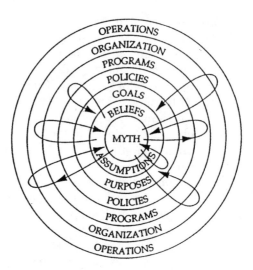

FIG. 1.3.   A school with an integrated vision.

school. The vision statement does not have an impact on student learning unless it is institutionalized in the various layers of school life. Schools that fail to confront their organizational structures' resistance to the vision remain dysfunctional.

Figure 1.4 helps identify and distinguish more clearly the leadership side of administrative work and the managerial side of administrative work. Much of the leader's work lies at the left side of the figure, whereas much of the manager's work lies at the right side of the figure, involved in the organization and daily operation of the school. The important work of institutionalizing the vision calls on the complementary skills of both leadership and management, the former to insist on bringing the vision forward into the practical functioning of the school and the latter insisting on bringing some kind of structure, predictability, and form to the vision. The figure brings the leader and the manager work into dialogue at the center of the figure. In a different context, Hill and Guthrie (1999) emphasized the integrative function of leadership, the work of bringing powerful perspectives and resources together so that their mutual interaction can produce the necessary effect. Here we see the integration of leadership and managerial work necessary for the re-creation of the school as a viable social institution, with the strengths of both approaches to administrative work coming together to effect what neither one of them singly could achieve. Obviously, we are talking not only of the integrative work of one person here, but a teamwork of all those in the school community who have talents in both areas.

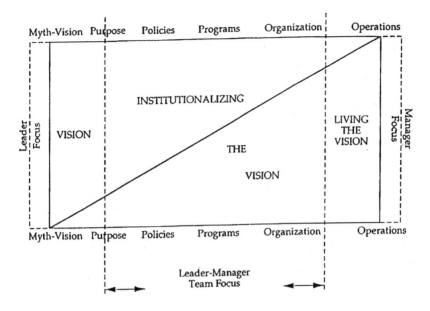

FIG. 1.4.   Bringing separated focus to a team focus.

Finally, Fig. 1.5 lays out in a more logical-sequential diagram the work of administrative leadership, moving from the visioning and purposing work through the restructuring work toward coordinating the daily operations of the school. Thus, we see the work of school renewal that Murphy (1999) urged as the core work of administrative leadership represented in a model of administrative leadership that elaborates that work in its reach and depth. The model strongly suggests that the work of school renewal cannot progress in more than a superficial rearrangement at the program and organizational level unless it is energized by a communal vision of who teachers and students are, what authentic learning involves, and what the social and academic purposes of schools are. The remaining chapters in Part One attempt to explore dimensions of the vision, employing the three themes of cultivating meaning, cultivating community, and cultivating responsibility. In the process of suggesting consideration of these themes as providing a fuller vision of what schools and therefore administrators should be seeking, I hope to include the other two concerns that Murphy (1999) identified as needing to be included with school renewal—namely, democratic community and social justice. In Part Two, I touch on the integrative work of administrative leadership—namely, the embodiment of the vision into the core structures that shape and sustain the daily operation of the school. In Part Two, it becomes more obvious that the transformational leadership

| ROOTS OF THE VISION | ARTICULATION OF THE VISION | INSTITUTIONALIZATION OF THE VISION | OPERATIONALIZATION OF THE VISION |
|---|---|---|---|
| Meaning associated with:<br><br>Human destiny<br>The nature of the individual<br>The nature of human society<br>View of the past and of the future<br><br>Frequently embedded in imagery, metaphor, myth, and story | Beliefs about:<br><br>- the human mind and how one knows<br>- how children develop as full human beings<br>- how children should be socialized<br>- varieties of learning<br>- moral values<br>- political values<br>- religious values<br>- what kind of future the young will face | Formal Organization<br><br>Policies<br>Programs<br>Procedures<br>- Graduation requirements<br>- Curriculum<br>- Course selection and assignment<br>- Grading criteria<br>- Discipline<br>- Student activities<br>- Staffing<br>- Budget<br><br>Informal Organization<br><br>Community spirit<br>Style of communications<br>Tone of relationships<br>Informal groups<br>Informal curriculum | Woodrow Wilson School<br><br>A school that opens its doors and looks like:<br>People coming and going to<br>- classes<br>- activities<br>- interactions<br><br>making up a fabric of experience<br>- meanings<br>- patterns<br>- rituals<br>- symbolic action<br>- celebration |
| | Formal Statement of the Mission of the School<br><br>Cultural purposes<br>Political purposes<br>Academic purposes<br>Moral purposes<br>Economic purposes<br>Social purposes<br>Religious purposes<br><br>Processes of Communicating the Vision<br><br>- Thematic purposing<br>- Rituals<br>- Celebrations<br>- Championing<br>- Heroes<br>- Rewards | | |
| MYTH | ASSUMPTIONS, BELIEFS | GOALS, OBJECTIVES | POLICIES, PROGRAMS, STRUCTURES | OPERATIONS |

FIG. 1.5.   The communal institutionalization of vision.

called for by Leithwood, Jantzi, and Steinbach, as well as (implicitly, at least) Elmore and Murphy, requires a healthy blending with transactional leadership (Bass, 1988) as the details of the vision get worked out in practical detail.

## RECAPITULATION

The ingredients for reform are known at least in general outline. The political mandate is there. Public opinion seems rather firmly behind school reform. Anyone familiar with large-scale organizational change, however, knows that the transformation of schools—one of the more conservative institutions in society—requires leadership on a broad and continuous scale for at least a generation. Persons at the forefront of these changes may find themselves embroiled in controversy with teachers' unions, special interest groups in the community, and fiscal conservatives who oppose increased spending for schools (Cusick, 1992). The task requires facility in building coalitions, arbitration and conflict resolution, and communicating an appealing vision of the human benefits to be derived from changes in the form and substance of schooling.

To exercise leadership in this climate of change requires deep convictions, strong commitments, and clear ideas about directions for change in the form and content of schooling. There should be no illusions about this. The people leading the way in school transformation must have thought and read their way through the complex issues at stake in school reform. They must be people who see a clear connection between the public program of schooling and the kind of society that will carry the human adventure into the future; that is, they will understand the human and technical challenges that the community faces and will bring the understanding of these challenges to bear on the design of the form and content of the schools they are redesigning.

Aware of the dangers and dysfunction of imposing policy from the top down, future administrators should also realize that their ideas about the shape and content of schooling must be tested in the forum of public debate. Such public debate is often a raucous, contentious, self-interested power struggle. One's bright ideas can be misunderstood, misinterpreted, distorted, ridiculed, and contested. One is subjected to personal accusations, verbal abuse, betrayals, threats to one's job, and various forms of raw hatred. Through all this, one must attempt to keep people talking about the issues, appealing to people's better sides, finding common ground, bargaining for more resources, bringing disparate interests together, and keeping one's dreams and hopes alive month after month, year after year.

Such a prospect is not for the faint-hearted or weekend enthusiast. Rather, it is for people who see the possibility for a better life for children and youth, who dream of a better tomorrow for all members of their society, and who have the inner strength of their convictions and ideals, as well as the humility to know that they need to join themselves to the ideas, talents, and energies of countless others if their hopes and dreams are to be realized. The school administrator of the future needs a different mindset and skills than the status quo administrator of the past; the dramatic challenges facing schools call for a different kind of vision and commitment. Schools are not served well by people who go into school administration primarily for the increased salary, the greater prestige and power in the community, or a heightened sense of self-importance, all the while assuming that schools are more or less fine the way they are. Those contemplating a career in educational administration need to make a sober assessment of their own talents, motivations, and dispositions for meeting the challenges in educational administration in the 21st century. Such an assessment is necessary before rather than after a decision has been taken to become an educational administrator. For those who do choose to pursue such a career, the foundational orientations provided in these chapters can expose them to exciting possibilities.

## ACTIVITIES

1. Write out your understanding of educational administration prior to reading this chapter. Compare your prior understanding with that of your classmates. Does that shared understanding of administration represent what you perceive as standard practice in the workplace?

2. Assess your motivation for choosing to move into administrative work. What personal and professional values energize your motivations?

3. Assume that the view of educational administration present in this chapter is to be used as the basis for standards of hiring and evaluating administrators in the near future. Assess your strengths and shortcomings for success in this kind of educational administration. What does this assessment suggest to you?

## REFERENCES

Apple, M. W. (1982). *Education and power*. Boston: Routledge & Kegan Paul.
Bass, B. M. (1985). *Leadership and performance beyond expectations*. New York: Free Press.

Bass, B. M. (1998). The ethics of transformational leadership. In J. B. Ciulla (Ed.), *Ethics, the heart of leadership* (pp. 169–192). Westport, CT: Quorum.

Bates, R. (1987). Corporate culture, schooling, and educational administration. *Educational Administration Quarterly, 23*(4), 79–115.

Burns, J. M. (1978). *Leadership.* New York: Harper & Row.

Cohen, M. D., March, J. G., & Olsen, J. P. (1972). A garbage can model of organizational choice. *Administrative Science Quarterly, 17*(1), 1–25.

Cubberly, E. (1916). *Public school administration.* Boston: Houghton Mifflin.

Cusick, P. (1992). *The educational system: Its nature and logic.* New York: McGraw-Hill.

Cyert, R. M., & March, J. G. (1963). *A behavioral theory of the firm.* Englewood Cliffs, NJ: Prentice-Hall.

Donmoyer, R., Imber, M., & Scheurich, J. J. (1995). *The knowledge base in educational administration: Multiple prespectives.* Albany, NY: State University of New York Press.

Elmore, R. (2000). *Building a new structure for school leadership.* Washington, DC: The Albert Shanker Institute.

Giroux, H. A. (1991). Curriculum planning, public schooling, and democratic struggle. *NASSP Bulletin, 75*(532), 12–25.

Griffiths, D. E. (1959). *Administrative theory.* New York: Appleton-Century-Crofts.

Hargreaves, A., & Fullan, M. (1998). *What's worth fighting for out there?* New York: Teachers College Press.

Hill, P. T., & Guthrie, J. W. (1999). A new research paradigm for understanding (and improving) twenty-first century schooling. In J. Murphy & K. S. Louis (Eds.), *Handbook of research on educational administration* (2nd ed., pp. 511–523). San Francisco: Jossey-Bass.

Leithwood, K., Jantzi, D., & Steinbach, R. (1999). *Changing leadership for changing times.* Philadelphia: Open University Press.

Lindbloom, C. E. (1959). The science of muddling through. *Public Administration Review, 19*(1), 79–88.

Louis, K. S., Toole, J., & Hargreaves, A. (1999). Rethinking school improvement. In J. Murphy & K. S. Louis (Eds.), *Handbook of research on educational administration* (2nd ed., pp. 251–276). San Francisco: Jossey-Bass.

Milstein, M. M., & Associates. (1993). *Changing the way we prepare educational leaders: The Danforth experience.* Newbury Park, CA: Corwin.

Mulkeen, T. A., Cambron-McCabe, N. H., & Anderson, B. J. (1994). *Democratic leadership: The changing context of administrative preparation.* Norwood, NJ: Ablex.

Murphy, J. (1992). *The landscape of leadership preparation: Reframing the education of school administrators.* Newbury Park, CA: Corwin.

Murphy, J. (1999). *The quest for a center: Notes on the state of the profession of educational leadership.* Columbia, MO: University Council for Educational Administration.

National Commission on Excellence in Educational Administration. (1987). *Leaders for America's schools.* Tempe, AZ: University Council for Educational Administration.

National Policy Board for Educational Administration. (1989). *Improving the preparation of school administrators: An agenda for reform.* Charlottesville, VA: Author.

Purpel, D. E. (1985). Introduction. In D. E. Purpel & H. Z. Shapiro (Eds.), *Schools and meaning: Essays on the moral nature of schooling* (p. XVII). Lanham, MD: University Press of America.

Senge, P. M. (1990). *The fifth discipline: The art and practice of the learning organization.* New York: Doubleday.

Sergiovanni, T. J., & Carver, F. D. (1969). *Organizations and human behavior: Focus on schools.* New York: McGraw-Hill.

Simon, H. A. (1957). *Administrative behavior: A study of decision-making processes in administrative organization.* New York: Macmillan.

Starratt, R. J. (1993a). *The drama of leadership*. London: Falmer.
Starratt, R. J. (1993b). *Supervision: A redefinition* (5th ed.). New York: McGraw-Hill.
Starratt, R. J. (1995). *Leaders with vision*. Thousand Oaks, CA: Corwin.
Taylor, F. (1911). *The principles of scientific management*. New York: Harper & Row.
University Council on Educational Administration. (1992). *Essential knowledge for school leaders: A proposal to map the knowledge base of educational administration*. Unpublished proposal.

# Chapter 2

# Cultivating Meaning

In this chapter, we address some of the problems and possibilities in the cultivation of meaning. In so doing, we touch on some of the most difficult and profound issues involved in schooling. As the chapter unfolds, the task of cultivating meaning may begin to seem impossible to some readers. The chapter ends, however, with the development of a foundational position from which educational administrators can approach the cultivation of meaning. To begin, let us consider some definitions.

## THE MEANING OF MEANING

Because we use the term *meaning* in several ways, it helps to know what we mean by meaning. Meaning can refer to what we want to convey, especially by language. Hence, one can say, "What I meant by that remark was that I disagree strongly with your politics, even though I like you as a person." Meaning also refers to a person's intention in saying or doing something, when the saying or doing has a symbolic or unspoken meaning. Thus, "It was clear to those present that he meant to humiliate the student in front of the principal." Another use of the term *meaning* refers to the denotation or connotation of words. Thus, people ask, "What does the word *hermeneutics* mean?" (seeking the denotation of the word). "What do teenagers mean when they say, 'That's cool.'?" is a question seeking the connotation of the word *cool*. Under other circumstances, we use the term *meaning* to signify that something was significant—that it carried some symbolic content for us. Thus, we say, "I found a deep meaning in the preacher's sermon."

In this chapter, the term *meaning* refers to the cultural and personal meanings that are attached to or embedded in events, circumstances, information, and symbols. Thus, the social studies teacher may ask students the questions, "What does the welfare system mean to you?" "How do you make sense of the American Civil War?" "Whose side would you have been on in the national debate over the Vietnam War?" "What does Newton's theory of gravity mean in the practical day-to-day matters of your life?" "What does a free market economy mean to a banking executive as opposed to what it means for an out-of-work coal miner?" All of those questions go beyond asking for factual information. They explicitly ask for a point of view, an interpretation, a placing of the topic in a perspective of some kind, relating it to some sense of values. The framework for meaning can be derived from the culture, from the study of other scholarly commentaries, as well as from personal experience.

Growing up in a third-generation, middle-class culture in the United States, young persons absorb attitudes and perspectives toward social practices such as conspicuous consumption (they simply have to have a certain brand of sneakers and blue jeans), competition (it is the American way; life is divided between winners and losers; winning is everything; life is a zero-sum game: My winning requires your losing), and responsibility (Take care of number one first; What is left over after that is for charity; Who are you to tell me what to do? This belongs to me, so I can do whatever I want with it; Everyone else cheats, so why can't I? It's not my fault that people are poor). A recent immigrant to the United States from Asia or Central America would have rather different attitudes and perspectives from their culture that lead them to attach different meanings to social practices. Different cultures socialize male and female children to place different meaning and value on various forms of social behavior.

Teachers' questions also ask for pieces of information. However, even in "factual matters," facts are described or explained by using frameworks of meaning. Hence, one might respond to the prior question about the welfare system that it is one way in which the state redistributes wealth. Another answer might be that it is the way the state keeps poor people in a condition of dependency. Both responses are factual, but their factualness is established by larger frames of meaning.

In some instances, the meaning may derive from something personal. The historical reality of slavery means something different to a descendent of slaves than it does to a person whose descendents were never enslaved, although both persons might know the same facts about the slave trade in the 16th century. The notion of sexual harassment means something different to someone who has experienced it than it does to someone who has not, although both might give the same dictionary definition of it. Does this imply that one can understand the meaning of something only if one experiences it? No. Meanings attain a kind of public status that most people understand, although each individual's understanding also contain unique colorations and intensities. Thus, meanings have a public status and a personal status.

One can study what certain actions, rituals, or symbols mean to people of a different culture and come to some understanding of their meanings. That understanding, however, normally does not have the depth and richness of meaning that it has to someone from that culture (Geertz, 1979). Anthropologists who immerse themselves in a culture may come closest to that depth of understanding, but even they will confess that their understanding never fully grasps the deepest meanings of the cultural phenomena of the people they study.

It seems fair to say that people of a common culture can come to some public agreement about what words, symbols, gestures, and natural objects mean. This is normally referred to as what those words, symbols, gestures, and natural objects *denote.* Thus, in certain English-speaking locales, a sign bearing the letters "WC" denotes a public toilet, although a foreigner might not get the connection between the literal translation of *water closet* and a toilet. In the United States, the word *bathroom* carries the same denotation, although a foreigner who comes from a culture where the toilet is always separated from the bathing area might find the term confusing. Symbols inscribed on traffic signs are supposed to denote a univocal meaning to everyone, giving them directions on how to proceed. Numbers attached to grocery items denote the same price for everyone. Terms such as *due process, binding contract, liability,* and *felony* denote precise meanings especially for lawyers; such terms soon enough come to have precise meanings for those who might need a lawyer. Terms such as *weight, mass, velocity, bacteria, nervous system, immune system, crystals, acids, carcinogens, toxic waste, biodegradables, biosphere, taxes, profit,* and *insurance* all have public meanings or cultural denotations. Clearly, schools are concerned with helping youngsters acquire these and a host of other public meanings, without mastery of which it would be difficult to engage in public life.

Words, symbols, gestures, and natural objects also carry additional meanings that color, shape, nuance, distort, elevate, or in some way add to the denoted meaning—the public meaning. This is the *connotative* meaning, which relates what is publicly signified to additional personal associations. Although some hypothetical persons who operate in a purely rational and logical fashion might apprehend the world only according to its denotations, most human beings develop a rich and complex web of connotative meanings associated with words, symbols, gestures, and natural objects. People in New York City and Washington, DC, carry connotative associations to the word *terrorists* that had not occurred to most of them before September 11, 2001.

Psychologists play word association games with patients to understand the affect they attach to objects, persons, or experiences in their lives. Poets employ images rich in connotation to convey their meaning. Politicians utilize, for better or worse, language and phrases that carry undercurrents of coded meaning for their followers. At a seemingly more prosaic level, ordinary conversations between ordinary people carry rich and complex patterns of meanings associated with experiences, persons, and objects, and a language of metaphor, intonation, and inflection that punctuates those meanings. Listen in on a conversation between two people sitting behind you on a train or sit at a bar and listen to the stories and interpretations expressed; you will hear layers of connotative meanings riding on the denotative meanings that people attach to experiences. It also becomes clear that the connotative meanings often exercise greater influence over people's interpretations of events as well as their subsequent actions and decisions.

## MEANING AND REALITY

One of the basic questions about meaning is its relationship to reality. Does the meaning something has for us correspond to the reality of that something? Differing political interpretations attached to U.S. military interventions in Vietnam, Panama, Iraq, Somalia, and Afghanistan indicate how different frames of meaning name the same event differently. What are the realities of those particular historical events and what do they mean? Most historians would say that, after all available documentary and evidential sources have been considered, the historian tries to provide an interpretation of what happened that is consistent with the cumulative record of evidence. Often, however, the sources themselves represent interpretations by various witnesses of what happened and why it happened. That is why history is always being rewritten and why there will probably never be a definitive history of any event.

The history of science, although shorter in time than the history of writing history, illustrates this perpetual rewriting. Science gradually builds a clearer body of knowledge, with each succeeding generation of scientists correcting the errors and misinterpretations of its predecessors. Hence, the meaning of *scientific discoveries* is constantly undergoing reinterpretation as new information, metaphors, and frames of reference are developed. Nevertheless, we find proponents of a new myth of science (Wilson, 1998) that claim a gradual, cumulative coalescence of scientific knowledge, all of which can be reduced to physics, which explains everything, including human behavior. The frameworks of physics, according to Wilson, are the primary, if not the only valid, sources of meaning. Berry (2000), among others, find this position intellectually overbearing, humanly barren, and ecologically disastrous.

In the field of literature, the arguments over meaning have perhaps reached their extreme limits. Does the text of the author correspond to some reality about human life beyond the text? Or is the text simply a revelation of the author's interior fantasy? Are all the characters merely a reflection of the author's own multiple personalities? Is the text, on the other hand, simply a reflection of the social history of the time, reflecting prevailing attitudes toward commerce, tradition, sex, war, nature, suffering, and a transcendent Being? Perhaps the text does not even have an independent meaning of its own, but rather has meaning only within the mind of the reader. This latter position places the reader as the constructor, reconstructor, or deconstructor of the text. The author's text is simply material out of which readers make sense for themselves. In other words, where is the text? Is the meaning of Joyce's *Portrait of the Artist as a Young Man* to be found in the social realities of the Dublin of Joyce's day? Is it in Joyce's interior battle with himself and his demons? Is it in the reader's reconstruction of Joyce's reconstruction of the social and religious realities of Dublin? Is it in the reader's critical deconstruction of Joyce's story? Is the meaning somehow to be found at all of these levels of composition?

The social sciences have been going through their own epistemological upheaval. Social scientists have questioned how much of social science is real science, in the sense that the natural sciences such as physics and biology are *real* sciences. Are social sciences, like the natural sciences, able to explain objective regularities in societies? Is social science able, in the process of reducing social phenomena to a few univocal variables such as class, power, or gender, to explain those social phenomena objectively, or does the reduction cause distortion to the point of misrepresentation? Over the past 30 years, the attempt to reduce social and human phenomena to quantifiable measures has increasingly come under attack, not only from philosophers and humanists, but from social scientists themselves (Foucault, 1972; Jennings, 1983; Lyotard, 1984; Rorty, 1979; Stake, 1976). Social scientists argue whether a country's statistics on its gross national product count for more than a country's artistic production, whether a country's industrialization should count more than a country's agricultural base, whether urban life is better than village life (Schumacher, 1973, 1977).

We see this argument carried on in the field of education between educators who organize their educational programs to produce higher scores on standardized tests of basic competencies and educators who propose a more authentic form of assessment tied to the local curriculum and more responsive to complex and multiform learning tasks. Educational research that attempts to measure statistically the impact of specific teacher protocols on learning tends to reduce teaching to decontextualized, uniform behaviors. This research is rejected by others, who argue that thick descriptive narratives of one classroom reveal more truth about effective teaching than a statistical study of several hundred teachers.

For the past 100 years or more, it was generally taken for granted in the social sciences that, through the study of psychology, economics, sociology, and political science, we could understand how society and human beings work. The findings of social research could then be used to create social policy. Governments could then, through social policy, construct a social environment that worked better. These assumptions have led to a massive rationalization of public life and growing interventions of the welfare state into everyday life through the multiplication of state agencies that oversee, prescribe, sanction, and remediate. For educators in the United States, an obvious example is the recent intervention of state and federal agencies in the operations of schools, especially in the imposition of curriculum standards and high-stakes testing, the reporting of testing results, and subsequent political commentary, with the threat of state takeover of failing schools.

More than a few scholars have commented on how often terminology developed in the social sciences that was intended as an interpretive tool, a short-hand kind of vocabulary to refer to complex realities being studied, gradually enters into the vocabulary of the general population and is assumed to define an objective reality. For example, the term *class* has been used by sociologists and economists to identify groups of people in society. We later find the word *class* used as a label that supposedly refers to desirable and undesirable qualities that people possess: "He's a real high-class person." "She's showing her working-class origins, unfortunately." "I'm proud to be middle class. Not full of airs like the rich; not ashamed of my status like the poor." We invent words to interpret new knowledge, and gradually the words invent us. Does the objective reality of *class* exist or is *class* a construct invented by human beings in their quest to bring meaning to social relations?

The human and social sciences represent a disciplined way to search for meaningful frameworks that help us interpret the human condition, guide the application of what we know, and illuminate the moral implications of our knowledge. Such searchings seem to be fueled by an awareness that the uses of knowledge in public life require a framework of meaning that is intimately tied to questions of what it means to be a human being in today's world, what a good society consists of, and what are our mutual responsibilities to the creation of such a society (Bellah et al., 1991; Habermas, 1971; Mills, 1959).

## MEANING IN THE CLASSROOM

Teachers in their day-to-day work cultivate the construction of meaning. Although they do not control the meanings their youngsters discover, accept, or create, they may strongly influence those meanings. What assumptions do teachers make about what is meaningful and where and how meaning is to be found? That, it seems, is an essential question all educators need to ask: What is a meaningful interpretation of contemporary human society: one that, on the one hand, offers hope and, on the other hand, owns up to the failed promises of modernity? Various interpretations are offered through the media, popular culture, and cultural and political ideologies of the left and right. Do schools attempt a credible answer? Do they at least attempt to help students study the questions?

For an unreflective educator, what is meaningful is what is in the syllabus and the curriculum guides. Why it is meaningful is a question that hardly crosses his mind. If someone were to ask, the answer would probably be: "Well, the central office curriculum coordinators in response to state curriculum standards have determined what has to be learned, so that must be what is meaningful." A more reflective educator might respond:

> Well, these learnings are what scholars in the field have determined to be most important. Science experts, historians, literary scholars, and so on have said that these understandings should be considered the essential and necessary scientific, historical, and literary understandings. Publishers consult these experts and translate their understandings into textbook chapters or course units, and our central office, or our departments, buy the textbooks.

However, textbooks rarely give a sense of the debates and uncertainties about where and how meaning and purpose are to be found. On the contrary, they tend to simplify the world of science, history, and literature into "beliefs about the way things are" (Duckworth, 1987, pp. 50–63). There seems to be an underlying assumption of most textbook authors that: (a) there is a right answer, (b) they know the right answers, (c) they know how to bring children to learn these right answers, and (d) these right answers help children in their education and the rest of their lives.

Schools that accept this unreflective rationale for teaching and learning accept the simplifications built into them, such as the following:

1. There is general agreement among "people who matter" (although not necessarily among experts) about what is meaningful—that what is meaningful appears in textbooks and curriculum guides and that learning means mastering the material (whatever mastery might mean) in the textbooks.

2.  The role of the teacher is to explain the textbook when necessary, and to get the children, through a variety of pedagogical stratagems and inducements, to memorize the material to the extent necessary to get the right answers on local and standardized tests.

3.  The role of the student is to accept the information provided in the textbook and curriculum guides and use this information to construct or recognize the right answers to questions on local and standardized tests.

Those who administer schools that accept this unreflective rationale for teaching and learning likewise accept these simplifications. Further, they accept as their own responsibility to see to it that teachers teach this curriculum and students are held accountable to produce enough right answers, as contained in this curriculum, to be promoted or graduated. Because the right answers are already known, it is simply a matter of getting teachers to develop sufficient motivational and explanatory techniques for students to *get* the right answers. Hence, the principal and other supervisors of teachers work with teachers to help them develop their bag of tricks and strategies to lead students to the right answers as given in the curriculum.

The problem with this strategy is that school knowledge and its acquisition is determined largely by someone other than the teacher and student. Whether that knowledge implies gender, racial, cultural, or class bias is never asked. When these questions are not asked, it is usually because of the assumption of legitimacy and power of the central office staff and of the publishing houses that their point of view concerning what things mean and how and where one finds meaning is the correct, the only, the most desirable, or the most politically acceptable point of view. When questions are asked and alternative meanings and methods of uncovering meaning are suggested, then advocates of these previously silent assumptions of legitimacy and power attack the supporters of alternatives (Nieto, 1992; Ogbu, 1992; Schlesinger, 1992). Those who support the administrative status quo in schools support a process of administering meaning, not cultivating meaning. This type of administration denies access to meanings that are not included in the state or district curriculum frameworks and the approved textbooks. The meanings that these frameworks and textbooks make available to students are prepackaged meanings representing a limited worldview.

## THE PROBLEM WITH RIGHT ANSWERS

When we learn, we make meaning. We do not learn information; we learn from information to make meaning. We extract the meanings encoded in information and align that meaning with previously constructed meanings.

Along the way, we make many *mistakes*, making things and relationships mean something that later experience and new information shows us they do not mean. Correcting previously constructed meanings is an essential part of the learning process.

Teachers help speed up the process of making meanings about the physical, social, and human worlds. They enable youngsters to participate in those worlds as agents whose destinies are entwined with the destinies of those worlds. Teachers help students correct learnings that hinder participation in those worlds. However, teachers normally do not do a good job of teaching students that this realignment, broadening, deepening transformation of earlier meanings is a never-ending process. We hear encouragement for the principle of "learning how to learn." We do not hear enough emphasis on the equally important principle "learning how to unlearn." Emphasis on this principle promotes the understanding that our making of meaning as individuals *and* communities is always a provisional enterprise. Our meanings always have to be revised for a deeper and broader understanding (Kuhn, 1970). When they teach the importance of unlearning as a necessary component of life-long learning, schools avoid the mistake of turning out young people who believe that the world really conforms to what their 10th-grade textbooks said it was.

The making of meaning is bound up with the community's self-identification in relationship to the physical, social, and human worlds. The immature individual's making of meaning cannot pursue its course independent of the community's sense of its relationship to the physical, social, and human worlds. Hence, schools present the community's meanings as the school's curriculum. However, schools also need to teach that these meanings are not frozen and totally exhausted in their current cultural expression. Hence, the work of the school also needs to promote the exploration of alternative expressions of standard cultural meanings or new applications of traditional meanings to different problems or questions. For example, feminist ways of framing questions now challenge traditional cultural meanings that previously framed those questions. Likewise, environmental concerns require the reframing of issues previously thought to be firmly understood (and settled) by other meaning frames. The reshaping of issues related to the conduct and economics of warfare—and the warfare of economics—may be required by new global alignments, the international community's need to suppress the production of nuclear and biological weapons, the redistribution of global sources of economic power, and the emerging global consensus on human rights. The realities of global scarcity and global environmental deterioration require a reformation of the meanings traditionally associated with market economics. A society whose schools do not equip its younger generation with the expectation that its current understanding of itself in relationship to the physical, social, and human worlds are limited and continually need to be re-imagined, re-fashioned, reformed is preparing itself for a dysfunctional future. It is placing itself more at risk than it was a generation ago, when a panel of national leaders thought the nation was at risk for not teaching enough students enough of the correct answers (National Commission on Excellence in Education, 1983).

Hence, when we speak of the work of the school as involving the student in the making and performing of meaning, we need to recognize the full measure of that task. Daunting as the agenda is, let us search for some approaches that may help us develop a foundation for this fundamental work of educational administration. I elaborate four foundational perspectives on which an administrator can build a vision of schooling that focuses on the cultivation of meaning. These four perspectives are: (a) the social production of meaning, (b) the generation of meaning in everyday life, (c) meanings within the cultural projects of civil society, and (d) learning and human concerns.

## THE SOCIAL PRODUCTION OF MEANING

First, we need to develop a reasonable stand on the nature of learning and the discovery/production of meaning. Learning is not something that takes place in isolation. Learning takes place within language communities whose lives are fed, led, inspired, and governed by traditions, worldviews, culture, and values. No individual learns independently of the community in which he or she lives. Even mature intellectuals who oppose their community's ideas, values, or traditions do so using the language and metaphors already available within the community.

Learning is a social activity that immerses the learner in a thick cultural stew of meanings. Add a little salt here and the meaning is colored by irony; add a little sugar and the meaning is colored by sentimental allusions. The knowledge makes sense only in a context of cultural presuppositions, assumptions, and prior personal knowledge. At any given moment, the meanings within the knowledge a learner grasps are limited and even slippery. The knowledge represents a temporary interpretive fix on a reality that is open to many interpretations. The production of meaning, whether by an individual or a group, is always limited and fallible.

Learning, therefore, is always interpretive, tentative, and subject to revision. No individual or group can achieve a comprehensive and exhaustive meaning of anything. The production or attainment of meaning is always cumulative yet limited, engaging yet partial, inventively new yet transitory. Learning becomes enriched when it involves more than one learner because the insights and perspectives of others can fill out the limitations, partiality, and tentativeness of the individual's knowledge. Differences of opinion and perspective reveal distortions; argument often requires returning to the material for a larger grasp of the meaning. The richest form of learning seems to take place in what the American philosopher Charles Pierce called a *self-corrective critical community of inquirers* (Bernstein, 1992). Within a community of learners, we have a better chance of arriving at richer, more complex interpretations of what is real and what is meaningful. Cultivating meaning then is a social activity in which learners share the burdens of inquiry and results of their efforts. That inquiry involves multiple texts, experiments, and perspectives in the generating of meaning. We treat the public and personal aspects of learning in chapter 9, where we look more closely at students' generation of meaning.

This foundation for an educational administrator is supported historically by the philosophical writings of Pierce, James, Royce, and Dewey—all quintessentially American thinkers—all of whom have influenced educational and social thought in the 20th century. We elaborate more on the school as a learning community in chapter 8.

## LEARNING AND EVERYDAY LIFE

A second foundational perspective for the work of cultivating meaning is to relate school meanings to meanings generated in students' experience of everyday life. The substantial work of Lave (1998; Lave & Wenger, 1991) on situated cognition has received considerable research validation in school settings (Brown, Collins, & Duguid, 1989; Newman & Associates, 1996; Wiggins & McTighe, 1998). That research indicates that "the activity in which knowledge is developed and deployed, . . . is not separable from or ancillary to learning and cognition. . . . Rather, it is an integral part of what is learned" (Brown, Collins, & Duguid, 1989, p. 32). Much of the work on authentic assessment of student learning promotes a form of student learning that is developed and expressed in concrete applications of learning to specific situations connected with the students' experience of life in the community (Newman & Associates, 1996; Wiggins, 1998; Wiggins & McTighe, 1998). Meanings grounded in life experiences have an immediacy and richness. Meanings explored in school can be illuminated and enriched through applications within the home and local community. This involves not only relating academic learnings to personal meanings found, for example, in family history, family responsibilities and loyalties, family celebrations, and cultural and religious traditions, but also relating school learnings to family economics, the technology used in the home, and the experience of nature in gardens, the cycle of seasons, and weather patterns. School meanings can also be related to experiences of neighborhood patterns (housing density, traffic patterns, commercial enterprises, health agencies), family occupations, health issues, life and property insurance, government services (or lack of them), neighborhood conflicts, neighborhood heroes, varieties of architecture, and community projects. In short, the total physical, technological, political, economic, and social realities of students' lives outside of school are rich sources of meaning that can provide a grounding for the various kinds of learning prescribed in the official curriculum. Ongoing discussions with students and their parents or caregivers will enable teachers and home-based adults to reinforce the learnings going on in both places. The shared cultivation of meaning in school and the home will generate social capital that strengthens the learning achievement of youngsters (Bloom, 1981; Coleman, 1987).

## MEANINGS WITHIN THE CULTURAL PROJECTS OF CIVIL SOCIETY

A third foundation for the fundamental work of cultivating meaning is the relation of school meanings to the large cultural projects of our current historical era and the cultural projects of our past history. For example, we often hear political and economic commentators speak of a new world order. What cultural work is needed to nurture this new world order? What new understanding of politics and economics will provide the scaffolding for such an order? How can the world community take responsibility for dealing with terrorists, genocide, pandemics such as AIDS? How can the world community take responsibility for the fragile ecosystem of the earth? How do we honor cultural differences in a crowded world that has shrunk in space and time? How do we settle conflicts in nonviolent ways? Although we cannot turn the fourth grade into a year-long discussion of the United Nations' agenda, we need to find ways to link what we learn in school to the weighty questions facing humanity.

Nationally, there are ongoing debates about resource allocation for public health, education, child and family services, affordable housing, national defense, space exploration, development of alternative sources of energy, nuclear waste disposal, law enforcement, and affirmative action for underrepresented communities. Relating any of these issues to the academic material under study provides multiple opportunities for youngsters to situate their learnings in wider frameworks of meaning.

There are other cultural projects facing states and regions that can be considered. For example, some states are wrestling with the question of what limits, if any, a community should put on political campaign spending. Other regions are dealing with the possibility of temporarily limiting the fishing in certain waters, thus threatening the livelihood and existence of coastal communities. Others face the question of prohibiting the use of automobiles and forcing commuters to rely exclusively on upgraded systems of public transportation. Still others face the challenge to keep open a local industry that provides a large percentage of its citizens with employment in the face of competition by companies with access to cheaper labor sources. Some states are wrestling with allowing or prohibiting genetically altered food production or genetic experimentation with human cells in hospitals. There are any number of significant public policy issues facing local, regional, national, and international societies, the analysis of which require the use of academic tools that students are mastering at various levels of sophistication.

We need to enable youngsters to feel an urgency of being prepared to participate in this agenda as adults. They need to feel connected to a significant discourse about the making of history. This continual highlighting of the significance of their learning also fuels the school's vision of the cultivation of meaning.

## LEARNING AND HUMAN CONCERNS

A fourth foundation for this fundamental work of educational administration is a stance that continually relates meaning, knowledge, and learning to a sense of something intrinsically human. This position sees learning as centered around questions of importance to human beings as human beings. What is important to human beings are answers to questions such as: How should I live my life? How can I maintain my autonomy, my identity as a singular individual who takes responsibility for myself and at the same time belongs to a community that grounds the meaning of my life? How should I govern myself? How should we govern ourselves? How can I get along with so and so, whom I do not like, who is so different from me? How can I find fulfillment in my work? How do I take care of my own needs while being responsive to people in greater need than I? How do I balance leisure with participation in public life? How do I make sense out of the complexity of economic and political institutions? How do I make sense out of the universe? What does it mean to say that I am responsible for what I know? The questions go on and on. They all have moral overtones.

For young children, the questions are more concrete: How do I make this thing work? Why did she call me a name? How do I please my parents? How do I make friends? How do I make up after a fight? Where does thunder come from? Why do adults get so angry? Many of their questions are attempts to situate themselves in a safe and predictable world that provides them with a sense of existential security (Becker, 1971).

This foundational position asserts that learning is neither neutral, disinterested, nor disengaged from the struggle to understand how to live as a human being. All of our relationships—whether with other humans, animals, inanimate nature, institutions, or primary groups—provide the natural and cultural space within which we define who we are (Bruner, 1990). We bring to these relationships, furthermore, a vague but enduring sense that our humanity is at stake in the way we respond to whatever we encounter—that somehow we are obligated to respond to whatever we encounter. In benign encounters, that response often is a spontaneous appreciation or wonder; in threatening encounters, the response is flight or self-protection. When the immediate threat is removed, we go back to look again, to figure out how to arrange conditions to minimize that threat so we can get on with our life.

There is a sense in which the pursuit of knowledge for its own sake expresses a noble human vocation. Although the life of a scholar can be tainted with self-serving, it nonetheless has a high moral purpose: to push back the frontiers of darkness and misunderstanding so that other humans may enjoy the fruits of new knowledge. The scholar nonetheless participates in the meta-narrative of learning and knowledge—namely, that humanity is on a journey in which we deliberately participate. Learning enables us to understand the journey and understand *ourselves* as we engage in the journey. Learning is what makes the journey a human journey, by producing interpretations about who we are and what the journey means.

Seeing the connection between learning and human concerns lends depth to the work of an educator. Bringing out these larger meanings embedded in classroom learnings provides a sense of purpose behind the work of teaching. The daily routines of the classroom can distract attention to these larger meanings and lead to a simplistic moralism or jingoistic rattling off of trite phrases. The best teachers understand the necessary rhythms between light-hearted banter, pragmatic skill exercises, the struggle with new ideas, and the dramatic moments of insight when the deeper, self-defining meanings rise to the surface. Leaders within the school capitalize on these talented teachers by having them demonstrate their pedagogy of cultivating meaning at professional development seminars.

## SUMMARY

With these four foundational perspectives on the cultivation of meaning, we may begin to discern the architecture of our educational vision. The work of educating is shaped by the understanding that meaning is socially produced and therefore requires attention to the cultural grounding of meanings and to the collaborative work of a community of inquirers. The work is shaped by an understanding that learning needs to be connected with the realities of everyday life. We recognize further how we cultivate meaning by connecting classroom learning to the major cultural projects facing civil society. The cultivation of meaning also implies that learning must be intentionally rooted in human concerns. These understandings provide the scaffolding for discussions with teachers about what is being learned in classrooms. They help frame evaluations of the current efforts to connect the school curriculum to the state and district curriculum frameworks. These four foundational perspectives on learning enable teachers to enrich student learnings while connecting to the curriculum frameworks. These perspectives help frame conversations with parents about what is important in the education of their children. They help redefine what is meant by school effectiveness.

These four foundational approaches to learning provide a sense of direction, but the landscape of meaning has not been cleared of all uncertainty. The landscape of meaning is presently a contested one. Educators find themselves in a period of historical transition between worldviews. In the next chapter, we survey this contested landscape to see both the problems and possibilities for cultivating meaning.

## ACTIVITIES

1. How can the four foundational approaches to learning be integrated with your school's effort to map instruction to state and district curriculum frameworks? Take one section of the required curriculum and apply the four approaches.

2. Talk with your teachers about the textbooks they use. Ask them to explain the assumptions the textbooks seem to make about the way students learn. Ask them what important topics are left out of the textbooks. Ask them whether the textbooks contain a point of view about human values.

3. Identify one or more teachers in your school who are relating classroom learning to the human questions suggested by the fourth foundational position—learning and human concerns. Talk with them about the kind of meanings they are encouraging youngsters to uncover.

4. Are any of the subjects or courses in your school related to a cultural project facing civil society?

5. Prepare a presentation for parents using the four foundational positions on learning described in the latter half of this chapter.

6. Are your classrooms and instructional spaces set up around the notion that learning is a social production? How would you change them to make them more conducive to this notion?

7. In your journal, reflect on how you would like youngsters in your school to interpret who they are and the meaning of their life's journey.

## REFERENCES

Becker, E. (1971). *The birth and death of meaning* (2nd ed.). New York: Free Press.

Bellah, R., Madsen, R., Sullivan, W. M., Swidler, A., & Tipton, S. M. (1991). *The good society*. New York: Alfred Knopf.

Bernstein, R. J. (1992). Pragmatism, pluralism, and the healing of wounds. In R. J. Bernstein (Ed.), *The new constellation: The ethical political horizons of modernity & postmodernity* (pp. 323–340). Cambridge, MA: MIT Press.

Berry, W. (2000). *Life is a miracle: An essay against modern superstition*. Washington, DC: Counterpoint/Perseus Books.

Bloom, B. A. (1981). *All our children learning*. New York: McGraw-Hill.

Brown, J. S., Collins, A., & Duguid, P. (1989). Situated cognition and the culture of learning. *Educational Researcher, 18*(1), 32–42.

Bruner, J. (1990). *Acts of meaning*. Cambridge, MA: Harvard University Press.

Coleman, J. S. (1987). Families and schools. *Educational Researcher, 16*(6), 32–38.

Duckworth, E. (1987). *"The having of wonderful ideas" and other essays on teaching and learning*. New York: Teachers College Press.

Foucault, M. (1972). *The archeology of knowledge* (A. M. Sheridan Smith, Trans.). New York: Harper Colophon.

Geertz, C. (1979). From the native's Point of View: On the nature of anthropological understanding. In P. Rabinow & W. Sullivan (Eds.), *Interpretive social science: A reader* (pp. 225–241). Berkeley, CA: University of California Press.

Habermas, J. (1971). *Knowledge and human interests*. Boston: Beacon.

Jennings, B. (1983). Interpretive social sciences and policy analysis. In D. Callahan & B. Jennings (Eds.), *Ethics, the social sciences and policy analysis* (pp. 3–35). New York: Plenum.

Kuhn, T. (1970). *The structure of scientific revolutions*. Chicago: University of Chicago Press.

Lave, J. (1988). *Cognition in practice*. New York: Cambridge University Press.

Lave, J., & Wenger, E. (1991). *Situated learning: Legitimate peripheral participation*. New York: Cambridge University Press.

Lyotard, J. F. (1984). *The postmodern condition: A report on knowledge* (G. Bennington & B. Massumi, Trans.). Minneapolis: University of Minnesota Press.

Mills, C. W. (1959). *The sociological imagination*. New York: Oxford University Press.

National Commission on Excellence in Education. (1983). *A nation at risk*. Washington, DC: U.S. Government Printing Office.

Newman, F., & Associates. (1996). *Authentic achievement: Restructuring schools for intellectual quality*. San Francisco: Jossey-Bass.

Nieto, S. (1992). *Affirming diversity*. New York: Longman.

Ogbu, J. (1992). Understanding cultural diversity and learning. *Educational Researcher, 21*(8), 5–11.

Rorty, R. (1979). *Philosophy and the mirror of nature*. Princeton, NJ: Princeton University Press.

Schlesinger, A., Jr. (1992). *The disuniting of America: Reflections on a multicultural society*. New York: W. W. Norton.

Schumacher, E. F. (1973). *Small is beautiful: Economics as if people mattered*. New York: Harper & Row.

Schumacher, E. F. (1977). *A guide for the perplexed*. New York: Harper & Row.

Stake, R. (1976, April). *Overview and critique of existing evaluation practices and some new leads for the future*. Paper presented at the annual meeting of the American Educational Research Association, San Francisco.

Wiggins, G. (1998). *Educative assessment*. San Francisco: Jossey-Bass.

Wiggins, G., & McTighe, J. (1998). *Understanding by design*. Alexandria, VA: Association of Supervision and Curriculum Development.

Wilson, E. O. (1998). *Consilience: The unity of knowledge*. New York: Knopf.

# Chapter 3

# Contested Meaning: Schooling Within the Legacy of Modernity

The day-to-day life of a school administrator allows little or no time for re-flection, for putting things in perspective. In the past few years, the daily and weekly schedule of school administrators has become longer and denser. Although still required to deal with parental complaints, student discipline problems, leaky roofs, budget overruns, reports for the state and local school boards, and arguments over faculty parking spaces, school ad-ministrators are also expected to take charge of the whole school improve-ment effort. That means bringing teachers' lesson plans into conformity to curriculum standards, initiating and supporting appropriate staff develop-ment efforts to develop teachers' capacities to bring all students to higher levels of achievement on state and district tests, as well as having teachers develop appropriate rubrics for student assessment and strategies for re-mediation programs for underachieving students (Strojny, 2002). Unfortu-nately, educators are swept up in the present policy and politics of national school reform, as well as the daily crises of the local school community, without realizing how larger cultural transitions are also at work under-neath the surface of the messiness and conflict of everyday institutional life.

The human philosopher Hegel is reportedly the author of the trenchant comment, "History is what takes place behind our backs" (Barrett, 1972, p. 3). Indeed, the chroniclers of present-day events, whether journalists or anchorpersons, are rarely able to distinguish between superficial events and events of lasting historical significance. We grasp what is happening "behind our backs" only when we have time to place events in perspective, to link events with a discernible pattern, and thus to form an interpretation that connects our micronarrative to the larger macronarrative. Particularly in

**43**

times of cultural transition, we are apt to dismiss the early signs of change as idiosyncratic, temporary aberrations in the smooth flow of public order. Thus, the first changes in accepted standards of taste, esthetics, political behavior, or lifestyles, as well as changes in scientific paradigms and philosophical perspectives are usually greeted with resistance, ridicule, condemnation, or various other forms of censure. After a while, however, certain cultural shifts begin to become more accepted, legitimate, and sensible, and they are eventually judged to be significant, promising, and enlightened.

We seem to be at a historical point when we in education need to take account of what has been happening "behind our backs," so to speak, in art, philosophy, social theory, technology, the sciences and humanities, and certainly geopolitics. We need to attend to the ways the world of scholarship as well as political and economic activity have been fundamentally refashioning the way we look at our world. Earlier frameworks, presuppositions, and bedrock principles have been challenged, modified, discarded, or reworked. Although an overarching sense of the emerging certainties may yet escape our grasp, we are beginning to realize that the old certainties are clearly inadequate, misguided, inappropriate, or invalid.

These old certainties make up what we have come to accept as the modern worldview. The assumptions behind this modern worldview are, by and large, the assumptions behind the certainties being taught directly or indirectly in our schools. Indeed, in most instances, proposals for school reform are based on the familiar beliefs of the modern worldview. The legislatures, business groups, and educational professionals proposing these reforms appear to be unaware of the shift that has been going on for well over half a century in art, philosophy, sciences, social sciences, and humanities, and how these shifts are now affecting global political alliances. The shift has been taking place behind their backs as well.

Peter Drucker (1989), a man usually a step ahead of his contemporaries, summarized the shift rather dramatically:

> Within the next decades education will change more than it has changed since the modem school was created by the printed book over three hundred years ago. An economy in which knowledge is becoming the true capital and the premier wealth producing resource makes new and stringent demands on the schools for educational performance and educational responsibility. A society dominated by knowledge workers makes even newer and even more stringent demands for social performance and social responsibility. Once again we will have to think through what an educated person is. At the same time, how we learn and how we teach are changing drastically, the result, in part, of new theoretical understanding of the learning process, in part of the new technology. Finally, many of the traditional disciplines of the schools are becoming sterile, if not obsolescent. We thus also face changes in what we learn and teach, and indeed in what we mean by knowledge. (p. 232)

## THE MOOD OF MODERNITY

Despite the caring and inventive efforts of individual teachers to engage their students in meaningful learning, schools, by and large, continue to reflect perspectives of early modernity that have come under increasing criticism from many quarters. Those perspectives were historically developed in Europe and the Americas during the period loosely identified as the *Modern World*, where most educators tend to place our present cultural reality.

The term *modern* often connotes "up to date," "progressive," "advanced," and, by implication, "better." A company involved in modernizing its production process would think of itself as becoming more efficient and effective, more intelligent in its use of resources, more rational in its strategic planning—in a word, becoming a better company. People described as adopting *modern ways* are thought of as discarding traditions (religious, political, economic, agricultural, aesthetic) that had become obsolete, anachronistic, or dysfunctional in favor of the more rational, scientific, and universal. Driven by these attitudes, the proponents of the ways of modernity were often involved in colonizing traditional societies, establishing commercial empires, or bringing disparate tribes and people under the umbrella of the nation state.

The modern world—the world of Europe, North America, and much of the Pacific Rim—gradually became the world of the welfare state, a world in which the ways in which people lived, worked, and interacted in public life were increasingly brought under the logical eye of rational inquiry and rational control (through political science, economics, sociology, education, public administration, social psychology, law enforcement, etc.). No matter that the welfare states were to be found in vastly different cultures called Japan, India, Canada, Germany, and the United States; the rationalization and bureaucratization of public life were the primary mechanisms of organizing the society. Schools in those states absorbed the ideology of modernity and were expected to produce thoroughly modern citizens.

At this point, it might be helpful to summarize the basic tenets of modernity.[1] In such an attempt, however, it would be important to observe the caution urged by Richard Bernstein who suggested that terms like *modernity* and *the modern world* are slippery, vague, and ambiguous. The term *modernity* should be understood more as a mood that, however amorphous, "exerts a powerful influence on the ways we think, act and experience" (R. J. Bernstein (1992, p. 11).

---

[1] In this overview of the modern and postmodern world, I have been assisted by the work of many scholars, notably Ernest Becker, *The Structure of Evil* (The Free Press, New York, 1968) and Richard Bernstein, *The Restructuring of Social and Political Theory* (University of Pennsylvania Press, Philadelphia, 1976). This overview reflects earlier material developed in *The Drama of Leadership* (Falmer Press, London, 1993).

The basic tenets of modernity might be summarized as follows:

- Science and technology, intrinsically good, are the fuel that drives society's engines.
- Objective knowledge, embedded in scientific discovery and technological invention, represents the truly legitimate knowledge of the world. This objective knowledge enables us to know all of life's realities.
- The individual is the primary unit of society; any theory of society must start with the sanctity of the individual and with individual rights and responsibilities.
- The individual, through the exercise of reason, is the source of intellectual and moral knowledge.
- The individual, guided by reason and self-interest, makes economic choices, the cumulative effect of which, when combined with the choices of other reasonable and self-interested individuals, result in the most widespread happiness of most of the members of that society.
- Under the aegis of science and human reason, human life is becoming progressively better.
- This progress is best guided by an intellectual elite who have developed expertise in the physical, social, and human sciences, and hence are best equipped to manage society's public affairs through their rational administration of state and corporate institutions.
- Democratically elected representatives of the people direct these elites to pursue the common good of society (or the nation or the people).

It is helpful to elaborate on some of these tenets of the mood of modernity to see why they may represent a naive point of view. We look at the tenets dealing with individualism, the impact of scientific rationality on our relationship with nature, our understanding of human nature, and the progressive character of modern history.[2]

**Individualism**

In the modern worldview, the individual occupies center stage. No longer do traditional authorities (tribal elders, popes, shamans, and sacred scriptures) determine what is right or true. In the theory or ideology of individu-

---

[2]This statement is attributed to the German philosopher Hegel by the French philosopher Jean Paul Sartre as recounted by William Barrett in *Time of Need: Forms of Imagination in the Twentieth Century*, Harper Colophon, New York, 1972, p. 3.

alism, the individual, by the exercise of reason, determines right and truth either by deductive logic or scientific proof.

Another view counters that the individual is neither the primary source of knowledge nor the primary judge of truth. Individuals are embedded in cultures and language communities. What is accepted as knowledge is socially constructed by these cultures and communities. Similarly, what is defined as morally right or wrong is determined by the community. One may not necessarily be happy with the location of knowledge and morality within the community—indeed, many go to great lengths to demonstrate that this knowledge and morality is an expression of power by elites within the culture; but the community, for better or worse, is the source of what is seen as true and right.

The modern mood posits the individual, not the community, as the basic social entity. The community is seen merely as a gathering of individuals. These individuals pursue their self-interests within limits spelled out and agreed to in a social contract. Thus, each individual surrenders some of his freedom to the state in return for protection against the intrusions of others on his basic freedoms. (Most of the thinking about these matters was done by men, with only men in mind, thus the use of the masculine.) In the economic sphere, the individual pursues personal gain in the free competition of the marketplace. As the recipient of a bounteous economic productivity, the individual can achieve self-realization in consuming a cornucopia of commodities. Through some presumed *hidden hand* behind the free market, each individual adopts a self-seeking, instrumental stance toward others and yet upholds a commitment to social harmony. When that harmony breaks down, the state assumes responsibility for the external regulation of social behavior.

However, the theory of economic and political individualism is disproved in practice. Political pressures by competing interest groups continually lead the state's regulation of social behavior toward concessions, compromise, and political expediency, rather than to a pursuit of an agreed on common good. Those without political influence are not protected by the state. Only when they organize to represent their interests (through workers' strikes, civil rights protests, voter registration drives, women's political action groups, etc.) does the state respond. The state, in short, is not the impartial overseer of a free-market, basically self-governing society; rather, the state is seen to be much more of a *product* of those who control the free market. The common good of the community indeed emerges from the self-interested activity of men in a free market, the postmodernist sarcastically observes, because the common good is defined by those who control both the market and the state. "What's good for business," as the saying goes, "is good for America."

**The Disenchantment of Nature**

Along with individualism, the modern mood enshrined rationality and science. Modernity believed that science enables humans to understand the laws that govern the operation of nature. As more and more knowledge has been accumulated about the natural environment, the abstract categories and vocabulary of science have come to dominate the language and imaginations of humans as they stand apart from and confront nature. The truth about nature is contained in scientific findings dealing with atoms, molecules, chemical compounds, and magnetic forces. These truths negate the primitive's world of spirits and totems, forces and mysteries, which require a reverential stance toward nature and brand such reverence as childish *anthropomorphism.* The poetry of brooding coastal waters, dancing stars, howling winds, raging storms, singing brooks, and winter trees as bare ruined choirs is entertaining, perhaps, but when all is said and done, these images are simply a subjective projection of the poet's fantasies. Science gives us real knowledge—knowledge about how to control nature: dams to control flooding, pesticides to control crop infestation, and antibiotics to control disease. Beyond the knowledge of how to control nature, we possess the knowledge of how to exploit nature for commercial purposes. Technology creates both the tools with which to exploit nature and the processes by which nature can be repackaged in consumable forms.

The modern expectations from the scientific study of nature and its subsequent technological mastery over and exploitation of nature has tended to develop in humans either a detached, indifferent attitude or, worse, an adversarial, superior attitude toward nature. With mass production and artificialization of nature, humans have lost direct contact with the primary natural processes of growth, decay, and regeneration; they have lost the sense of the interdependence of natural processes in the environment. Nature has ceased to provide the modern person with metaphors for understanding his or her own natural processes. What may be worse, science may have destroyed man's sense of dependence on nature or any sense of stewardship toward natural environments. Humans have come to accept increasingly artificial environments as their natural environment. Their environment is more and more a mediated environment. In such mediated environments, free-floating image and stimulation (e.g., MTV and the advertising media), not stable meaning frameworks for sustained human striving, become the primary social and psychological realities.

**The Disenchantment of Humanity**

The success of the natural sciences led the human and social sciences to imitate them. More and more of the social, cultural, economic, and political worlds were subjected to scientific analysis. To reduce the complexity of the sociocultural world, however, the scientific method had to search for a limited number of variables or categories that could explain at least most of the social and interpersonal behavior of humans (Wilson, 1998). Social scientists applied the methods of the natural sciences to dissect the personal and social worlds by means of reductionist categories such as *drive, need, instinct,* and *motive.* Organizations were viewed as large machines driven by a few variables such as authority, profit, hierarchy, status, goals, and efficiency. Laws of the financial market were derived for economics (e.g., supply and demand, cost–benefit equations, risk equations).

The human and social worlds became rationalized. That is to say, all social and interpersonal behavior could be analyzed and broken down into rational explanation. The social world became disenchanted, emptied of aesthetic, ethical, and human value. The Emperor's clothes were seen to be a metaphysical fabrication of fictional threads. The social sciences came to be seen as the source for explaining pretty much everything that happened inside of and among humans in society. It was explained as a matter of power, socialization, mass propaganda, market forces, alienation, and anomie, of self-serving political alliances, the necessary bureaucratic organization of life to serve the goals of efficiency, predictability, and order.

Under the microscope of the human sciences, even human beings became disenchanted. Once their problem had been diagnosed, scientific or technical solutions could be applied to return people to a state of equilibrium where desire was balanced by release. There was no mystery to creativity, genius, or madness; the human soul or spirit was simply a cultural or religious fiction. The existence of a subject encountering other subjects in interpersonal dialogue was denied by the explanations of reductionist psychology and social psychology. Humans as economic agents were reduced to consumers and producers, all quantifiable in economic formulas. Humans as political agents were looked on as electors whose self-interested votes were gathered by political rhetoric and simplistic platitudes. Humans as citizens became objects of public policy and must be uniformly obedient to the dictates of the state. Humans as biochemical objects were seen as systems of neurologically interrelated cells. In short, humans were reduced to an assemblage of things; they no longer existed as natural entities in their own right. The notion of a human person disappeared into component systems of drives, microbes, cells, genetic codes, and neural reactions; a unit of purchasing power; a unit of production; a unit of taxable income; an assemblage of carbon, hydrogen, oxygen, and small amounts of other minerals.

Thus, we have the ultimate irony of human beings finding themselves estranged from themselves by the very process of attempting to understand themselves. Either the human person, the self as a unity, is a subjective fiction unable to stand up to rational and empirical criteria for being defined as real, or the claims for rationality are undercut by a humanism grounded in an irrational intuition of the truth about human beings. One or the other or both of these assertions have led to the legitimating of nihilism, egoism, and anarchy. Such attitudes are expressed by artists and architects in the playful intermingling of esthetic elements previously claimed to be rationally incompatible—in a recreationally defined, consumer-driven social Darwinism. In a cynical mockery of the orthodoxy of work, the truly modern person defines *achievement* through a manipulation of either the stock market, banking system, legal system, political system, or welfare system. These attitudes generate a reactionary return to religious fundamentalism that seeks to establish communities untainted by the qualities of the modern world; they have been used to justify tribal and international warfare by means of terror and weapons of mass destruction.

### The Myth of Progress

Modernity assumed that history is a unidirectional process moving forward or upward. Civilization was seen as advancing by stages. Relatively self-subsistent tribal societies steeped in superstition and tradition gradually became united with other groups and *advanced* to urban centers, which developed trade, monetary systems, more cosmopolitan culture, more centralized governing structures, and more specialized legal and police systems. Civilization then *advanced* to nation states and empires; government became separated from religion, and commerce was largely in private hands. National identity was thought to hold primacy as tribal, religious, and ethnic cultural features evanesced. Everyday life became interwoven with and regulated by a complex of social institutions. These advances, of course, went hand in hand with advances in rationality, science, and objective knowledge of the world. Human beings were thought to be better off: Infant mortality declined due to advances in nutrition, water purification, medicine, and sanitation; housing, transportation, education, and the productivity of the workforce all improved. In other words, the myth of progress asserted that as history unfolded and moved forward, guided by advances in human knowledge and science, people became happier, wiser, and more fulfilled.

The modern worldview saw science and technology, now wedded to capitalist industry and invention, moving forward under the banner of democracy, leading to greater freedom for the individual, greater rationality in civic and international affairs, and greater harmony among peoples. It is not difficult to understand how these myths of individualism, technical rationality, and progress hardened into an ideology that placed the industrial West in a superior position to the underdeveloped rest of the globe and rationalized economic, political, and military expansion into those lands to bring them the blessings of this higher civilization. It was the West's mani-

fest destiny to bring progress to the colonies. America was the new prom-
ised land overflowing with the milk and honey of material abundance for
those who would embrace the civic religion of democratic capitalism.

The myth of progress, however, cannot stand up to the evidence of two
world wars and numerous regional wars that have unleashed massively destructive weaponry against both combatants and citizens. It cannot stand up
to the evidence of extermination camps, racial and ethnic demonization,
ethnic cleansing, torture chambers, widespread political imprisonment,
state surveillance of all citizens, and terrorism both real and symbolic. Beyond the violence of war and political oppression, one finds widespread evidence of impulsive and random cruelty among racial, ethnic, and religious
protagonists. Almost daily, reports of domestic violence and child abuse
compete with the now familiar headlines of widespread drug abuse, prosti-
tution, and pornography. Gun-carrying children have replaced stereotypi-
cal gangsters as impulsive killers in the popular imagination. More recently,
international and homegrown terrorists spread anxiety in a world that was
supposedly moving into ever brighter and promising vistas.

The engines of progress—business corporations, government institutions, cultural institutions, and the elites who run them—are often shown
to be subject to a scandalous lack of rational or moral integrity. Hardly a day
passes without some report of corporate fraud, government venality and de-
ceit, vindictive use of power, disregard for the environment, religious big-
otry, inattention to public safety, unsafe products, false advertising claims,
price rigging, insider trading, accounting fraud, sexual harassment, or
reckless investment by *trust* institutions. The public is exposed to behavior
previously expected from the low life lurking in the seamy atmosphere of
the underworld, now being exhibited by supposed beacons of the community. "This is progress?" we ask.

In response to the modernists' faith in reason, science, the benevolent
hidden hand of the free market, the progress of history, and the freedom of
the individual, many contemporaries question the trustworthiness of any
absolutes or orthodoxies. That attitude can be summed up in a series of
"don't trust . . ." statements:

- Don't trust the government.
- Don't trust the banks.
- Don't trust the market.
- Don't trust the police.
- Don't trust your doctor.
- Don't trust your priest, minister, rabbi, mullah.
- Don't trust your lawyer.
- Don't trust the university.

- Don't trust logic, statistics, scientific proof.
- Don't trust the corporation you work for.
- Don't trust mass-produced products.
- Don't trust advertising.
- Don't trust politicians.
- Don't trust your investment broker.
- Don't trust the media.

This sense of alienation articulates a mind stripped of illusion. There are no absolute truths, no universal principles. Nothing is pure; all is tainted by uncertainty egoism and calculated manipulation. The postmodern person knows the truth, and it is not kind or gentle. Listen to the music of the youth culture. Observe the attitudes of adolescents toward the adult world. They have picked up the message of alienation. Yet schools, by and large, continue to teach as if the certainties of the modern worldview define the way the world is and provide the enduring frameworks of meaning.

## MODERNITY CORRECTING ITSELF:
## REFLEXIVE MODERNITY

This widespread skepticism, however, has to acknowledge that the modem world has not been a complete failure, a narrative of only terror and be-trayal. The landscape is also dotted with successes, with examples of moral courage, instances of generosity and sacrifice, and the small but significant kindnesses that ordinary people extend to one another. Some corporations exhibit great concern for their workers and their customers; some are pro-ducing quality products and exercising social responsibility. Science and technology have produced many breakthroughs in medicine and manufac-turing that have benefited millions of people. Access to the information highway—the key to economic development—has spread around the globe. Many government agencies have provided many good services to people. Firemen, rescue workers, and neighborhood volunteers have stepped for-ward at moments of extreme danger with heroic actions. Not all politicians break their campaign promises. The evils of the modern world, although frighteningly real, have to be weighed against the evidence of human good-ness that flourishes despite the evil.

Nevertheless, the way we look at the world has shifted profoundly. Al-though we still believe in human ideals, we are not as confident about their eventual realization. We recognize the need for courage and long-term commitments to a future that is by no means guaranteed. Now that we have some sense of the shift away from naive optimism to awareness of the struggle, where do we as educators go from here? How do we attend to the task of administering meaning in a world so uncertain about which meanings to embrace?

The question of whether we have reached a definitive split between the modern world and the postmodern world, or whether modernity has moved onto a more mature, reflexive plane, has been debated among scholars. Without discounting the critique of the postmodernists, I tend to side with those who argue that the world is moving toward a reflexive modernity in response to an earlier, more naive modernity (Beck, Giddens, & Lash, 1994; Delanty, 2000). By critically reflecting on the excesses of early modernity, we can temper their tendency to absolutize rationality, individualism, objective knowledge, historical progress, and indeed the unquestioned beneficence of modernity. Looking at our present condition as comprising not a definitive break with modernity, but rather a development in a continuum with early modernity, we can be both critical and hopeful. Giddens' (1998) interesting proposal of a "Third Way" in political economy is a good example of a European attempt to move social and economic policy beyond the competing absolutes of socialism and capitalism toward a more inventive cobbling together of the ideals and strategies of both systems in a democratic society. Our critique does not mean that we jettison any and all attempts to arrive at rationally satisfying and compelling positions, although we acknowledge that all positions will, sooner or later, need revision and modification. Neither does our critique negate the importance of individuality and personal autonomy, although the sociocultural context of the human person is seen more clearly as coming into play in both self-definition and moral definition.

As Beck, Giddens, and Lash (1994) implied, reflexivity is a necessary characteristic of late modernity because the inventions of early modernity have produced such problematic, unanticipated consequences. Every premise of early modernity—whether cultural, economic, or technical—is expected to be questioned and, in the light of critical analysis, reformulated. This reflexivity is the source of late modernity's inventiveness. It is also the source of its anxiety. With few certainties to guide invention, no one knows ahead of time whether the invention (e.g., genetic engineering) will be more harmful than beneficial. Thus, the reflexivity of late modernity must be a shared cultural activity that can lead to a more consistent reflexive choosing to act, as well as a consistent awareness of codependency in relationships. Mutual reflexivity, especially when linked to systems thinking, leads to an increased sense of coresponsibility for the social and institutional consequences of choices as indeed we see in the best efforts at school renewal (Leithwood & Prestine, 2002). This characteristic of reflexivity surfaces again in our exploration in later chapters on community and moral excellence, as well as the chapter on learning.

For the contemporary educator, there remains the hard work of absorbing the "new realities," as Drucker reminds us, of creating a synthesis of the new and old worldviews (with the awareness that not everything in the old worldview should be discarded, and that not everything in the new should be accepted), and of bringing the mission and purposes of schooling into alignment with this new synthesis. Then comes the inventive work of constructing an appropriate curriculum and pedagogy for the school of the future.

The redesign of schooling cannot wait for a research and development team of education experts to design a prototype of such a new school in a laboratory somewhere over the course of a 5-year period. Schools have to be redesigned even while they are functioning in the old ways. It is like redesigning an airplane while it is on a protracted series of flights. When the plane lands, a new set of wings is fitted on. At the next landing, a new tail rudder replaces the old one. On the next landing, new engines are installed. In flight, the pilots and navigators carry out their new training protocols and fine tune the new systems as they go. That is not, of course, the way the airline industry is run, but it is the way the educational industry is run. School administrators responsible for cultivating meaning have to manage this refitting, retooling, and retraining while the school is in flight, and when it lands for the summer or between semester breaks, they have to replace dysfunctional pieces and install new ones.

I am not proposing any specific new designs. Rather, I suggest that educational administrators can cultivate the pursuit of meaning in this time of transition primarily through engaging teachers and parents in the process of creating and enacting a vision for their school that responds to their local context. The beginnings of a way out of the ruins of a discredited modernism are already at hand, although the shape and direction of its flowering is inchoate and indeterminate at present. The way out is to go forward, neither clinging stubbornly to the absolutes of early modernity nor jettisoning wholeheartedly the agenda of the Enlightenment. Rather, the way forward is to explore new understandings of the natural, social, and human worlds, and to bring new meanings to the learning process. On such understandings a new vision of schooling can be forged.

## VISION

I propose that an essential work of administration is to construct a preliminary vision for the school and engage the rest of the school community in the process of developing a common vision for the school. This would be a fundamental way to direct the school community toward the cultivation of meaning.

The development of a collective vision of where the school should be going is fundamental to the work of an educational administrator. This kind of activity involves both process and content. Developing a collective vision involves sharing ideas, clarifying and understanding the various points of view reflected in the community as well as the beliefs and assumptions underneath those points of view, negotiating differences, and building a consensus. Developing a collective vision also involves the content of that vision. Administrators do not possess the total content of this vision—no one does—but they should be willing to lay out their own attempt at articulating the content of a vision.

A credible vision of education must begin with the sense of the transition between early modernity and the later, more reflexive modernity. A vision of education that reaches beyond the critique of modernity must be based, paradoxically, on the very reasoned inquiry, scientific study, and scholarly theories that early modernity championed. Fortunately, within the natural and social sciences, as well as the humanities, there is emerging a view of nature, society, the human person, and knowledge that reverses the naive, reductionist determinism of earlier natural, social, and human sciences. These developments can be found in the recent work of many scholars—work that, to my mind, has been ably summarized by Turner (1991).[3] Although a thorough presentation of this work is beyond the scope of this chapter, a brief summary is offered to point out how dramatically these emerging views recast the human adventure, and therefore the kind of education that is called for. This is an education that places human beings and human social life within the dynamics of the natural universe, not outside of it, opposed to it, or orphaned by it. Isolated individualism is thus transformed by the intrinsically relational nature of all reality, rationalism is transformed by a field theory of intelligence, the myth of progress is transformed into the myth of social responsibility, and

---

[3]Besides the work of Frederick Turner, *Rebirth of Value: Meditations on Beauty, Ecology, Religion and Education* (State University of New York Press, Albany, 1991), additional sources include: Sir John Eccles, Roger Sperry, Ilya Progogine, and Brian Josepheson, *Nobel Prize Conversations* (Saybrook, New York, 1985), Stephen W. Hawking, *A Brief History of Time* (Bantam, New York, 1988), Vladimir Lefebre, "The Fundamental Structures of Human Reflection" (*Journal of Social and Biological Structures, 10,* 1987), James Lovelock, *Gaia: A New Look at Life on Earth* (Oxford University Press, Oxford, 1979), Lynn Margulis and Dorian Sagan, *Microcosmos: Four Billion Years of Microbial Evolution from Our Microbial Ancestors* (Summit, New York, 1986), Ilya Prigogine and Isabelle Stengers, *Order out of Chaos: Man's New Dialogue with Nature* (Bantam, New York, 1984), Ingo Rentschler, Barbara Herzberger, and David Epstein (Eds.), *Beauty and the Brain: Biological Aspects of Aesthetics* (Birkhauser, Boston, 1988), Thomas I. Scheff, *Microsociology: Emotion, Discourse and Social Structure* (University of Chicago Press, Chicago, 1990), George A. Seustad, *At the Heart of the Web: The Inevitable Genesis of Intelligent Life* (Harcourt Brace, New York, 1989), and Danah Zohar and Ian Marshall, *The Quantum Society* (Flamingo, Harper Collins, London, 1994).

the hidden hand of self-seeking economics is transformed into the cooperative economy of the global community.

## EMERGING VIEWS OF NATURE, SOCIETY, AND THE HUMAN PERSON

The new view of the natural universe is one of a free, unpredictable, self-ordering evolutionary process. Throughout the long history of cosmic and terrestrial evolution, the basic theme that all natural scientists find is reflexivity or feedback. It appears as though the universe is continually experimenting, discarding what does not work and keeping what does. The experiment is nonlinear and therefore generates new future states that, while folding earlier forms into themselves, are not predictable but only describable after the fact (Turner, 1991).

The generative feedback process is exemplified in the evolution of life forms and perhaps most clearly in our own evolution. The feedback principle shaped the long history of our biological development, and indeed it is the origin of our own reflexive self-awareness and self-reflection. Humans seem to be naturally designed for learning and creativity. Human reflexivity enabled us to speed up the evolutionary process, so to speak, of the universe's slow process of reflexive experimentation. Collectively engaging in the feedback of our own learning and creative experimentation through the free exchange and criticism of ideas, we can assist the journey of an intrinsically intelligent cosmos into fuller transcendence of itself (Berry, 1999).

Psychobiology, neurology, paleogenetics, paleoanthropology, archeology, and other scientific specialties point to deep structures in the human brain and body that exhibit this reflexivity. Between the last phases of human biological evolution and the initial phases of human cultural evolution, there appears to have been an overlap of between 1 and 5 million years. During this time, we were in the process of domesticating ourselves. The overlap of more than 1 million years suggests that our own cultural evolution was a major influence on the genetic material that in its later stages constituted our human species (Turner, 1991). In other words, cultural and genetic evolution during this time engaged in a mutually shaping relationship; indeed, cultural evolution may have driven biological evolution. What emerged was a species equipped to learn through creative exploration and expression. What is natural to the human species suggests the kind of education that should stimulate and develop this talent.

What also emerged during this evolution was a naturally satisfying response within the human brain to beauty. Traditional archeology tended to present human prehistory in pictures of hulking males hunting and making tools. More recent paleoanthropology complements this picture by identifying women as the culture bearers. Their legacy was weaving and sewing, language and conversation, the daily rituals of gardening and cooking, children's lullabies, and evening storytelling—in short, the gradual creation of a reflexive esthetic sense.

The theme of reflexivity is also postulated for the planet earth in the Gaia hypothesis (Lovelock, 1979). This theory proposes that the enormous networks of mutual interactions between the organic and inorganic elements of the earth's surface make up a living, reflexive, organic system. As in the case of a small living organism, this larger organism reacts to threats it perceives in its environment. Humans make up part of this organic system; we are dependent on this ecological environment and tamper with it at our peril. Gaia is our *mother*; we are part of this larger whole and bear responsibilities to that larger source of our life. If we damage the source of our life, we may in turn be destroyed as one of nature's experiments that failed.

Some physicists even postulate an *anthropic principle*, which is reflexivity extended to a cosmic scale. This principle of quantum theory stipulates that, for the universe to become actual, it had to produce a human knower whose observation of the universe would force the universe to collapse from the realm of the possible into actuality. Thus is human knowledge implicated in the evolution of the universe toward the human.

This thinking is a far cry from the reductionism and determinism of earlier forms of science. Turner (1991) summed it up well:

> In the new science of the late Twentieth Century, theoretical physics can find common ground with oriental mysticism; free, self-organizing systems are plausible not only in the human world, but throughout the world of matter; our common inheritance with the higher animals has become for us a source of strength and health, not a restriction on our freedom; and our human creativity now appears to be only the most intense form of the generous creativity of nature. Meanwhile, we have begun to see how a more sophisticated technology can act in harmony with nature and even begin to heal the scars that our earlier and cruder technologies have bequeathed us. (p. 46)

We hear echoes of this observation in remarks by Vaclav Havel (1994) when he received the Philadelphia Liberty Medal on July 4, 1994:

> Paradoxically, inspiration . . . can once again be found in science, in a science that is new—post modern—a science producing ideas that in a certain sense allow it to transcend its own limits. I will give two examples . . . [He cites the anthropic cosmological principle and the Gaia hypothesis and then continues.] The only real hope of people today is probably a renewal of our certainty that we are rooted in the earth and at the same time, the cosmos. This

awareness endows us with the capacity for self-transcendence. (*The New York Times*, p. A27)

We might add that this new awareness offers us the ground for a vision of the educated person.

## A NEW UNDERSTANDING OF KNOWLEDGE

Besides the transformation of modernist science toward a new view of the cosmological history of the universe and human evolution, there has emerged a new understanding of knowledge itself. Within the mood of late modernity, we discover a series of insights concerning the nature of knowledge as a sociocultural construct. Learning is seen as involving the learner in knowledge production. Learning is understood as inescapably involving the self's own narrative—the self's self-creation and realization. Learning is also seen as the individual's cultural production in relationship to communities of language and memory. These insights are embedded, to be sure, in the large theme of reflexivity elaborated earlier, but they need to be developed sufficiently for us to see how they can become additional ingredients of our vision of a new way of educating.

## KNOWLEDGE AS A HUMAN AND SOCIAL CONSTRUCT

We saw in previous chapters that knowledge is no longer seen as a one-to-one correspondence with *the thing out there* independent of the knower. Rather, knowledge of some external reality is understood as a conceptual or metaphorical interpretation of that reality, a partial grasping of some aspect of that reality. That partial grasping, however, involves the internal mental operation of a cultural being—a member of language community, a person with a life history and previous learning experiences, and a historical context in which the learning is taking place (a context that is favorable or unfavorable, threatening or nurturing, anxiety filled or relaxed, with friends or strangers, easily related to recent experiences or something totally new, etc.)—all of which predispose the knower to apprehend that external reality within a tapestry of prior meaning, value, and affective frameworks. What is known, then, is something that, although it exists in relationship to an external reality, is a human and social construct. It is a human construct in that it is produced by a human being with specific prior personal and cultural experiences. It is a social construct in that it is shaped by the language and culture of the society that the knower inhabits and by the immediate social context of the classroom. It is in relationship to external realities such that any action based on this knowledge must take that reality into account. If I jump out of a 20-story building, my knowledge of gravity tells me to expect certain consequences.

## SPATIAL AND TEMPORAL IMPLICATIONS
## OF KNOWING

We now recognize that knowledge is not an isolated piece of information, but rather that every piece of knowledge means something in relation to the larger meaning paradigms within a culture. A rock painting of a kangaroo in a cave in the Northern Territories of Australia means something to an Australian Aboriginal tribal elder and something quite different to a European tourist. To an archaeologist or anthropologist, the same rock painting means something different than it would to a White, Australian schoolboy. In the act of apprehending the significance of the rock painting, each person also tacitly positions herself in relation to that rock painting. For some, it positions them as members of a culture quite different from the aboriginal culture. For others, it positions them in time as members of a race of people whose cultural artifacts date back around 40,000 years, suggesting that the observers are somehow part of that 40,000-year journey.

When I learn something in science—say, the physics of gravitational force—tacitly I know something about myself in relationship to that piece of information. I know something about how gravity affects me. I know that I am in a gravitational field that places me in relationship to the heavenly bodies of our galaxy. Similarly, when I learn something about the food chain in certain oceans, I know, again tacitly, something about myself—about how I live in a natural environment of various kinds of food and as part of a food chain that sustains the food I eat. In other words, everything I learn about the world I live in teaches me, although usually at a subliminal level, something about myself. Knowledge positions me in a place and time within a network of relationships.

## KNOWLEDGE AND SELF-KNOWLEDGE

In a real sense, then, we can say that whenever I learn anything, I am simultaneously and of necessity learning something about myself. If, in the continuing process of learning, I am repositioning myself again and again in relationship to temporal and spatial realities and to my culture, I am continuously reproducing myself. The self I am coming to know is more and more involved in a variety of relationships to the realities of the world I am learning about. For example, if I make a new friend, there is something new about me: My experience is now enlarged by my friend's experience, my responsibilities to other people are realigned to take account of my responsibilities to my new friend, and my new friend discloses a new appreciation of myself that I did not have before. A new enemy may also challenge me to create and understand new aspects of myself. If my ethnic community is Italian, Irish, or Chinese, then as I learn the history of my people, I take on a growing understanding of myself as belonging to a specific cultural and political history; I become enlarged by belonging to a cultural and historical community. I am not alone; I am part of something much bigger than myself.

As I reflexively re-create myself during new learning about my world through my active participation in a language and cultural community, the results are not always beneficial to my growth as a human being. If the cultural worldview of the language community that educates me believes that nature is an inexhaustible resource available for exploitation and consumption, then the meaning of the food-chain lesson may create a self-understanding that justifies my relationship to nature as an exploiter. If the worldview of my language community believes that women are inferior to men, then what I learn about women in history and literature may create a self-understanding that places me in a domineering relationship to women. In other words, the worldview that stands behind the explicit curriculum of the school carries all kinds of messages that in turn form the self-understanding of the individuals who learn that curriculum (Newman, 1992).

Usually learning in schools implies that we are learning about reality as it is, rather than learning about how our cultural community has come to interpret reality. If schools communicate that what we learn is the way things are, then we come to identify school learning as objectively defining reality. Gradually, this kind of fixing of reality into what schools teach us about the culture's interpretation of reality leads naturally to our expectation that this is the way reality *should* be, or at least that this is the way reality always has been and always will be. To change the way reality is presented in school (e.g., by changing the perspectives for interpreting the relationships between classes of people, between the sexes, or between the races; changing the definition of biological life; providing a contrary interpretation to a moment in history) can be seen as a violation, a dangerous interruption of life's natural regularities. Thus, do controversies over "sensitive topics" rise to the surface at school board meetings and in letters to the editors of local newspapers.

## KNOWLEDGE AS INTERPRETATION

One of the insights driven home by the late modern mood of critical reflexivity is that language and knowledge are not neutral. Categorizations fix people and things in hierarchies, in superior or subordinate positions in relationships to other people or things (Freire, 1970). Think of the terms *welfare* and *tax incentives*. The first term carries many negative overtones; the second connotes quite different relationships between the state and private individuals. Both, however, signify financial benefits bestowed on some people by the state in the interests of the common good. In our culture, one is supposed to be ashamed to be on welfare; in contrast, receiving tax incentives is a sign of privilege. When youngsters learn these things in school, they are positioning themselves in a meaning system that has already made cultural judgments on their position in the social order. Such knowledge creates self-definition. In reproducing such knowledge, youngsters reproduce definitions of themselves.

Those definitions are, as implied in the language the school uses to teach them, relational. Hence, my self-definition places me in some kind of pecking order in relation to others in the classroom and the community. Whether the distinctions are related to wealth, gender, sexual preference, race, ethnic heritage, physical size, neighborhood, age, IQ scores, athletic ability, and so on, youngsters pick up the value preferences within the culture and the subculture that the school teaches. This is the tacit curriculum, which even teachers are not usually aware they are teaching.[4] What is worse, the students are not aware that they are absorbing biases, stereotypes, and ethical judgments implied in classroom language. The process of self-definition, and hence of self-creation, seems to proceed effortlessly and without conceptual explanation. For the youngster, life simply unfolds and presents new information and experiences every day.

This does not mean that some of the learning is not painful. However, it is usually communicated in such a way that it seems simply to explain impartially the way the world runs. There is no singling out of an individual as an object of someone else's evil intentions. The individual is simply part of a group (women, poor people, Asians, corporate stockholders, etc.) that exists in this relationship to the rest of the members of society.

It must be understood, as well, that the process of learning involves the continuous re-creation of the world. With every new understanding, I add something new to the tapestry of my understanding of the world. Some-

---

[4]This curriculum and its deep cultural assumptions are documented by many scholars. To mention a few: Robert Dreeben, *On What Is Learned in School* (Addison-Wesley, Reading, MA, 1968), Philip W. Jackson, Robert F. Boostrom, and David T. Hansen, *The Moral Life of Schools* (Jossey-Bass, San Francisco, 1993), Paulo Freire, *Pedagogy of the Oppressed* (Continuum, New York, 1970), Orit Ichilov, *Political Socialization, Citizenship Education, and Democracy* (Teachers College Press, New York, 1990), Susan Hynds, *On the Brink: Negotiating Literature and Life with Adolescents* (Teachers College Press, New York, 1997), C. A. Bowers and David Flinders, *Responsive Teaching: An Ecological Approach to Classroom Patterns of Language, Culture, and Thought* (Teachers College Press, New York, 1990), and Thomas S. Popkewitz, *A Political Sociology of Educational Reform* (Teachers College Press, New York, 1991).

times tacitly, sometimes with brilliant clarity, this new understanding causes me to realign the relationships among the various elements of this tapestry. These new understandings of the world are not something I create out of nothing. They are new understandings shaped by the language, images, and meta-narratives of my cultural and language community. When I learn, for example, about the Nuremberg trials after World War II, and the crimes for which the accused were on trial, I learn something new about the limits imposed by the international community on the conduct of warfare. I have to realign my understandings about warfare, about the rule of law, about racial and religious intolerance, about the depth of cruelty and barbarism humans are capable of. In all of this, I learn about the world I inhabit, and imbibe moral lessons that shape later interpretations of warfare and the possibilities of my involvement with warfare, about intolerance and my complicity in it, about the rule of law and my support for it.

I also learn an interpretation of history from within my own historical community. Had I been born in Germany, I would perhaps be offered a different interpretation of those events in history. As I grow older and study other military campaigns involving my country, I also learn that some *war crimes* are never prosecuted because the political chemistry needed to prosecute them is suppressed. I learn that intolerance includes subtle as well as overt forms of violence, and that the law tends to serve those who control its exercise. My relationships to the realities of warfare, law, and intolerance continue to shift and, as they do, a different me emerges, yet it is a me that continues to be shaped and, to some degree, controlled by my cultural community.

Another aspect of knowledge is that it becomes a tool for future knowledge. Through knowledge acquired earlier, I come to new experiences with ways to interpret those experiences, almost with expectations of what those experiences will mean. Prior knowledge predisposes me to interpret new things in the categories of prior interpretations. Prior knowledge becomes implicated in the new knowledge. I rarely, if ever, come to an experience without sensory and perceptual habits and dispositions that shape what I know. Knowledge of the way certain games are played enables us to quickly interpret how other games are played. However, knowledge of cultural definitions of kinship, masculinity, sportsmanship, authority, heroism, and the like provides me with an even deeper understanding of the ritual and symbolic meaning behind the games. Beyond the shaping influence of perceptual habits are habits of belief. What I know is what I believe.

Modern physicists challenge us to recognize that our theories about the physical world affect those realities. When we use a wave theory to study the motion of particles, they behave like waves. When we use a particulate theory, they behave like particles. In one sense, we produce the knowledge and then the knowledge produces reality, including ourselves.

This dialectic, of course, does not take place in a social vacuum; rather, it includes corrective feedback loops that tell us whether the knowledge we are producing and using to produce other realities is related to what appears to be out there. Teachers, parents, and peers let us know whether our knowledge and interpretations are crazy. The fact remains, however, that in this continuous process of creating knowledge, we continuously create our world. Sometimes the world that is created gets out of control, as it did in the death camps of Nazi Germany, in the gulag prisons of Stalinist Russia, and the terrorist training camps of Afghanistan. But those uses of knowledge only show us unmistakably how the process works. In the United States, the constitutional checks and balances among the executive, legislative, and judicial branches of government (as well as a free press and public opinion polls) provide some assurance that the social reality our knowledge produces will not lead to extremes. (However, native peoples, women, African and Mexican Americans may not feel so assured.) Similarly, for the scholarly community, the open exchange and critique of new knowledge is supposed to control the realities that knowledge can produce.

## RECAPITULATION

At this point, perhaps we should pause and see what we have in front of us. We have traversed the landscape of contested meaning: the disillusionment, cynicism, and skepticism engendered by the critique of the promises of early modernity. In the search for a new vision of education in the present chapter, we have discovered that the critique, although telling, has not been fatal. Science has survived—although considerably less arrogant, and with a more profound respect for the mysteries it explores. The state has survived—although considerably more transparent in its best and worst performances. Human reason has survived—now more open to multiple interpretations and seen as both limited and inventive. The individual has survived—seen now in a more organic relationship to the natural and cosmic environment and with greater social responsibilities.

Meaning has survived—understood now as emerging from a more dynamic relationship between open-ended values (not deterministic principles) embedded in self-correcting, reflexive natural and social realities. The human person constructs and performs meanings out of experience with those natural and social realities, meanings that yet rely on the cultural and language communities for their legitimization. We thus understand knowledge as a cultural product that, in its transmission, affects the self-understanding of learners. In its apprehension by the learner, knowledge becomes integrated—usually quite tacitly—into an individual and personal worldview that in turn—for better or worse—produces interpretations and shapes new realities.

With these understandings, we can begin to build a vision of a curriculum of meaning. I suggest that we build this vision around one focus: the students, not the teacher, as the primary workers in the learning process. This focus, to be sure, is embedded in our changing understandings of the natural, human, and social world as it is being developed in the natural and social sciences and the humanities (embedded, one would hope, in state and district curriculum standards). A focus on the students as the primary workers enables us to create the basic ingredients of a curriculum or meaning.

Despite the need to rethink and re-create the learning process in today's schools, educators are challenged by some to return to a world of earlier certainties, whether those certainties are grounded in science and rationality or in a religious tradition, albeit a civil religion of small-town friendliness and redemption through hard work. They are challenged by others to emphasize intellectual skills, technological literacy, or a simplistic patriotism whose only horizon is economic superiority in a global market. None of these choices offers an appropriate interpretation of the challenges the country faces in the 21st century, and none provides a framework for school policy. This is not to say that schools should not promote friendliness and hard work, technological and economic literacy, as well as patriotism. These elements of the school agenda, however, need to be placed in a broader framework, one defined by the quest for and creation of those meanings that deal with the larger human journey, which transcends national boundaries, economic competition, and the desire for ever more sophisticated technology (Hynds, 1997). This defines for us a curriculum of meaning, a curriculum that incorporates and goes beyond the state curriculum frameworks. A concern to understand and participate in that larger journey, both as individuals and communities, should frame all else that we do in schools.

The following chapters in Part One continue to elaborate on the elements of our potential vision of education. Our cultivation of the meanings behind our relationship to the natural and cultural worlds also involves the cultivation of a new kind of community and standards of moral excellence. Meaning is constructed in community; community does not emerge without a shared search for common meanings. Neither can community thrive without a moral excellence. In turn, moral responsibility must mean something in the larger understanding of the human journey. Thus, the themes of cultivating meaning, community, and moral excellence will come to be seen as organically related to each other and mutually interdependent.

## ACTIVITIES

1. In your journal, list all the people and institutions you decided not to trust well before you read this chapter. If you believed in the world-

view of early modernity, how did your trust erode? Share your reflections with your study group.

2. Identify at least five examples of early, naive modernity still prevalent in your school.

3. In your study group, discuss whether you currently teach according to the perspectives of this chapter and what that looks like in practice.

## REFERENCES

Barrett, W. (1972). *Time of need: Forms of imagination in the twentieth century.* New York: Harper Colophon.

Beck, U., Giddens, A., & Lash, S. (1994). *Reflexive modernization: Politics, tradition, and aesthetics in the modern social order.* Stanford, CA: Stanford University Press.

Bernstein, R. (1992). *The new constellation: The ethical-political horizons of modernity/postmodernity.* Cambridge, MA: MIT Press.

Berry, T. (1999). *The great work: Our way into the future.* New York: Bell Tower.

Delanty, G. (2000). *Modernity and postmodernity.* London: Sage.

Drucker, P. F. (1989). *The new realities: In government and politics/in economics and business/in society and world view.* New York: Harper & Row.

Freire, P. (1970). *Pedagogy of the oppressed.* New York: Continuum.

Giddens, A. (1998). *The third way: The renewal of social democracy.* Cambridge: Polity Press.

Havel, V. (1994, July 8). The new measure of man. *The New York Times*, p. A27.

Hynds, S. (1997). *On the brink: Negotiating literature and life with adolescents.* New York: Teachers College Press.

Leithwood, K., & Prestine, N. (2002). Unpacking the challenges of leadership at the school and district level. In J. Murphy (Ed.), *The educational leadership challenge: Redefining leadership for the 21st century* (pp. 42–64). Chicago: University of Chicago Press.

Lovelock, J. (1979). *Gaia: A new look at life on earth.* Oxford: Oxford University Press.

Newman, F. M. (1992). *Student empowerment and achievement in American secondary schools.* New York: Teachers College Press.

Strojny, M. H. (2002). *Changes in the roles and responsibilities of Massachusetts elementary school principals as a result of the Educational Reform Act of 1993.* Unpublished doctoral dissertation, Boston College, Chestnut Hill, MA.

Turner, F. (1991). *Rebirth of value: Meditations on beauty, ecology, religion, and education.* Albany, NY: State University of New York Press.

Wilson, E. O. (1998). *Consilience: The unity of knowledge.* New York: Knopf/Random House.

# Chapter 4

# Educating for Community: Modernity's Challenge

In this chapter, we take up the second major theme of the new center of educational administration: cultivating community. As we approach this theme, we have to realize that the school community we might cultivate is a far distance from the community of the neighborhood school of the earlier part of the 20th century. That is because the experience of community, and the way we think about community both in the popular media and the academy, has changed over the past half century. Cultivating community in schools today means taking account of social forces that not only erode the former notion of community, but require the cultivation of a new kind of community that functions with different psychological and social dynamics (Bernstein, 1992). That is, if we wish to cultivate a community in school that responds to the sociocultural dynamics in the larger society and, indeed, realistically prepares youngsters to carry on a reasonably fulfilling life in that society, then educators need to attend to the "curriculum of community" with different understandings of what community means in this period of late modernity. This chapter pursues the problematic nature of early modernity's promotion of isolated individualism and the artificial community created by a social contract among self-seeking individuals. The chapter moves to an analysis of the invasion of the life world by the forces of mass administration and mass production and their effects on the more traditional experience of community. Finally, the chapter takes up the challenges of late modernity to community, challenges embodied in the increased pace and complexity of social life, the instability of family life, career obsolescence, and the border crossings among race, gender, religious, and class identities. These analyses are necessary to reveal how the tectonics underlying the traditional notions of community have shifted, apparently irrevocably. The following chapter attempts a response to these shifts and develops some of the newer ingredients for the construction of community in late modernity.

## RECENT PROPONENTS OF COMMUNITY IN EDUCATION

Although the theme of community does not occupy center stage in the literature on school renewal, it has been championed by some well-known scholars. In some cases, the theme of community emerges from a focus on caring as a primary value in the educational process. The works of Beck (1994) and Noddings (1992) are examples of this point of view. Others such as Becker (1967), Bricker (1989), and Ichilov (1990) dealt with community in connection with the democratic purposes of schooling. Still others, such as Purpel and Shapiro (1985) and Starratt (1994), connected the building of community in schools to the moral purposes of schooling. Bryk and Driscoll (1988), Smith (1993), and Peterson (1992) linked concern for community in schools specifically to the making of a learning community. One of the more influential recent books, Sergiovanni's (1994) *Building Community in Schools*, grounded the discussion of community in the distinction between *gemeinschaft* and *gesellschaft* as developed by the German sociologist Ferdinand Tonnies in the late 19th century. Sergiovanni also developed the beginnings of a moral grounding for community and then went on to link community with the dynamics of the learning community.

All of these recent works, however, seem to assume that within our culture the notion of community is nonproblematic—that with more care, attention, and leadership, what we have understood as community can be restored. Perhaps the work of Bowers (1987), although not so much concerned with community as I define it here, goes to the root of the problem by attacking the cultural assumptions behind the classical liberal worldview—assumptions about rationality, the individual, and human history as continuous, linear progress. These assumptions, as we saw in chapter 3, have been seriously challenged by the historical record of the 20th century and the critique of postmodern philosophers and social theorists. Bowers, however, attacked these assumptions primarily because of their disastrous cumulative effects on the ecology of the planet and called for a change in perspective that would locate humans within an ecological web of intelligence and life much closer to the Gaia proposal.

Furman (1998) and Merz and Furman (1997) have likewise criticized the treatment of community in schools as fundamentally problematic. They contrasted the more traditional notion of community as dependent on and generating sameness, with its attendant implication of ignoring or suppressing otherness of difference. Rooting their critique in feminist poststructuralism, these authors elaborated a postmodern sense of community that not only acknowledges diversity of culture, gender, and lifestyle, but that postulates such diversity as a necessary condition for community—a condition that generates a healthier, more robust community while honoring individual autonomy. My difference with their analysis is that the issue of sameness as a defining characteristic of community is not a modern phenomenon, but can be found even more manifest in medieval or feudal communities. Nonetheless, their critique signals an awareness that a late modern construction of community can correct some of the less desirable aspects of earlier communities, and that communities in late modernity have to be far more inventive and flexible as they reflexively construct themselves.

## COMMUNITY AS A PROBLEM

Once again, let us take an idea journey so that we can understand the depth and complexity of the issue. As with our treatment of meaning, we need to see community in the light of the transition from early modernity to reflexive modernity.

One of the major beliefs of early modernity was that the individual was the primary social unit. This belief held that individuals create artificial social contracts by which they agree to surrender some of their freedom to an artificially constructed state in return for protection from others' invasion of their rights to property and the free pursuit of their own self-interests. From the philosophies of Thomas Hobbes and John Locke, there emerged a theory of *possessive individualism*, as MacPherson (1962) ably documented. Popkewitz (1991) and Smith (1993) both treated MacPherson's work as illuminating the basis for modernism's ideology of individualism and the effects of this individualism on school arrangements. Individuals were thought to possess themselves as their own private property. Hence, their talents, such as intelligence, business acumen, creativity, and artistic potential, belonged to them independent of their relationship to the community. These talents were to be developed for the self-realization of the individual, for his or her material betterment. This belief in possessive individualism was tied to a social philosophy of *laissez faire*. As Popkewitz (1991) commented:

> A common theme of possessive individualism is that society is improved through the efforts of its individual members to better their [own] positions through participation in the polity through work, and through the exercise of the entrepreneurial spirit. (p. 142)

Through a hidden hand of economic and political providence, society would somehow progress under the collective efforts of individuals, using their owned talents for self-serving purposes within a free marketplace of economic and political striving. In this perspective, community is simply made up of self-serving individuals who use the community for their own individual purposes.

The modern move toward individualism was a reaction against the smothering of individuality and individual initiative by more traditional communities of the tribe or clan, or of the medieval feudal communities governed by religiously legitimated orthodoxies and hierarchically arranged systems of power and class. Within those communities, individuals were assigned a place, were expected to function within that place, and were required to keep that place. Individual social advancement or free inquiry were smothered by custom, tradition, and religious authority.

The fear of this kind of domineering community is still with us. Not a few contemporary scholars in the field of education are wary of introducing the theme of community into schooling for fear that a strong community stifles dissent, smothers creativity, and ostracizes difference. They warn about romanticizing the notion of community and the danger of seeing only its potentially beneficent effects. Bricker (1989) attempted to strike a middle ground between individualism and communitarianism by situating knowledge as socially grounded in society, and therefore as providing individuals the rules of rationality and the knowledge that enables them to make free choices. He seems to place himself within the classical liberal position, however, when he stated in his last chapter that: "Autonomous persons should be understood as being neither totally emancipated from society, nor totally bound to it; rather, by making use of the opportunities provided to them by society, *they are able to live lives of their own*" (Bricker, 1989, p. 97; italics added).

What contemporary critics of community in schools fail to see is that individualism has been romanticized as well. The free, autonomous person who lives a life of his or her own does not exist except as a hermit in an imaginary wilderness. We are at a point in our cultural and political history where the ideologies of individualism and communalism are increasingly seen to be dysfunctional. There is a search for a more mature realization of community in which autonomous individuals can be at home and indeed be free precisely as engaged members of a supportive community (Becker, 1968). Dewey was ahead of his time when he said: "I believe that the individual child is a social individual and that society is an organic union of individuals. If we eliminate the social factor from the child we are left with an abstraction; if we eliminate the individual from society we are left only with an inert and lifeless mass" (Dworkin, 1959, p. 22).

The modern logic of individualism, however, reveals that, in its own relentless, reductionistic, rationalizing of the individual, the individual becomes *a fiction,* and that in two senses of the term. As we saw in the last chapter, modernity—studying the person from a variety of scientific subspecialties—demonstrated that:

- The individual was an isolated economic unit that could be predicted and controlled as both a producer of wealth and a consumer of commodities.
- As a political being, the self-interested, power-and-security-seeking individual could be reduced to a vote, a recipient of public services, a producer of tax revenue, an object of public policy, and a statistic in the prison system, the health care system, and the foodstamp program.
- In psychology, the individual could be reduced to an organism of drives, needs, and wants controlled by positive and negative reinforcement or subconscious mechanisms.
- In social psychology, the individual was simply a positive or negative influence on the activity of the group, a predictable pattern of behavior depending on the type of socialization he or she was exposed to, or a free-floating self shaped in response to the perceptions of others in the immediate social landscape.
- In biology and its subspecialties, the individual was a system of neurons, microbes, and DNA genetic factors.
- In physics, the individual consisted of a reaction to and a component of various energy field forces.

In the drive to rationalize the physical and social universe, science reduced the individual to compartmentalized units either of subsystems or macrosystems. Under the collective analyses of modern sciences, the individual human being as an objective, unitary reality effectively disappeared. The individual, in short, was a fiction—an imaginary composite that, on the surface, might appear to enjoy free will and interiority, but that under the objective scrutiny of the natural and social sciences was reduced to much simpler components.

Moreover, the sociology of knowledge interprets the individual as a socially constructed phenomenon. In that sense, knowledge is a fiction (from the Latin verb *facere,* to make): It is something made. The word *fiction* is often given the meaning of "purely fictitious," something purely imaginary and fanciful. However, fiction can also mean something that is made as a tool to understand. In that sense, the terminology used to describe the individual—self, human person, soul, subject—can be seen as socially useful symbolic terminology constructed within a sociocultural context to identify and name a human reality as an identifiable, dynamic unit of a social group. It is the group's or species' way of identifying members of the group. In naming this unit a self, person, and soul, the group names something that may be a quality of that unit (intelligence, autonomy, flexible adaptability, reflexivity, etc.); in naming it a self or person, however, the group also confers a psychosocial reality on that unit. The group creates the individual, so to speak, as a self.

The individual, once aware of being named a subject, person, or soul, comes to reproduce that quality in him or herself. The individual responds to the expectations of the group. The individual is socialized into becoming a subject, a source of various activities, by the group. As the individual responds to this socializing process, the individual creates him or herself as this individual, a member of this group who calls him or herself humans, Italians, Chinese, Californians, or Cubs fans. Thus, modernity again ends up, through its analysis of the sociology and the anthropology of knowledge, asserting that the individual is a fiction. Now, however, the insight goes much deeper. The individual is seen not so much as a fiction made up of simpler units, but a fiction that, while initially called forth by the group (especially by its parents), subsequently creates her or himself and makes and remakes that self through continuous sociocultural interactions with the group.

Although this theory of the total fabrication of the individual, first by the group and then by the individual in continuous interaction with the group, may appear to deny the creation of an individual soul by God, as some theologies would seem to require, it is important to remember that social scientists are not talking to theologians or thinking from within theological frameworks. Rather, they are attempting to capture, within the empirical methodologies of social science, what goes on in the ordinary socialization process of children.

The problem of early modernity, however, is that it successfully socialized the individual also to become independent from the group (MacIntyre, 1981). In freeing the individual from the tyranny of the group, it also orphaned the individual, casting him out into a wilderness of other predators, leaving him to learn the hard lessons of survival on his own, forcing him to enter into a social contract with other predators, but leaving him alone with only his immediate nuclear family as the source of intimate exchange. (I use the masculine form here intentionally because this kind of socialization has been applied especially to men.) This isolation of the individual becomes more apparent under the relentless pressure of an administrative apparatus that has grown to such proportions that it has invaded the most private realms of personal life.

## THE LIFE WORLD VERSUS THE ADMINISTERED WORLD

The life world is the world of natural human relationships: the face-to-face life of people within a family and extended family, the world of intimacy and friendship. In native societies (often patronizingly labeled *primitive*), the life world encompasses everything: the child's birth in the home, the raising and socialization of children, education in the myths and traditions and history of the community, rites of passage at various stages of life, religious rituals, the world of work and commerce, and immersion in the rhythms of nature and the seasons.

With the coming of modernity, especially in the 19th and 20th centuries, another kind of world began to emerge—a more artificial world of the state and of commerce. Public life became fragmented, compartmentalized, and rationalized through the public administration of the state. The state began to regulate banking, education, food production, use of airwaves, travel, commerce, law courts, and dumping of garbage. The world of commerce became separated from the home. Workers worked in factories and firms where work was governed by goals of efficiency and maximization of productivity, not by kinship relations, the rhythms of nature, or the cycles of the religious calendar.

The world of mass production and mass administration gradually but relentlessly intruded more and more on the life world of family and neighborhood. The government increasingly regulated the life world through laws governing marriage and divorce, compulsory schooling of children, provision of health care and public housing, administration of pension funds, and monitoring of retirement incomes. The commercial world commodified more and more of the life world, replacing family agriculture with the supermarket, herbal healing with the chemist, and the village square as the hub for news and gossip with newspapers, society columns, talk shows, and TV newscasts. Even romance became commodified through dating services, wedding consultants, honeymoon packages, and marriage counseling. Day-care centers, child psychologists, social workers, and TV programmers took over much of the socialization of youngsters.

The life world of face-to-face relationships where human beings engage in conversations, negotiate conflicts, and express how they feel about aspects of their lives, where people laugh and joke with each other and commiserate over common sufferings; the life world where people make things for one another, such as clothing, meals, and toys for children; the life world where people experience nature first hand through planting, watering, weeding, and harvesting, where youngsters see birth and dying as natural events, where one can arrange flowers and eat food one has grown in one's own garden; the life world of sickness and recovery, of tragedy and pain and loss, of the joys of intimacy, the satisfactions of friendship, the loyalties of family, the singing and dancing to celebrate days of remembrance and days of scared events—this life world has been increasingly *colonized*, as Habermas (1970) pointed out, by the artificial world of rational order, the manipulations of desire and fantasy through advertising, the reduction of individuality to predictable uniformity in state policy formation, and the quantification of interpersonal relationships and work and leisure, which are then entered into cost–benefit formulas and calibrated in the development of economic and political policies. The mind set of this artificial world affects private citizens, business executives, and public officials.

This is not to say that the natural life world is all sweetness and light. It is also a world of jealousies and hatred, of parental violence against children, and of madness and cruelty. That part of the life world deserves public regulation and therapeutic attention. Yet we should remind ourselves when reading the educational reform proposals of state and corporate blue-ribbon committees that their worlds are also affected by greed, lust for power, self-serving rationalization, and not a little insanity.

## THE IMPACT OF MASS ADMINISTRATION ON SCHOOLS AND STUDENTS

By the end of the 20th century, the colonization of the life world by the artificial world of mass administration and mass commodity production and consumption had clearly affected all aspects of schooling. Students are treated as things—as intellects who are expected to absorb required information and then reproduce it, untouched by their own sentiments and experiences, on exams. Achievement in school means meeting uniform standards set for everyone, not a personal response to the curriculum. Students are to be controlled. Their sexuality is an embarrassment. Their physical energy is distracting. Their rebellion is to be smothered. It is as if they are the adversary. Students hear the unspoken message: "No thinking for yourself, thank you. We don't need your uniqueness or your creativity, only your conformity to our agenda. Leave your personal life at the school house door. Inside this building we own you."

What results from all this? A massive alienation of young people from schooling. Students recognize the trivialization of learning. Academic studies have less and less to do with their life world. Their hopes and fears, their longings and uncertainties are not addressed. Instead their schooling experiences are managed, controlled, commodified, and artificialized by those in authority.

In this artificial world of mass administration and mass production, schooling is understood as management of inputs and outputs, efficient delivery of services, and productivity in terms of test scores. It makes perfect sense to officials of government and industry to colonize the schools, demanding that schools serve national economic policies. In their minds, schools are there to further the interests of the state and commercial enterprise, for that is what for them defines public life. Hence, school administration is expected to mirror government and business administration, and schools are expected to resemble the efficiency of corporations (Callahan, 1962).

These proposals would reduce schooling to predictable, controllable, uniform elements of policy implementation. State and commercial executives would define what skills are required, and the schools would be expected promptly to turn our compliant workers with the required skills.

## SOCIAL DARWINISM IN SCHOOLS

If we consider the present practice of education in most schools, we can hear clear echoes of possessive individualism. Success in school comes through competition among individuals using their talents for the top grades. Ranking students by grade point averages means that some will come out on top at the expense of those lower on the scale; having winners, after all, implies having losers. Those who get good grades clearly used their talents to better themselves. Those who fail either did not have the talent or did not work hard enough. In either case, no one else is to blame for their ranking in school. In this system, collaborative learning arrangements are resisted because teachers find it difficult to assign individual grades when the product is the result of a group effort. Schoolwide goals may proclaim the promotion of the fullest development of *each individual's* talents. Nevertheless, that development takes place within a system of competition for grades and competition to get into the better colleges. This system of individual competition places the individual against other individuals and encourages the use of talents as one's own possession. The system encourages a selfish concern with one's own betterment, with little or no concern for those whose chances to get ahead diminish with one's advancement.

The direct and indirect messages that schools communicate do not socialize youngsters to see democracy as a way of bringing people together to create a community of neighbors and friends who want to share a mutually satisfying public life. More often democracy is presented as a system of protection of individual rights: The democratic process is a way to protect property and encourage legislation favorable to one's own concerns. Freedom is not seen as the opportunity to share life and possessions with others in the community; rather it is seen as freedom *from* other people, from their intrusions into the individual's life of owning and consuming material goods.

As generation after generation of youth have been socialized to be independent of the community, independent of parents and extended family obligations, independent of tradition, the successes of individualism associated with modernity begin to turn sour, to turn pathological (Garbarino, 1995). In freeing student achievement as a student's possession to be used in competition against the group, students are left to learn the hard lessons of survival on their own. In other words, students are assumed to enter into a social contract with the school as an artificial community where relationships tend to be predominantly functional and defensive. Ironically, the disregard of students' need for community has brought an equally problematic reality, the isolated and alienated individual. His freedom has become his prison. He finds himself standing alone against the horizon of an impersonal social world; defiant, perhaps, in his confidence of his own wit and inventiveness; entertained, perhaps by his possessions; nevertheless, despite associates, even some siblings, ultimately alone.

Should we wonder that children raised in this environment of thoroughgoing individualism employ violence so easily when they feel disrespected? If the bonds that tie humans together are purely functional and utilitarian, then a sense of profound alienation develops when relationships with teachers and peers appear dysfunctional or hostile. Bullying, scapegoating, humiliation of failing grades, name calling and peer insults, the humiliation of appearing ignorant and stupid before one's classmates, the constant harassment of adults enforcing rules around the school, the public shame of detentions and suspensions, the easily interpreted messages of disparagement bordering on contempt—all this in an environment of competition, the staging of prestige for star athletes and star academics, the constant pressure to produce, the official predictions that one will not amount to anything without good grades—forces youngsters alienated and angry with their treatment into a group pariah status at school that feeds on itself and erupts in violent retaliation.

The damage is done not only to the surly and violent outcasts, but likewise to those who carry off the prizes within the competitive system because their achievements signal their socialization into the ideology of possessive individualism. They are getting ready for a lifetime of competition within the economic jungle, trapped by the illusory symbols of wealth and possessions into a quest that offers no satisfying conclusion, neither for themselves nor their opponents in the competition.

Another possibility, of course, is that educators build genuine communities that connect the world of teaching and learning with the life world of the community. I am not suggesting that it is possible to return to the organic community of the primitive life world. The world of state government and commercial enterprise is here to stay. The two worlds, however, do not have to be antithetical. In fact, they could enhance the values of each other. The life world, after all, requires some administration—family budgeting, negotiating of conflict, and distribution of labor. Commercial transactions in the life world are an everyday reality as families purchase food, clothing, and other household necessities. Technology has enhanced some aspects of the life world as, for example, in the availability of cultural productions through electronic media and the enhanced communication with family members on any part of the globe. However, nonexploitive dialogue between these two worlds—dialogue that serves the human interests of people—requires a profound transformation of the assumptions behind the world of mass administration and mass production.

Unless educators confront the colonization of the school by the logic of mass administration and mass production, their efforts to build a genuine learning community are frustrated. The school community can counteract that type of thinking by establishing continuous connections between the learning being promoted in the school and the life world of the students and the community. This learning probes both the possibilities and challenges of living in a mass-administered society and a world of mass production and consumption—especially the dangers that arise when that world is severed from concern for moral striving, personal responsibility, responsibility to the environment, and the human quest for both freedom and community. In other words, the curriculum should include the work of uniting the two worlds, allowing neither the artificial world of mass administration and mass production to dominate the human agenda, nor the humanistic agenda to ignore the demands of civil society and economic productivity.

## LATE MODERNITY'S CHALLENGE TO COMMUNITY

Beyond the challenge of cultivating a curriculum of community that raises issues with the colonization of the life world by the forces of mass administration and mass production, schools find even further challenges to community in late modernity's frenetic and complex globalizing society. In conditions of late modernity, traditional conceptions of community are no longer appropriate (Cogan & Derricott, 1998; Demaine & Entwistle, 1996). The traditional, publicly established order of references for identity and community (Taylor, 1989), or what might be referred to as the landscape of the cultural metanarrative, can no longer be counted on to situate either the self or community. Modern persons are ontologically and culturally homeless (Berger & Berger, 1973). In addition, traditional phenomenological markers for a sense of community or indeed of self, such as living in one place over several generations, belonging to one class, to one culture, involved in a specific type of work, belonging to one religion, one language group, or even one family—none of these can be taken for granted any longer (Gilbert, 1997). The fast pace of change, the shrinking of distances, the media exposure to instantaneous worldwide news, the explosion of knowledge on the information highway, the diffusion of allegiances across many virtual and imaginary communities, globalization of commerce and entertainment and terrorism, multinational alliances, migrations, and technological invention—these postmodern conditions destabilize, dilute, and dissolve the traditional community and, in so doing, destabilize the traditional self (Giddens, 1991). In turn, individuals in late modernity are freed from the definitions and constraints imposed by place, religion, family, and job and are engaged in a more improvisational and fluctuating invention of identity. The self is freer to be whoever he or she wants to be.

Some of this invention concerns external appearances that signal identity or at least how one wants to be perceived. Thus, people go to health clubs to reshape their bodies, to give them a new sense of themselves, filled with new energies and renewed self-confidence. Adopting a new style of clothing gives oneself a new look, a new feel about oneself. Joining new clubs, traveling to different places, trying out a new spirituality, reading self-help books, attending assertiveness seminars, joining support groups—all these are paths that the individual explores in the reinventing of him or herself. Moreover, individuals belong to more and more associations and groups (professional associations, investment clubs, ballroom dancing clubs, civic associations, book clubs, quilting circles, bowling teams, volunteer groups, political parties), and thus move through multiple communities, sometimes in the same day. Those communities provide unique associative bonds, some more intense and deeply touching than others. Membership in many of those groups can be fairly transitory due to changing jobs or residences; other memberships atrophy because of loss of interest or emerging new interests.

The external sociocultural supports within which individuals and communities forged a relatively stable identity and life course, within which communities established customs and patterns, traditions, and norms for guiding their collective life together have disappeared for most of the industrialized West. Lacking those supports, individuals and communities have to engage in a much more active and flexible creation of themselves and their social relationships (Giddens, 1991). Because membership in many communities no longer requires long-term commitments, extended induction periods, repetition of traditional rituals and conventions, nor adoption of a particular role, individuals have to create relationships without much of the more traditional institutional and cultural scaffolding that provided the outward trappings of an institutional or group identity, within which one could establish relationships by employing traditional formulas of greeting, adopting traditional topics of conversation, and so on. This means that relationships must be forged through improvisation, but without a clear script or perhaps the wrong script to improvise on. Irving Goffman (1959) would have to write a different book on the presentation of self in everyday life were he to attempt such a project within the present context of late modernity.

Lacking more stable norms and traditions, individuals and communities are engaging in more and more short-term, pragmatic agreements about their personal and social relationships. This takes place not only in the workplace and political arena, but also in the family. Elkind (1994) spoke of the postmodern family home as a busy train station where both children and parents check in for brief moments to catch their breath and touch base before rushing off to their next commitments or activities, whether that is serving on the local school committee, flying off to a corporate meeting on the opposite coast, coaching little league, taking the weekly exercise class, driving Laura to her soccer game, or taking Larry to the Cub Scouts.

Furthermore, social conflict is much more an everyday reality as tribal and regional groups attempt to protect the sources of their identity against dilution and domination by other cultural groups and language communities. Globally and locally, identity politics replaces the more traditional and ambiguously benign rhetoric of democratic community, in either its conservative or progressive forms. Neither classical liberal individualism, nor the traditional communitarianism, nor indeed a hybrid of these ideologies provide any longer a workable foundational framework for organizing and guiding a workable contemporary community (Gilbert, 1996).

Schools face the fallout from this thinning of family and community ties in the attendant loss of social capital (Coleman, 1987). Parents work longer hours, often dropping their children off for preschool and picking them up after the after-school program on their way home from work. Add to these children of employed parents the children of unemployed parents, children who bring to school additional debilitating conditions such as severe poverty, the effects of family dysfunction, neighborhood violence and gangs, substance abuse in the home, and the problems of depleted social capital increase. Finally, schools also have an increasingly multicultural student body to accommodate, often recent immigrants and second-language learners.

The accumulated impact of these influences work against the public character of schools and their mission to prepare young people for participation in social, civic and political life (Goodlad & McMannon, 1997; Marshall, 1964). The school reform agenda has all but neglected this aspect of schooling in its unrelenting focus on academic achievement. Even if it were possible for schools to increase academic achievement while totally neglecting the community and citizenship aspects of schooling, few would argue the desirability of schools graduating students whose scores on national and international tests ranked among the top of industrial nations, but who had no sense of their social and political responsibilities, let alone their civil and human rights (Goodlad, 1996).

In the next chapter, we build on this analysis of the problematic nature of modernity's construction both of the isolated individual and the artificial community, and of the tensions between the intimacy of the life world and the impersonality of the public world. The continued fragmentation of individual identity and stable communities in more contemporary times under conditions of late modernity further reveals the deconstruction of individuality and community. Yet modernity's insatiable quest to understand the basic elements of natural and social reality through the methods of the natural, social, and human sciences ironically has led to those sciences correcting some of the assumptions of early modernity about the natural and social worlds. Indeed, contemporary natural, social, and human sciences have begun to reveal a transforming perspective on the individual–community dialectic, which in turn suggests a fresh focus for cultivating community in schools.

## ACTIVITIES

1. List all the commercial transactions your school system conducts with companies selling mass-produced products. In what ways can you say that these companies have colonized the schools?
2. List all the state and local ordinances, laws, rules, and policies that govern the school's life. In what sense can you say that the school has been colonized by systems of mass administration? Contrast public and private schools in this regard.
3. Identify some of the more alienated student groups in your school. Place yourself inside their mindframe now that you have read this chapter. What does it look like?

## REFERENCES

Beck, L. (1994). *Reclaiming educational administration as a caring profession.* New York: Teachers College Press.

Becker, E. (1967). *Beyond alienation: A philosophy of education for the crisis of democracy.* New York: George Braziller.

Becker, E. (1968). *The structure of evil.* New York: The Free Press.

Berger, P. L., & Berger, B. (1973). *The homeless mind: Modernization and consciousness.* New York: Vintage Books.

Bernstein, R. J. (1992). *The new constellation: The ethical-political horizon of modernity/postmodernity.* Cambridge, MA: MIT Press.

Bowers, C. A. (1987). *Elements of a post-liberal theory of education.* New York: Teachers College Press.

Bricker, D. (1989). *Classroom life as civic education.* New York: Teachers College Press.

Bryk, A., & Driscoll, M. (1988). *The high school as community: Contextual influences, and consequences of students and teachers.* Madison, WI: National Center on Effective Secondary Schools.

Callahan, R. E. (1962). *Education and the cult of efficiency.* Chicago: University of Chicago Press.

Cogan, J. J., & Derricott, R. (1998). *Citizenship for the 21st century: An international perspective on education.* London: Kogan Page.

Coleman, J. S. (1987). Families and schools. *Educational Researcher, 16*(6), 32–38.

Dworkin, M. S. (Ed.). (1959). *Dewey on education.* New York: Teachers College Press.

Demaine, J., & Entwistle, H. (Eds.). (1996). *Beyond communitarianism: Citizenship, politics, and education.* New York: St. Martin's Press.

Elkind, D. (1994). *Ties that stress: The new family imbalance.* Cambridge, MA: Harvard University Press.

Furman, G. C. (1998). Postmodernism and community in schools: Unraveling the paradox. *Educational Administration Quarterly, 34,* 298–328.

Garbarino, J. (1995). *Raising children in a socially toxic environment.* San Francisco: Jossey-Bass.

Giddens, A. (1991). *Modernity and self-identity: Self and society in Late Modern Age.* Stanford, CA: Stanford University Press.

Gilbert, R. (1996). Identity, culture and environment: Education for citizenship for the 21st century. In J. Domaine & H. Entwistle (Eds.), *Beyond communitarianism: Citizenship, politics, and education* (pp. 42–63). New York: St. Martin's Press.

Gilbert, R. (1997). Issues for citizenship in a postmodern world. In K. Kennedy (Ed.), *Citizenship education and the modern state* (pp. 65–81). London: Falmer.

Goffman, I. (1959). *The presentation of self in everyday life.* Garden City, NY: Doubleday Anchor Books.

Goodlad, J. I. (1996). Democracy, education, and community. In R. Soder (Ed.), *Democracy, education, and the schools* (pp. 87–124). San Francisco: Jossey-Bass.

Goodlad, J. I., & McMannon, T. J. (Eds.). (1997). *The public purpose of education and schooling.* San Francisco: Jossey-Bass.

Habermas, J. (1970). *Toward a rational society* (J. Shapiro, Trans.). Boston: Beacon Press.

Ichilov, O. (Ed.). (1990). *Political socialization, citizenship, education and democracy.* New York: Teachers College Press.

MacIntyre, A. (1981). *After virtue: A study in moral theory.* Notre Dame, IN: University of Notre Dame Press.

MacPherson, C. B. (1962). *The political theory of possessive individualism: Hobbes to Locke.* London: Oxford University Press.

Marshall, T. H. (1964). *Class, citizenship, and social development.* Chicago: University of Chicago Press.

Merz, C., & Furman, G. C. (1997). *Community and schools: Promise and paradox.* New York: Teachers College Press.

Noddings, N. (1992). *The challenge to care in schools.* New York: Teachers College Press.

Peterson, R. (1992). *Life in crowded places.* Portsmouth, NH: Heinemann.

Popkewitz, T. S. (1991). *A political sociology of educational reform.* New York: Teachers College Press.

Purpel, D. E., & Shapiro, S. (Eds.). (1985). *Schools and meaning: Essays on the moral nature of schooling.* New York: University Press of America.

Sergiovanni, T. J. (1994). *Building community in schools.* San Francisco: Jossey-Bass.

Smith, G. A. (Ed.). (1993). *Public schools that work: Creating community.* New York: Routledge.

Starratt, R. J. (1994). *Building an ethical school: A practical response to the moral crisis in schools.* London: Falmer.

Taylor, C. (1989). *Sources of the self: The making of the modern identity.* Cambridge, MA: Harvard University Press.

# Chapter 5

# Cultivating a Mature Community

The previous chapter clarified the present-day tension between community and individual. We find ambivalence toward both notions in schools because schools reflect the tensions of a society in transition between the early modern and late modern worlds. This chapter attempts to expand our understanding of the individual and community dialectic by re-imagining community using more recent findings within the natural and human sciences.

## NEW UNDERSTANDINGS FOR RE-IMAGINING COMMUNITY

We begin the 21st century with the tensions between individualism and communitarianism as an apparently unresolved and irreconcilable problem. Some would have us go back to the premodern notion of community, in which individuality and autonomy were absorbed in a communal identity (MacIntyre, 1981). Others continue to pose the freedom of the individual as the bedrock of our national identity. Rather than demanding an either/or solution to the tension, our challenge is to create an ecology of community that promotes the richest form of individual human life within the richest form of community life (Becker, 1967). We are closer now to understanding community in a large enough sense to fashion such an ecology. Advances in the natural and human sciences ground new understandings of the symbiotic interconnection of all natural systems on the planet (Lovelock, 1979), a growing understanding of the reflexivity of cultural systems in their own complexification (McCarthy, 1996), and a new awareness of the continuum of intelligence in its tacit or inchoate state in subatomic physics and in its increasingly more obvious presence from lower to higher life forms to its flowering in human systems of understanding (Bateson, 1979; Bohm, 1981; Ferris, 1988; Swimme & Berry, 1992; Zohar & Marshall, 1994). These understandings provide the building blocks for constructing a richer understanding of community.

This challenge in our schools is a reflection of the challenge facing our society at large—namely, the creation of richer forms of community life within civil society. As we said earlier, this does not require wholesale rejection of the achievements of modernity or an anarchy of isolated critical enclaves (whether from the right or left) in a revolution against the excesses of modernity (MacIntyre, 1981). It is impossible to return to a premodern state of affairs, attractive as Aristotelianism appears (Taylor, 1989). We can only move forward, learning the lessons that both Aristotle and history teach us. This journey requires, however, a transformation of our limited understanding of both the individual and the community.

## COMMUNITIES OF MATURE INDIVIDUALS

Achieving or performing community is only partially realized at best. It involves a struggle. Why? Because we, although incomplete as individuals, want to be the center of attention, respect, admiration, and control. We desperately need, as Giddens (1984) suggested, a sense of ontological security—a sense that the world is not going to snuff out our life in the next moment or the next day. We want to be secure in our basic physical needs for food and shelter. We want the world to be predictable. For the world to be predictable, we must somehow, even if only in our fantasy, control it. We must arrange it to suit our needs. One way we do this is by inventing science. Science, we think, places us in the driver's seat. Knowledge of nature enables us to control it.

We also need to feel secure in our social world. We are always checking that social world to see how it is responding to us. The tape at the back of my head is always running: "How do I look? Am I saying the right thing? Am I being noticed? Are these people friendly or unfriendly, attentive to me or bored with me?" I must control my social world because that world is what defines me. It can disapprove of my actions and punish me by redefining me as stupid, dumb, crazy, or bad (Goffman, 1959).

The pulls toward self-sufficiency and self-gratification are strong. They are some of the survival instincts we inherit by being a child of nature and the cosmos. The universe appears indifferent to our needs and desires, unforgiving of our excesses, and capricious in inflicting the calamities that fall on us from nature. My life can be snuffed out in an instant by an earthquake, destroyed by a mosquito, ruined by a drought, or made miserable by a bacterial invasion. The universe does not weep over my demise or misfortune. Some humans never make it past the first 3 weeks of life; some are born with severe physical or mental disabilities. Nature appears to respect only one law: adapt or disappear. Dysfunctional species disappear. Add to the impersonal disinterest of the universe and the struggle for survival of all life forms a social environment of competition for scarce resources (whether those resources are oil, money, or a mother's attention), and we begin to recognize the depth of the survival instinct and its roots in the human psyche. This instinct, embedded in the genetic material of our chromosomes and the quantum mechanics of our nervous system, prompts an aggressive self-interest.

Yet there is a second instinct that is more mature and therefore more intelligent and more human: the instinct toward connection, toward an other, whether that other is a spouse, companion, extended family, clan, or nation. This instinct is a more intelligent and creative development of the survival instinct. It is an instinct carried in the learning of atomic, chemical, and organic structures: connect, bond, unite, and become stronger through complexification. Complexification leads to increased adaptability and creativity for new forms of self-reproduction. That bonding at the inorganic and organic levels grows toward the reflexive self-awareness of attraction.

This dynamic of attraction, connectivity, complexification, stabilization in a new form, and then new transformation through new connections is indeed the most basic law of the universe. As life-forms within the universe, we experience that law in the depth of our being. It leads us to seek connections in order to live and, indeed, to be human. We only come to experience our humanity through our connection to other humans—at first with parents, then with siblings and relatives, and then with the kids next door. These connections shape us, feed our sense of who we are. We do not enter into relationships as fully formed individuals. Rather, our relationships continuously nourish and form us.

We need to be connected to other human beings as much as we need food to stay alive. Thus, we enter the dynamic of being attracted by other people by their wit, talent, good humor, and honesty. We reciprocate by attempting to make ourselves attractive by showing forth socially appealing qualities. From that reflexive self-awareness of attraction grows the creativity of making oneself more attractive (the bright colors of some flowers, the fantastic plumage of some birds and their complex birdsong, the daily makeup and weightlifting, and the wearing of perfume, designer clothing, and even university degrees).

At the higher levels of social bonding, one encounters various forms of love: symbolic expressions of cherishing that are expressed in language, touching, and gestures (the gruff handshake between two tradesmen; the cradling of infants in their mothers' arms; the entwining of lovers; the placing of a flower on the grave of a dear friend).

At more general levels of bonding, there is a more expansive awareness and experience of love. The sociology of everyday life, the sociology of the professions, feminist studies, biographies, and popular history, help us appreciate how much one depends on the gratuitous generosity of countless people whose work makes social life possible (the farmers who produce the food, the builders who build the shelters, the planners who anticipate the complex needs of a modern city, and the countless men and women who attend to the daily maintaining of transportation, communication, financial, health, and education systems). Added to their fidelity in maintaining the infrastructure of society are the efforts of scholars and artists to probe the mysteries and complexities of the natural, human, and social worlds. They tease out and express the meaningfulness of life and its underlying beauty and terror.

Although the social world we live in is far from perfect, it is this social life that feeds us—that nourishes our sense of our individual and social identities. This social world can be seen as a gift that is gratuitously given to us. There grows a gradual appreciation that deeply embedded in the ambiguity and muddiness of social life is a massive, incoherent, yet clearly spoken collective act of love. All the effort that goes into making sociocultural life (as opposed to the self-seeking efforts of those who manipulate social arrangements to their own benefit at the expense of others) in the present, and even more so during the past centuries of struggle, can be seen as a gratuitous act of love.

We celebrate this collective act of love by remembering the public heroes of the past: The young men and women who gave their lives in battle to defend the country's future; the founding fathers and mothers of the republic; the states-people, inventors, artists, and saints whose achievements and creations continue to shape our sense of ourselves. Beyond the public heroes is the mass of humanity, whose daily performance of their work in factories and farms, universities and government offices, hospitals and homes, sustained the sociocultural fabric of past generations. These are the ordinary heroes of human history whose biographies were written in the hearts of friends and families, but who never made it into the official histories of their times. However, their lives as well as the lives of public heroes express a self-giving, a struggle on behalf of human destiny and human dignity against the forces that would destroy us. We live off this inheritance; their self-giving enriches us. They provide us examples of how we might repay the gift by adding the gift of our own lives' work to it, whether that involves raising children whose experience of love enables them to reproduce that love in their adult lives, fidelity to the highest quality of our craft, or the search for a new medicine, a new symphony, or a new world order.

At these higher levels of awareness of social bonding, one becomes increasingly aware of the gratuitous gift of nature in all its variety, complexity, inventiveness, and sheer abundance. Our bodies are extraordinary creations, the result of millions of years of patient experiment. We are the result of the efforts of cosmic dust reaching for the dream of life, the struggle of life to become more and more in charge of itself, and the amazing flowering of atoms into human intelligence over eons of cosmic time. Whether our religious beliefs posit a transcendent God or Creator, or whether we leave the existence of some divine force outside of or above the universe as an open question, we are still confronted with the awesomeness of the existence of life and its almost infinite variety as a natural miracle.

As we saw in chapter 3, the sciences continue to discover the enormous intricacy of the structures and processes of life forms and the interpenetration and mutuality among levels of life systems, from the biochemistry of DNA to the neurochemistry of consciousness to the social ecology of cultural rituals that create and sustain meaning. What this inheritance points to is a universe that is ultimately benign despite its apparent indifference to dead-end experiments and despite the chaos and randomness embedded in its very intelligibility. This awareness of a benign universe—a mothering universe, if you will—leads to thankfulness for this patient, mutely eloquent, self-giving process that has given birth to us and to a planet in which we find a home and all the ingredients for a full and rich life. It also leads to a sense of responsible membership in a community of life, so that the gift becomes enriched not diminished by my history, by our history.

## THE INDIVIDUAL'S RESPONSE TO COMMUNITY

Through this growing awareness of being bonded to and gifted by successive levels of community, we see how love generates love—how our affective, cognitive, and personal participation in community reveals to us deeper and richer insights into love as the center of these communities. Therefore, love is a response to community—a reciprocal gift of life to the welfare of the natural, social, and human communities we inhabit. In that giving, we more fully realize the meaning, identity, and purpose of our lives as human beings (MacMurray, 1970).

From this vantage point, we understand the instinct for individual survival as immature, small-minded, and self-defeating. We also see how immature communities are (tribes, cities, states, nations) that close in on themselves, mistakenly believing all other communities to be inferior to them in strength, intelligence, cultural achievement, or nobility, seeing all other communities as threats to their hegemony or simply to their survival. The more mature community embraces the community of humanity, the community of life, and the community of being, and finds through that bonding an increased wisdom and strength that are the seeds of its own transformation.

## THE STRUGGLE FOR A MATURE COMMUNITY

That is the game, epic, metanarrative, tragicomedy that is played out in everyday life. The instinct for individual self-survival pulls us in one direction; the instinct for connectedness and complexification, the attraction to loving relationships, pulls us in another. Sometimes the two instincts become confused. Often the two pulls are entangled in the same choices and actions. Sometimes one is used to rationalize the other ("The arms race is necessary for world peace"; "We need more prisons to promote the security of the community"; "A healthy economy requires an unemployment rate of 6%").

When we speak about cultivating community, we are not imagining a sugarcoated, utopian reality. Rather, we are speaking of attempting to build an environment where the pulls and tugs between these two instincts provide the very stuff of the social learning agenda—an environment that is noisy; conflicted; filled with ambiguity; muddied by the traditional vices of anger, lust, envy, contentiousness, and greed; and yet encourages trust, openness, loyalty, integrity, generosity, courage, and love as responses. Nevertheless, this struggle for a community goes on within larger communities where the selfish influences of individualism control vast resources of institutional and political power. The influence of this power will not evanesce simply by our wishing it to. Neibuhr (1932) criticized this naivete when he observed:

> . . . most . . . social scientists . . . seem to imagine that men of power will immediately check their expectations and pretensions in society as soon as they have been appraised by the social scientists that their actions are anti-social. (p. xvii)

Neither can those who cultivate such a community stand above the struggle in paternalistic self-righteousness. They enter the struggle as wounded healers, as humans who experience and openly acknowledge the pulling and tugging of the two instincts in themselves. In concert with teachers, parents, and students, cultivators of community engage in the struggle and pain of calling forth the larger, more generous, more mature instincts.

## THE ISSUE OF CITIZENSHIP

The concept of this more mature community requires a rethinking of our notions about citizenship and concomitantly of our notions about education for citizenship (Kymlicka & Norman, 1993). Previously, citizenship was seen as a role made up of limited activities required of isolated individuals who shared responsibility for the social contract. Remember that the individual was seen as the primary unit of society. The duties of the citizen, then, were to see that the social contract was maintained and the justice envisioned in this contract was upheld (a justice, primarily of legal protections of private property and constitutional rights and of legal punishments for violators of private property broadly conceived). The upholding of the social contract was achieved through participating in the election of those who would support the social contract thus understood. Because the common good was identified with the freedom of individuals to pursue their own self-interests (limited by the rule not to interfere with the legitimate interests of others), it was assumed that the state (and other do-gooders) would not interfere with the natural course of events that would result from everyone pursuing their own self-interests because that would naturally result in the best arrangements for everyone.

There would be room for charity to be extended to the destitute and mentally incapacitated, of course, but that was a matter of personal choice, not of social policy. Because citizens were only minimally a community, and much more a collection of private individuals with rights that pertained to them as individuals, being *civil* to one another meant extending the minimal signs of a superficial goodwill toward the other.

In contrast, citizenship can be understood in terms of building up the community—proactive activities that create fellow feeling among people. For example, the proactive citizen gives time and work to a serious discussion of possible solutions to widespread poverty or to the search for a better public educational system. Within the general culture, however, these activities are not seen as normal citizen activities. On the contrary, the individualist would proclaim that one's work, time, and energy belong to oneself and are to be used for one's own betterment. Everybody is responsible for looking after themselves. We should not take that responsibility away from people. If we start that, before we know it those do-gooders will be interfering in our private affairs.

Such a view of citizenship, as the minimum public participation needed to keep the social contract functioning, is based on the faulty premise of the individual as the primary unit of society. As we are coming to understand better, the primacy of the individual over the community or of the community over the individual is a false dualism. It does not have to be an either/or, win/lose relationship. We are coming to understand that communities are stronger and richer when they are made up of individuals of diverse talents and potentials. Likewise, we see that individuals are stronger and richer when they are bonded into networks of people who offer different perspectives on life, when they complement their own talents with the community's cornucopia of other talents, when they associate with others who stretch them beyond the limits of their isolated perspectives. We are also beginning to understand that individuals are sustained at every level by love—the explicit love of family, friends, spouse, and children, and the tacit love behind the generous gift of the work that sustains social and human life made by countless others in everyday life. We are starting to understand that this love, when expressed both explicitly and inchoately, creates community and gives it continuity, consistency, and value.

In this view of community, the individual is enriched simply by membership in the cultural, economic, and political life of the community and finds even greater fulfillment in responding to the community (now in the person of a beloved friend, now in the person of neighbors, now in the form of a voluntary association, now in the form of his or her career) with loving service. Through that loving service, the community is enriched and, reflexively, the individual re-creates/performs him or herself. The individual becomes a more expansive being, a more complete being by being more closely bonded to a member or group in the community or to the community itself. Through engagement with the community, the individual ceases being isolated, alone, and unconnected to anyone or anything.

Civil libertarians argue, however, that the individual has the right to choose to be alone; that every person enjoys a fundamental freedom to isolation from community involvement, the freedom to be selfish, the freedom to go off in the woods, like Thoreau, and thumb his nose at the community. This is indeed a constitutionally protected freedom. Sometimes a separation from the community for psychological, moral, or political reasons is necessary for a while. Such isolation from the community, however, especially on a permanent basis, has never been seen as a desirable state of affairs for humans. Most civil libertarians, while maintaining the right of the recluse to live that way, think of such behavior as odd and eccentric. Even in prisons, solitary confinement is seen as one of the most punitive sanctions against a person who has already been removed from normal social relations.

The normal life of humans is found in community. Even when Thoreau removed himself from his human community, he sought a deep communion with nature. He studied the rhythms, patterns, and eccentricities of nature and grounded his own identity within the web of nature's life. Perceiving the gift of nature to humans, he gave nature back to us in his writings, thus connecting us to our natural community of life.

## AN EXPANSIVE VIEW OF CITIZENSHIP

Citizenship should be a proactive involvement in the life of the community—an activity that seeks to give back to the community what the community has already given to the individual: life, talents, capabilities, energy, and love. Citizenship can take as many forms as there are relationships in the community (volunteering on a neighborhood child-care committee, serving on a faculty grievance committee, working in a clothing factory, designing a new highway bridge). In this regard, I differ with Levin (1990), who maintained that we need one kind of education for citizenship and another kind for work. Levin posited citizenship as democratic participation in the pursuit of citizens' rights (note the echo of classical liberalism). The role of worker, according to Levin, requires quite a different set of attitudes—namely, obedience to the owner or foreman, the surrendering of our rights of free speech, free assembly, and so on to the authority of the employer. Our work and our relationship with fellow workers is carefully spelled out in the contract whereby we sell our labor to the owner—a contract far different from the social contract we enjoy as citizens.

On the contrary, work can be another way of exercising citizenship. I am not simply working for an employer, I am also working for the clients of the company, the customers. Through my work, I join with the others in my company and those countless other citizens who help make the institutions of society work. The products or services I render contribute to the well-being of my society. Furthermore, if the products I produce or sell were to harm or disadvantage society (e.g., unsafe automobiles, defectively tested medicines, environmentally contaminating chemicals), I have an obligation as a citizen to speak up to my employer. If the employer refuses to respond, then I am obliged to go to the proper authorities and report it.

Another way of thinking about citizenship is to imagine the individual citizen, when he or she is proactively engaged with others, as being the community in microcosm. By this I mean that in all my relationships I should be acting out the ideals and values of the community. Acting as a *good citizen* means pursuing in all my relationships those ideals that my community stands for—at least in the minimum observance of those customs of civility, traditions of etiquette, minimal rules of social exchange, and legal requirements. If I were representing my neighborhood at some regional gathering, I would want the other participants to see me as a good representative of my neighborhood, not as someone who flaunted all the values my neighborhood stands for. That is why members of teams who represent their country at the Olympic competitions are held to exacting standards of sportsmanship and social behavior. For that moment and in that place, they *are* Italy, China, France, or Brazil. The kind of citizenship we need to promote is not a self-centered focus on my rights as a member of such and such a community, but rather a citizenship that stands for the values and ideals of his or her community. This, of course, assumes that citizens know what their communities stand for and have come to cherish those values and ideals. When this happens, the individual becomes, in microcosm, the community in action, serving itself, knowing itself, healing itself, and celebrating its nobility and its destiny. The individual, in his or her immediate circle of family, neighbors, and coworkers, becomes the community seeking a fuller expression of itself.

Education in this kind of citizenship involves a discussion of the kinds of meanings embedded in the community's understanding of itself. It also involves the practice of those ideals and values in specific and concrete ways within the school setting. Teachers can devise learning activities that require exploration and performance, within the school itself, of justice, caring, democratic processes, nonviolent negotiation of conflict, debate on public policy, sharing of talent for the building up of community, and so forth. Unacceptable behavior is seen not so much as breaking a rule imposed by the administration, but as failing to live up to a value that is cherished by the community. This response to deviant behaviors, when reinforced over years of schooling, changes the youngster's perception of the ground for moral action away from thinking of the obligation imposed on him as an isolated individual to obey this abstract rule or principle, and toward thinking of his connection to his community and how that behavior enhances or diminishes the community's life. We move from a kind of Kantian abstract ethics of duty to an ethic of citizenship, of proactive participation in the life of the community.

Preparation for citizenship is still one of the mainstream, traditional purposes of public education. That purpose is served not only by civics courses dealing with the structures and processes of government, but also by exposing youngsters to the arena of public policy—its formation and implementation in laws and regulations; exposing them to the major issues contested in public debate: ecological preservation; alternative energy sources; full civil rights for various groups disadvantaged by social and political structures; government regulation of global corporations; international agreements on investments in global economic and technological infrastructures; ownership of the airways, the oceans, the rainforests, the Internet; international responses to terrorist organizations; genetic engineering of food, livestock, medicine, human organs; immigration rights and responsibilities, to name a few. Many of these public policy issues can contextualize the academic curriculum content, thereby ensuring a greater student interest in these topics.

The purpose of preparation for citizenship has traditionally included learning to live with people whose class, race, religion, and ethnic background differs from one's own. Although traditional assumptions about schools serving a melting pot function have been shown to be naive, the deeper dream of *e pluribus unum* still remains a social and political ideal that schools are supposed to serve (Whitson & Stanley, 1996). Given the stridency of identity politics in the present, schools can no longer assume that minimum social harmony between antagonistic groups happen automatically simply by placing these groups under the same roof for 7 hours a day; they have to work at making it happen—indeed, strenuously work at making it happen. As Goodlad (1996) reminded us, schools need to teach the rudiments of political democracy, but they also need to teach social democracy and, beyond those two, the democracy of the spirit. That kind of teaching requires attention to building community at the school for its own sake, as a good in its own right, as an essential learning experience for young people growing up under conditions of late modernity when the identity of the individual and the formation of community have to be reinvented. Education for a productive life remains a primary purpose of schooling, to be sure, but it must share the stage with education in and for community.

## SELF-GOVERNANCE

One of the fundamental questions facing the individual as well as the community is "How shall I/we govern myself/ourselves?" This question covers a whole host of decisions, from how one controls the schedule of digestive relief, to how one gets a fair share of the family platter of macaroni, to how a school makes out a class schedule, to how a family makes out a monthly budget, to how I respond when an opposing player in the neighborhood basketball game knocks me down from behind. In the formation and building of community within a school, the processes by which a community governs itself, and the corresponding processes whereby individuals govern themselves, are crucial.

I am not referring to the drawing up of a student book of rights, nor of a faculty/parents bill of rights (although that may eventually be treated in a much larger and continuous development of processes of self-government). The formation and building of community should start with questions: What kind of a community do we want to be? What do we value most about the prospect of our life together in this school? When a new class comes into our school, what do we want them to know about us as a community? What do we want to be thought of by people in the wider community?

Discussions of these questions bring to the surface the values that members of the school community hold sacred. These values are articulated in stories (precision of philosophical definition is not the goal of these discussions) that provide typical examples of behaviors that reflect those values.

These discussions (which should include parents and school board members as well as students and teachers) should produce the choice of two or three central values by which the community wishes to distinguish its life. The school may want to adopt a motto or coat of arms expressing these values. These values can be embossed on a school flag, pins, or emblems, and written into a school song or school pledge. All these symbolic representations become ways for the community to remind itself what it stands for. Membership in the community brings with it general obligations to enact those values in the daily course of the school week or school year. School awards for outstanding contributions to the living out of those values can become a semester or end-of-year occasion.

Encouragement of a generalized, proactive exercise of membership is far more important in the activity of self-governance than a book of rules and prohibitions. The community governs itself by pursuing those human ideals that make living in that community desirable and humanly fulfilling. In reality, the interpretation of these values as justifying or rationalizing certain behaviors is a daily process of negotiation. There will be a pull toward self-centered behaviors. There will be normal misunderstandings between people and arguments that tear at the fabric of the community. It is the community's daily work and responsibility to heal divisions, provide space for differences of opinion, and allow for a plurality of cultural expressions while calling the members to honor and pursue those common human values that unite them.

Besides the honoring of central values that unite the community, there is a need for explicit policies and procedures for handling grievances, arbitrating disputes, and setting community goals. This, of course, requires constituting a body or group that has the authority to set the general frameworks by which the community conducts its business (calendars, budgets, work schedules, delegation of responsibilities, standing committees, etc.). This authority within the school is exercised in conjunction with the authorities of the local community and state who have jurisdiction over aspects of school life. Hence, if the school establishes a student court, that court's jurisdiction needs to be defined in reference to the civil law as well as the internal procedures of deciding disputes within the school. For example, the student court may have something to say to a student who is caught selling drugs within the school, but it also has to recognize the civil jurisdictions of law enforcement agencies in the larger community over such illegal behavior. The school may have an internal budget committee, but that committee has to function within the resources and limitations set by local and state agencies. The school budget committee may have little discretion, for example, in limiting expenditures for children with special needs.

Involving the school community or representative committees of the community in *administrative* decisions helps cement ownership of the practical decisions necessary to run its affairs. Whenever possible, however, these decisions should be related to those large values by which the community wishes to govern itself and not simply to the technical values of efficiency and expediency. Self-governance involves self-administration, but it is not to be equated with it. Governance involves not simply the administration of scarce resources or restricting of unacceptable behavior; it also involves those proactive choices that go beyond expediency to reach out in more generous ways to our fellows—not so much in the pursuit of some abstract virtue, but simply out of a caring for the person, a desire to share a part of our life more fully with that person or persons.

A community governs itself proactively by seeing to the necessary services required of all or some members of the community. These services include the communication of news and public opinion, assistance to disabled members, health and sanitation services, commercial services, and so on. In the school community, every person should be involved in some kind of service activity. This might involve working on the student newspaper, putting out the daily bulletins and announcements, serving as big brothers or big sisters to underclass students, serving as peer tutors, working with maintenance crews on special cleanup projects, serving on peer conflict-resolution teams, or working on the student court. These service activities can be cycled periodically so that students experience serving the community in a variety of ways.

Service activities that reach outside the school into the larger community can be options for the older children as well. Every child should learn the lesson that their quality participation is needed by the community. That lesson, repeated over 8 to 12 years of schooling, can create a life-long habit of community participation.

Self-governing is about self-control, to be sure, but it is also about channeling one's actions in a certain direction, and that channeling may be narrow or expansive. Governance may involve a choice to go beyond what administrative guidelines suggest to the more generous choice of self-giving. Hence, a teacher may follow administrative guidelines in providing her class with crayons and colored paper from general supplies. She may also pay out of her own pocket for a pair of eyeglasses for a child in her class whose family cannot afford them. A school may provide administratively for cooperative learning arrangements; a group of students may decide to govern themselves in a way that, besides following the administrative arrangements for cooperative learning, sets up an after-school tutoring service for younger students who are having academic difficulties or an after-school enrichment program for children whose parents are working. They govern themselves just as surely by choosing to go beyond the normal administrative arrangements of the school as by complying with those normal administrative arrangements. In that case, they are exercising their rights to help others.

Under the influence of modernity's ideology of individualism, our culture does not see that kind of proactive building up of community as part of the democratic process. That is because deeply embedded in our notion of democracy is the notion of possessive individualism, which uses democratic procedures to protect this possession, this property of *my life*, by which I stand apart from the community of other separate property owners, by which standing apart I exercise my basic freedoms. Freedom is not seen as the freedom to share my life and possessions with others; it is seen as freedom from other people, from their interference with my life, from their intruding on my living my life the way I want to live it. The rights of free speech, assembly, and owning property, however, can also be understood as necessary rights for building community, as necessary to a form of proactive citizenship on behalf of a democratic community.

## COMMUNITY AS CURRICULUM

While promoting the ideal of a mature community, educators must also work with youngsters—perhaps the majority of teenagers—who experience the social world as fragmented, impersonal, transitory, and untrustworthy. As Delanty (2000) suggested, following the leads of Castoriadis (1987) and Maffesoli (1996), community is imaginary, not in the sense of pure fancy, but as a projected state of affairs that has affective influence on people or groups that are contemplating cooperating together. We speak of the European Community. Europe is clearly a collection of distinct nation-states whose history reveals more conflict than cooperation. By referring to the larger construct of *community*, these nation-states suspend their differences to invent a greater reality. European Society will not do; it must be European Community. Community implies *solidarity*, a togetherness around common interests, *trust* that members will hold to their agreements, and *autonomy* on the part of the members responsibly acting in the social world (Delanty, 2000). Community does not smother differences. Here community relies on and prospers due to differences. Similarly, we speak of the *university community*. That community is made up of diverse academic departments who guard their territory and integrity quite passionately, although within those departments there are fierce disagreements over research methodologies and theoretical interpretations. Nonetheless, there is a solidarity around the pursuit of understanding—a trust that each scholar pursues that understanding according to legitimate methods and an honoring of the individual scholar's autonomy to conduct the search.

These guiding principles of community—solidarity, trust, autonomy—can provide the scaffolding for cultivating community at school. Cultivating community means that it is always something out in front of us, something that each day we construct, however fallible and messy. In appealing to their sense of community, we invite youngsters to work toward it.

The curriculum of community is not one course or a cluster of courses. Rather it is a sequence of multiple learning activities spread out over the whole K–12 curriculum. Some of these learning activities take place in the classroom through deliberations of how the class will comport itself; some are explicitly connected to learnings in the academic subjects such as geography, history, literature, science, world languages, and art; some take place on the playground, in the cafeteria, or on the school bus; some might be learned in group communication exercises run by the guidance department or homeroom teachers; some may be learned in school-sponsored special events for grandparents and parents. The curriculum of community is likewise taught by the establishment and maintenance of a school honor code, by the establishment of and frequent reference to schoolwide core values, by the daily engagement of student conflict-resolution teams, in activities conducted by the student government and student court, in school-sponsored community service activities, through big-brother, big-sister arrangements, through peer tutoring programs, through the dramatization of student issues in dramas, musical comedies, and artistic displays, and through special assemblies where civic community issues are deliberated. The curriculum of community is explicitly taught in all the co-curricular activities of the school as well, through the exercise of teamwork and contributing to a sense of pride in the school.

Much of the curriculum of community grows out of the community issues students bring to school, such as conflicts over cultural expressions of pride, identity, attitudes toward authority; perceived inequalities in the way different groups are treated; learning styles; relationships with teachers; perceived humiliations in classrooms and corridors; explicit bullying, intimidation, disrespect, stereotyping, insults, name-calling; student property and theft; parental involvement; and student privacy and record keeping.

By and large, adults in the school tend to make all the decisions about what should be done or not done about these issues. As a result, students have little or no voice in how the school regulates behavior around these issues. Furthermore, students are thereby prevented from involvement with shaping the values by which they might preserve and protect public and private spaces in the school. Their only cultural activity within the school is more or less compliance with adult-imposed regulations or more or less resistance to these regulations. They have no voice in shaping their learning environment. Adults complain that youngsters in school never think of anyone else but themselves while they deny them the opportunity to think about their mutual responsibilities to one another.

The building and sustaining of community will have to deal with the messy side of community as well as its more uplifting side. Thus, students will need to learn how to disagree, resolve misunderstandings, settle disputes nonviolently, and repair broken relationships. They will also have to work to overcome prejudices they have learned at home, how to place their own interests aside to help someone else. That is hard work, learned only over multiple experiences in a solicitous and supportive environment. This work needs structured and programmatic support. It needs teachers to provide the scaffolding for students to move from what they know to what they do not know. It needs teachers who take student mistakes as opportunities to learn, rather than opportunities to punish.

School leaders concerned to build community as one of the primary curricula of the school would encourage students, first and foremost, to compose the curriculum of community—to name those learnings that are important and essential to them. As that curriculum was being composed, the adults in the school could be invited to join with the students to explore some planned sequence of proactive learning experiences that would engage that curriculum. Following those discussions, students could draw up a list of learning activities that older students might teach to younger students. Adults in the school might develop their own collective notebook of actual and potential learning activities, perhaps arranged in some developmental sequence—activities that could make up the curriculum of community that they agree will be taught by everyone in the school, including the students, support staff, cafeteria workers, and custodians, applying those learnings consistently in the various interactions among children at various grade levels. Every year, faculty, staff, students, and parents could add new suggestions to the notebook of learning activities.

Obviously, this curriculum would be constructed over several years by the educators, students, and staff at the school with the help of parents and district professionals. It would grow out of a commitment to make the school a humane and socially nurturing environment in which the pursuit of academic learning would go hand in hand with social learning. The curriculum would build on the basic experiences of people being present to one another, learning to trust one another, to talk to one another and share stories. It would progress to more intentional and explicit focus on the active establishment and maintenance of a culture and of structures that support community.

The curriculum of community flows from understanding community in late modernity as a complex, multidimensional, fluid, contested, and pragmatic phenomenon. It is built on and sustained by relationships of interpersonal mutuality (Kerr, 1996), a mutual presence to a shared common work or activity (Boyte & Kari, 1996), shared responsibilities and rights of membership, and mutual commitments of loyalty. This curriculum recognizes that community has to be actively constructed every day by the members of that community because the agreements of today may sew the disagreements of tomorrow. It also recognizes that a contemporary community inescapably involves diversity and the politics of identity, and so it builds in structures and processes to negotiate and honor difference, to find common ground, as well as time and space for a variety of interests. In all this, it insists on processes of deliberation. Finally, this curriculum explicitly attends to the institutionalization of communal self-governance, thereby sewing the seeds for more adult participation in a democratic community.

## SUMMARY

We have seen how administering community involves a refashioning of the term into a richer, more expansive idea. This more expansive idea of community is called for as we enter the 21st century with its concepts of the global village and a planetary community of life. It is an idea of community that is called for not only by the critique of individualism, but by the growing contributions of women scholars, scholars from our increasingly multicultural citizenry, the many scientists who provide a new view of the planet and the cosmos. Once again, we see that the message of the first chapter has been underscored. Educational administration is not for the fainthearted. It is not for those who cannot sustain the intellectual effort to understand, study, and attempt to verbalize a sense of community that is still being formed within our culture. It is also not for authoritarians or rugged individualists. Rather, it is for those who have the courage to make a career in a profession that is finding its way in a time of transition, the courage to forge a vision of schooling that honors a mature sense of community and educates youngsters in its imperfect realization. This curriculum cannot be ignored on the excuse that there is already too much academic material to be mastered in an already crowded school year. Mastering that academic agenda without preparing youngsters for participating in a new kind of community renders that academic learning problematic, if not dangerous. That is why we have to look at the cultivation of meaning and the cultivation of community as inescapably intertwined.

## ACTIVITIES

1. In your journal, describe how democracy is understood and taught in your school or school district.

2. Generate five schoolwide activities that could be initiated within a month in your school that would increase your school's sense of community.

3. In your study group, brainstorm administrative initiatives that would improve the sense of community at schools.

4. The author presents some fanciful ideas about the individual belonging to a variety of communities—cultural, national, natural, and cosmic to which a response of bonding and participation, rather than withdrawal and protective isolation, is the more mature response. In your study group, discuss how strongly the cultural understanding and ideology of individualism might inhibit your own school embracing this expanded sense of community.

5. In your own words, prepare a statement on the school as a self-governing community. Present this statement to your faculty for their response and commentary.

## REFERENCES

Bateson, G. (1979). *Mind and nature: A necessary unity.* New York: E. P. Dutton.

Becker, E. (1967). *Beyond alienation: A philosophy of education for the crisis of democracy.* New York: The Free Press.

Bohm, D. (1981). *Wholeness and the implicate order.* London: Routledge & Kegan Paul.

Boyte, H. C., & Kari, N. N. (1996). *Building America: The democratic promise of public work.* Philadelphia: Temple University Press.

Castoriadis, C. (1987). *The imaginary institution of society.* Cambridge: Polity Press.

Delanty, G. (2000). *Modernity and postmodernity.* London: Sage.

Ferris, T. (1988). *Coming of age in the Milky Way.* New York: Doubleday Anchor Books.

Giddens, A. (1984). *The constitution of society.* Berkeley, CA: University of California Press.

Goffman, I. (1959). *The presentation of self in everyday life.* Garden City, NY: Doubleday Anchor Books.

Goodlad, J. I. (1996). Democracy, education, and community. In R. Soder (Ed.), *Democracy, education, and the schools* (pp. 87–124). San Francisco: Jossey-Bass.

Kerr, D. H. (1996). Democracy, nurturance, and community. In R. Soder (Ed.), *Democracy, education, and the schools* (pp. 37–68). San Francisco: Jossey-Bass.

Kymlicka, W., & Norman, W. (1993). Return of the citizen: A survey of recent work on citizenship theory. *Ethics, 104,* 352–381.

Levin, H. M. (1990). Political socialization for workplace democracy. In O. Ichilov (Ed.), *Political socialization, citizenship, education, and democracy* (pp. 158–176). New York: Teachers College Press.

Lovelock, J. (1979). *Gaia: A new look at life on earth.* Oxford: Oxford University Press.

MacIntyre, A. (1981). *After virtue: A study in moral theory.* Notre Dame, IN: University of Notre Dame Press.

MacMurray, J. (1970). *Persons in relation.* London: Faber.

Mafessoli, M. (1996). *The contemplation of the world.* Minneapolis, MN: University of Minnesota Press.

McCarthy, E. D. (1996). *Knowledge as culture: The new sociology of knowledge.* London: Routledge.

Neibuhr, R. (1932). *Moral man and immoral society.* New York: Charles Scribner's Sons.

Swimme, B., & Berry, T. (1992). *The universe story.* San Francisco: Jossey-Bass.

Taylor, C. (1989). *Sources of the self: The making of the modern identity.* Cambridge, MA: Harvard University Press.

Whitson, J. A., & Stanley, W. B. (1996). "Re-minding" education for democracy. In W. C. Parker (Ed.), *Educating the democratic mind* (pp. 309–336). Albany, NY: State University of New York Press.

Zohar, D., & Marshall, I. (1994). *The quantum society.* London: Flamingo/HarperCollins.

# Chapter 6

# Cultivating Responsibility

## INTRODUCTION

In this chapter, we turn to our third theme at the center of educational administration: cultivating responsibility. Initially it will be helpful to situate this theme within the analysis earlier provided by Murphy (1999) of the three possible centers for educational administration. Murphy identified education for social justice as one of the three core themes which could ground or center educational administration. Although Murphy preferred school improvement as the center, he saw concern for social justice in education as implicated in the effort at school renewal. A sizable number of educators and parents, however, would use a different vocabulary in attending to the theme of "responsibility," namely, those espousing "education for moral character." The initial sections of this chapter, therefore, will be devoted to summaries of these apparently competing schools of thought so as to highlight how the theme of cultivating responsibility speaks to both, and provides, I would argue, a deeper and broader perspective for educational leadership. The later part of the chapter will be devoted to presenting what I mean by "responsibility," followed by a brief analysis of how it is learned, followed by illustrations and applications drawn from the schooling context. This chapter is intended to provide the grounding for the succeeding two chapters that complete Part I of the book.

## EDUCATION FOR SOCIAL JUSTICE

The situation of schooling for children of the poor in the United States, and in other developed countries, has been well documented, and the record points to fundamental inequities (Connell, 1993; Hodgkinson, 1995; Land & Legters, 2002; Larson & Murtadha, 2002). When educators speak of education for social justice, this is the most basic place to start. Schools as major social institutions of society are, for the children of the poor, unjust institutions. As Connell (1993) pointed out, schools are major public assets that benefit children from middle and upper class backgrounds much more in comparison to the benefits derived by children of the poor. He argued that equal access to educational opportunities is an issue of distributive justice. Kozol (1992) documented the savage inequalities in school resources, teachers' educational backgrounds, facilities, and learning environments in multiple school systems serving poor children. Land and Legters (2002) and Hodgkinson (1995) cited depressing statistical evidence of the relationship of poverty to poor academic achievement and school failure.

Connell points out that, beyond distributive justice of equal access to learning, there is the question of the content to be learned, and the assessment of that content. Within curriculum itself, one can find class and gender and cultural bias. The organization of curriculum reflects the perspectives of dominant groups in society. Thus, as children approach the learning task, what they are required to learn is a form and substance of knowledge that reflects the class, gender, and cultural bias of those who organized it (Goodson, 1985). Those children who share the class, gender, and cultural backgrounds of those who constructed the curriculum and its assessment will more readily and easily learn that curriculum; the converse is true of those children who do not share that background. When the majority of teachers who "deliver" that curriculum to children as though the knowledge contained in the curriculum objectively describes the way the world is and indeed should be, the imposition of an hegemonic curriculum tends to be fixed in place. This sets up an additional form of educational injustice, namely, that schools have disproportionately favored White, middle and upper class, English language males.

Beyond disadvantaging poor children, schools also disadvantage—no matter what their class—females, special needs children, racial and ethnic "minority" children, second language learners, and children of recent immigrant parents (Blomgren, 1998; Gordon, 1999; Macedo, 1998; Martin, 1998; Nieto, 1992; Stringfield & Land, 2002; Swartz, 1996). This happens through placing these students in dead-end programs that limit their opportunity to engage a more rigorous curriculum with students of various abilities and backgrounds; through placing them with teachers whose expectations of their abilities are very low, who unwittingly teach them in ways that demoralize, miseducate and alienate them, and who lack the empathy to motivate and relate to children who come from different backgrounds than themselves; through placing them in learning environments with a decontextualized, abstract curriculum with no scaffolding to their own cultural experiences; and through engaging a curriculum whose implicit cultural, political, class, and male assumptions are translated into connotative language and imagery that subtly or quite explicitly cast people who are different from the mainstream in a less favorable light. In other words, schooling not only is biased in regards to class structure, but also in regards cultural differentiation, as Lois Weis so trenchantly observed (Weis, 1996). Thus, education for social justice must confront not only the structural inequality that negatively affects the schooling experience for poor children, but the cultural inequality that negatively affects both poor children as well as other children. Although some variance in student achievement may be tracked to home background, other variance is attributable to underresourced, biased, and underperforming schools. Insofar as lower achievement is due to within-school variables, one may say that children are being treated unjustly by their school, whether or not a particular teacher in that school intends that treatment explicitly.

## RESPONSE TO INJUSTICE

In the research on education for social justice, there are a variety of responses to unjust schools. Some would simply accept the curriculum and organization of schools as it is and work to have minority and poor children and females succeed within such schools. This seems to reflect the attitude that, "despite the odds, we can show the complacent majority that we are as good as they are and can succeed in their game even when the cards are stacked against us." Thus, many minority parents and educators choose to knuckle down and get their children to work hard at passing the state high-stakes tests, even though they know that the tests are not necessarily a fair or authentic test of what their children know and have learned. The challenge is to succeed even if it means following the "White man's rules," and conforming to a Euro-American biased curriculum. The attitude is: "If this is what it takes to succeed in the mainstream of society, then this is what we will do. Leave the cultural and gender identity stuff to the home and the cultural community." They want no relief from the so-called rigor of the school improvement agenda. They accept no excuses for poor achievement. They tend to emphasize effort-based achievement in the face of unequal resources. They see an opportunity for increased social capital generated by conjunction of the similar aspirations of other minority and poor parents and the aspirations of state policies for school improvement.

Other educators (Allen, 1999; Hynds, 1997; Nieto, 1992) encourage students to name and confront the experience of injustice in their own lives, even while they are engaging the official school curriculum, whether in social studies, language arts, or the performing arts. Connecting the curriculum to issues in their own lives enables them to draw relationships between the stories and historical accounts in their textbooks and similar themes in their own experience. Furthermore, in writing about and analyzing those themes, students are developing a command of the language, exercising higher order thinking, and mastering the methodological and academic skills required in the syllabus. They are also finding their voice, sharpening their sense of themselves as gendered, cultural, productive and reproductive persons (Martin, 1998; Nieto, 1992), and gaining an appreciation of the sociopolitical context of their lives. This kind of education for social justice conducts two parallel curriculums: one deals with mastering the official curriculum on which they will be tested; a second curriculum concerns establishing their own identities as social and cultural persons who are finding their way in a world poisoned by prejudice, power relations, and stereotyping, yet a world of possibilities for those with courage and inventiveness.

A third response to unjust schools attempts not only the two parallel curriculums, but adds a third curriculum: the learning of social responsibility. These educators engage the traditional curriculum in order to enable their students to succeed on the state high-stakes tests; they also use the traditional curriculum to stimulate the additional learnings involved with cultural, sexual, and social identity; they go beyond these learnings toward a third curriculum that draws out lessons about the structures and processes within the larger society by which social justice is thwarted or promoted. Berman and La Farge (1993) provided examples of attempts to raise issues about social responsibility in a variety of academic subject areas at a variety of grade levels. By and large, teachers use standard curriculum topics to surface deeper questions and issues, often pointing to the way social injustice is perpetuated through political and institutional structures. These lessons generate discussions about a variety of options open to citizens for confronting social injustice in responsible and effective ways, ways that deal not only with the symptoms, but with underlying institutional supports for injustice. These kind of lessons can be taught in both affluent suburban schools as well as urban and rural schools serving poor and minority children. This kind of teaching is encouraged by a national organization of educators called Educators for Social Responsibility. That group continues to publish material that schools may use in their efforts to promote social responsibility (Kreidler, 1994; Lieber & Lantieri, 1998).

Another group of educators that provides assistance to schools attempting to promote social responsibility employs materials illuminating common practices of stereotyping and scapegoating found in society. Their program, "Facing History and Ourselves," uses the Holocaust story to bring the lesson home (*Facing History and Ourselves*, 1994, 1999). In many Catholic schools, especially at the high school level, similar programs in social justice education have been initiated (Dobzanski, 2001; O'Keefe &

Haney, 1998; Oldenski, 1997). Sometimes these programs are coupled with an active community service program: for younger students it would involve various forms of service within the school such as assisting in cleaning up the cafeteria, peer tutoring, peer conflict mediation, running a school store, assisting the maintenance crew on various projects; for older students, this would involve working in soup kitchens, tutoring in after-school programs in the inner city, serving the needs of house-bound seniors, helping at a center for homeless families, and so forth. In some schools, it even involves working with an agency or church community in a third-world country. Students are encouraged to process their community service experiences through the lenses of critical inquiry and social justice in their social studies or religion courses in order to identify underlying societal and cultural beliefs and practices that sustain conditions of injustice. In these latter instances, education for social justice has moved well beyond making the schools more just to encouraging students to look at injustice in the larger society and consider the causes and effects, as well as weigh alternative public policy responses.

## EDUCATORS FOR SOCIAL JUSTICE

This kind of education calls for different kinds of educators, and for different kinds of educational leaders, reflecting greater sensitivity toward the diverse talents, interests, backgrounds and difficulties various children bring to the schoolhouse doors. This kind of leadership would seek to develop a culturally responsive teaching faculty (Gay, 2000; Villegas, 1991) with the sensitivity to read how students are responding to curricular and classroom events, and the flexibility to improvise a variety of instructional patterns, groupings, and scaffoldings. Administrators focused on social justice issues at school would seek early diagnosis of student learning issues, and develop with the teachers a variety of remediation efforts targeted to the specific needs of specific children, targeting and arranging resources for supporting early intervention strategies. This kind of leadership would seek to include various student groups in discussing improvements in the institutional supports for the learning environment, including grading, assemblies, library resources, co-curricular options, field trips, community service, and so forth. Administrators concerned to redress institutional injustice would initiate comprehensive systems of communication with parents, especially with underrepresented parents, seeking their suggestions about their participation in the life of the school, listening to their concerns, and providing continuous information about developments at school and with their children.

Notice in the above analysis, however, how often the administrative response to issues of social justice in schools has to come back to essential issues of teaching and learning and to all those supports for the central work of learning and teaching. Granted, the focus on education for social justice requires that educational leaders approach the taken-for-granted aspects of curriculum and teaching, learning and assessment with a much more critical frame of mind. Yet, this same critical frame of mind would appear, as Murphy (1999) has suggested, absolutely necessary for involvement in the school improvement focus of educational leadership. The critical issues center around improving student learning, no matter who the students happen to be, working with teachers to devise new strategies and design new learning activities that will more readily engage the students, connecting the curriculum to the lives of students, and rearranging schedules, spaces, assignments, grading systems, motivations and reward systems—all in the service of improving the quality of learning for all students. Deeply ingrained in the school improvement agenda is the emphasis on all children, and the emphasis on closing the achievement gap. Much of the work of school improvement involves a concentrated focus on reaching those students for whose academic success the school had previously not taken responsibility. The underperforming student, whether culturally or racially different, whether struggling with some handicapping condition, whether from "the projects" and neighborhoods dominated by gangs and drug activity—their lack of success was attributed to their family, cultural and class background. Now the school improvement agenda has taken that responsibility upon itself. When students do not learn, schools have to point the finger at themselves and find better ways to bring about quality learning for them. Thus, the concern to transform the school from being an unjust institution for a sizeable population of students finds common ground with the concern to improve learning for all students—the heart of the school improvement agenda. Connell (1993) made the same point, though from the other side of the field, when he insisted that a curriculum for social justice provides a deeper and broader education for both disadvantaged and advantaged students by exposing them to the voices of silenced or oppressed people within the accepted curriculum, thus enabling both groups of students to see the more complete social reality, and to consequently take a position of greater responsibility toward that complete social reality.

## EDUCATION FOR MORAL CHARACTER

A parallel concern with ethics, justice, morality, and responsibility is voiced by a community of educators representing different traditions in education. Character Education, Education for Moral Development, Education for Family Values, Character Development—these are some of the labels applied to this tradition. Often associated with the so-called Religious

Right, or religious fundamentalists, this tradition is much older and broader (Tyack & Hansot, 1982), even though one might fairly characterize the tradition as more conservative than the tradition of Education for Social Justice. Although originally viewed as a backlash to the psychologizing of moral education through values clarification (Hunter, 2000), character education in its many forms (Character Counts! Coalition of the Josephson Institute of Ethics; Character Education Partnership; the Community of Caring; the Jefferson Center for Character Education; the Character Education Institute; the Teel Institute for the Development of Integrity and Ethical Behavior; the Hartwood Institute's curriculum based on world literature; the Boy Scouts' *Learning for Life*; Bennett's [1994] *The Book of Virtues*, etc.) actually uses pedagogical principles that most progressive educators would espouse. Thus we find them advocating reflecting on the values contained in stories, discussing with other students how they would respond to value conflicts, talking over moral issues with their parents, discussing points of difference in other students' values, relating the enactment of specific values to one's sense of self worth, and so on (Hunter, 2000).

Often this tradition emphasizes socializing youngsters into adult moral values. That is, they propose an environment where the espoused values of the community are embedded in the whole school environment, where rules are clear, where sanctions for violations are both known in advance and applied, and where adult models of moral behavior provide exemplars for imitation. There is a clear acceptance of the adult authority role, and the need to inculcate obedience to authority. On the other hand, I know of no educator in this community that wants to promote the exercise of arbitrary authority, or slavish obedience. There is always room for due process, for participation in the formation of the rules, and for moral reflection. One can find isolated examples of teachers and administrators exercising arbitrary authority over children in progressive as well as traditional schools. One should not thereby conclude that the teacher or administrator represents what that system's educational philosophy stands for.

This form of moral education tends to indoctrinate youngsters into espousing moral principles which are seen as universal and deeply embedded in the universal requirements for human society. These principles include honesty, respect, fairness, loyalty, kindness, compassion, justice. Some would call these principles, when internalized, "virtues," or habitual ways of acting. Schools provide multiple opportunities to identify these virtues in others and to practice them in different contexts so that they do become habitual. When schools and parents work together to promote those virtues, children and youth are enveloped in a form of social capital which facilitates their socialization into virtuous living. Lickona (1991) and Ryan and Bohlin (1999) provide examples of families and communities supporting the school's effort to build virtuous character by engaging the young in similar exercises outside of the school.

One of the more eloquent spokespersons for this tradition, Henry Johnson (1987), made it clear that teachers do not have to import moral lessons into curriculum content. "It is not necessary to inject moral content or ethical questions into the study of history or literature or science, they are there already because there are moral and ethical dimensions in every sort of human experience as it is lived" (p. 88). He likewise asserts that schools as forms of human community, involving multiple and complex human relationships, imply moral tasks and moral questions, as does any human community. Indeed, he pointed out, the school's central task, the development of intelligence and the acquisition of knowledge rest on moral commitments to truthfulness, open and fair inquiry, and equitable opportunities to learn. Thus, Johnson argued, there is no need to debate the possibility for moral education; education is intrinsically involved with moral issues. It is a contradiction in terms to hold for a morally neutral form of education (Johnson, 1987).

## CAN THESE TWO TRADITIONS TALK TO ONE ANOTHER?

Strictly speaking, neither tradition talks to the other. One tradition stresses social responsibility; the other stresses individual responsibility. Education for Social Justice starts from the premise that schools are unjust, that they disadvantage children of poverty, bilingual and bicultural children, females, children with special needs, and racial and ethnic minorities. Educators for Social Justice want *all* children in schools to have an equal opportunity to learn and to succeed. Therefore, they want both equalization of resources (funding, curriculum materials, qualified staff, facilities, and administrative support), and compensatory resources (social workers to assist parents, specialized remedial services, cooperation with other community resources such as hospitals, employment agencies, housing and recreational personnel). A quality learning experience in school includes the students' accessing knowledge to pass high stakes tests, but also the opportunity to validate their sexual, cultural, and racial identity within the learning agenda of the school, engaging a curriculum that connects with the students' lives and realistically prepares them to participate in the larger world.

Educators for Character Development do not assume that the school disadvantages students in these ways. Rather, they assume schools disadvantage students by attempting to remain morally neutral, or by allowing relativistic moral perspectives to go unchallenged in the name of diversity. They see the rise in teen pregnancies, drug use, school violence toward both adults and peers, cynicism toward and alienation from the adult world, and they ask what response schools should make. They tend to see the schools reflecting the permissiveness of the wider society, thus neglecting one of their traditional responsibilities, namely the teaching of right and wrong and respect for legitimate authority, the work of socializing morally responsible human beings. They tend to expect that all students will conform to mainstream (White, middle-class) norms of behavior, and to see alternative or different expressions of identity as deviant, or at best, inappropriate.

Looking at where these two traditions start from it is hard to see how they could talk to one another. Yet, both traditions do have something to say to one another. Where the character development educators would emphasize self-respect and respect for others, educators for social justice could encourage the learning of those virtues specifically in Black–White relations, in male–female relations, in relations between affluent and poor, and in labor and management relations. Where educators for social justice would critique class, racial, and gender distortions in the history curriculum, they could appeal to the character educator's demand for principles of honesty and fairness in the pursuit of truth. Where character development educators decry sexual promiscuity, educators for social justice would find similar concerns in the critique of feminist educators of male privilege and domination. In other words, though each tradition uses different vocabularies and different starting points, their concerns overlap and provide grounds for authentic sharing of ideas. Furthermore, the efforts of educators for social responsibility stretch personal and interpersonal virtues of the character development educators toward virtues of citizenship and political involvement. The principles of fairness, compassion, honesty stressed by character development educators have multiple applications in the civic arena. Similarly, character development educators can challenge the identity politics of groups seeking social justice to treat their opponents with fairness and compassion, avoiding demonizing the opposition, thus opening space for authentic conversation, compromise, and potential reconciliation.

Hunter (2000) argued rather persuasively that morality defined as character has over the course of the 20th century been transformed into a subjective, individualistic morality, more concerned with therapeutic solutions to moral lapses, than to relating morality to an objective order of things. He decries the equation of psychology with cosmology—making the psychologically healthy growth of the individual as the basis for all moral imperatives, rather than humans being subjected to the moral imperatives imposed by God or some laws of the cosmos. Lacking any universal moral principles that could be objectively established by philosophical or theological argument, Hunter argues that the contemporary American culture, as a collective, is morally rudderless, split into a practical moral relativism by the plurality of moral opinions that accept no consensus. Curiously enough at the end of his illuminating analysis, he proposes that groups might indeed find common grounds for public agreement on important moral issues (for example in opposing racism) *within* their traditions, even though the principles within their tradition for doing so might not at all resemble the arguments for opposing racism in other traditions. This suggestion, I believe, applies to the potential dialogue between the education for social justice community and the education for character development community.

## CULTIVATING RESPONSIBILITY

Although finding common ground for dialogue and cooperative educational policy among these two communities, I want to explore the possibility of grounding their conversation in a deeper and broader theme which lies at the heart of what both groups are trying to propose—the theme of responsibility. I want to first develop an argument around the meanings of the terms "responsibility" and "being responsible." Then I want to translate the theme of cultivating responsibility as cultivating the ability of people to respond, to be response-able. I will cite psychological theory and research on child development that makes my argument reasonable (not necessarily absolutely convincing). I conclude by suggesting that the theme of cultivating responsibility satisfies the demands of both communities of educators treated above, although potentially muting much of the rhetoric and vocabulary that both groups find inflammatory or offensive in the other's position. Furthermore, those in leadership positions who have to advocate for this core work of schools will find the vocabulary of responsibility to have a more broadly receptive audience in the civic community, than the vocabulary of either of the other two positions.

Moran (1996) presented a helpful overview of responsibility as the core term for developing a new grammar of ethics and morality. His historical analysis indicates how philosophers have wrestled since the 17th century with the problem of an ethics and morality divorced from belief in a Supreme Being who could be the ground and authority for all ethical and moral principles, or membership in a church whose scriptures and doctrines would similarly provide a grounding for moral principles. He concludes, correctly, I believe, that, at least in the industrialized West, there is no possibility for the general public to agree on any absolute, whether absolute certainty, absolute authority, or absolute power on which to base a realistic theory of ethics and morality. He cites Kierkegaard's metaphor of the swimmer who tries to float on the waves while maintaining one foot on the ocean bottom. One either has to let go of the ground and swim, or drown in the attempt to stay anchored on the bottom. Moran is not opposed to the relativism of no longer being anchored in absolutes. For him that does not mean that "anything goes" in morality. Rather, he sees the postmodern or late-modern world having to move toward shared responsibility in listening to and responding to all the various voices who are themselves seeking a way. Listening to and responding—this is the aural–oral metaphor on which the word responsibility rests.

Responsibility is essentially a relational characteristic of human intercourse. It is grounded in our social nature, and is revealed in the actual process of our development as authentic persons. Responsibility is what emerges from our daily negotiation of our relationships; if these relationships are going to work in any humanly satisfying and reasonably predictable fashion, then we have to take responsibility towards those relationships and for those consistent actions that make them work.

Beyond interpersonal responsibilities but affecting their definition, one can also approach responsibility from a sociocultural perspective as "a construction of social systems organized by human beings. (Responsibility) involves informal understandings of the expectations of a culture, societal norms about appropriate conduct, legal requirements for behavior, and individual conceptions about the relationships among people" (Shaver & Schutte, 2001, p. 36). Socially constructed understandings of responsibilities, often fluidly dependent on specific circumstances, become embedded in social institutions.

No longer do we have a *commonly accepted* textbook or scripture that can tell us how to manage our lives. Living in a pluralistic and contentious world, human beings have to take responsibility for working things out because we cannot agree on whether there is an absolute or on whose absolute will be *really* absolute. This was the conclusion also reached by the respected theologian Martin Marty (1997) when he reviewed the problem of defining the common good in an America fractured by identity politics. His recommendation was not to seek agreement on general abstract principles, but to listen for the common ideals to be found in people's stories as the basis for accommodation. Appreciation of one another's stories provides the basis for developing relationships, which, in turn, leads to taking responsibility for sustaining those relationships by some consistent pattern of reciprocity. Such a moral endeavor to live "responsibly" will be messy, but it appears to be our only realistic option, unless we wish to return to tribal and ethnic enclaves of like-minded believers, a possibility raised by MacIntyre (1984) whose work also confirms the lack of any widespread agreement on absolutes.

Besides suggesting a workable approach to ethics for adults, responsibility as a pedagogical policy is also attractive. Because it is grounded initially in relationships, children and adolescents can readily understand its significance based on their immediate experiences of relationships within the family and their circle of friends. In contrast to the complex treatises on ethics such as the carefully reasoned but abstract and dense prose of Rawls' *A Theory of Justice* (1972), a more simple and more common sense development of the theme of responsibility provides a workable framework for the education of the young, workable for them and for those teaching them. It sidesteps the issue of absolutes and religious doctrines, neither denying nor affirming their legitimacy, leaving those issues to be dealt with by parents and their religious affiliations. The practical lessons of taking responsibility will have their own positive and negative consequences, more in the tradition of Rousseau's naturalistic pedagogy of Emile (1979), and will lead through repetition in many circumstances to a gradual understanding of workable general principles involved in taking responsibility or being responsible.

## A BRIEF OVERVIEW OF THE CONTOURS OF THE THEME *RESPONSIBILITY*

When we say that a person has "a sense of responsibility," what does that mean? The phrase seems to convey that the person understands *to whom* he or she is responsible and *for what* she or he is responsible. Moran (1996) also used this distinction, although I differ in minor ways from his development of those distinctions. In traditional social discourse, one might say that a spouse is responsible *to* her or his spouse, and that sense of responsibility means that the spouse is responsible *for* action that respond to the demands of marital fidelity, mutual affection, truth telling, support under difficult circumstances (the traditional terms of "I will honor you all of my days, for better or for worse, in sickness and in health, till death do us part" part of the marriage agreements, or "contract"). The spouse is responsible *to* the person, the total person of the beloved; the spouse is responsible *for* maintaining all the agreed-on aspects of the relationship that define them as married to each other, as well as for negotiating developing aspects of the relationship that were not explicitly expressed in the initial agreements, but may have been implied (for example, caring for an aging parent of one of the spouses).

In the above example, we see that the term *responsible to* conveys a continuous state of obligation or accountability; put more positively, a continuous state of attending to the other person, a continuous state of caring and loving. The term *responsible for* conveys a continuous set of actions to which one is obliged by the relationship; put more positively, a continuous set of actions to which one obliges him or herself, guided by the unfolding relationship. The term *responsible for* also can convey responsibility for performing a specific action or series of actions. The husband confesses to the wife, "I'll take responsibility for letting the cake burn. I got caught up watching the ball game." The remorseful driver admits, "I was responsible for the deaths in the accident I caused by drinking too much at the party and falling asleep at the wheel." The phrase *responsible for* in these two examples refers to actual behaviors.

A parent has a sense of responsibility about the parent's children. That means the parent is responsible to the children and responsible *for* protecting, feeding, educating, loving, socializing, supporting the children. In both cases, being responsible carries that double notion of being responsible to someone or something and being responsible for acting in certain ways toward that person or thing. Responsibility, however, is not restricted to interpersonal relationship. Besides, a mutual relationship of caring between a person and another person, responsibility can imply a relationship between a person and a group (soccer team, family, local gang or posse, quilting circle), a person and an organization (local parish, school, voluntary association, place of employment, a neighborhood safety committee), a person and a cultural activity (one's craft, profession, avocation), or even to something more abstract such as "the environment," "democratic principles," and "the least advantaged members of my society." The responsibility is to someone or something, and implies a responsibility *for* doing or behaving a certain way *consistently, for* observing a code of behavior (what is implied by behaving consistently). Conversely, one can have a responsibility to an evil person, a dictator, a gang selling drugs in the neighborhood, or a dishonest company. There, one's responsibility is to oppose that person, gang, or company. Opposition can take many forms, and thus one can act responsibly in a variety of ways. We will encounter this aspect in chapter 8 when we deal with the ethic of critique.

Barnard (1938), in his enlightening treatment of executive responsibility, reminded us that people hold multiple responsibilities simultaneously. These multiple responsibilities flow from the different relationships they have with persons and things. Barnard posed this example. "Mr. A., a citizen of Massachusetts, a member of the Baptist Church, having a father and a mother living, and a wife and two children, is an expert machinist employed at a pump station of an important water system" (p. 267). We can apply our analysis of responsibility to this example. Mr. A. is responsible to the state of Massachusetts, to his church community, to his parents, to his wife and children, to his craft as a machinist, to the company that employs him, and to the public being served by the water system. Each relationship carries its own distinct set of responsibilities, responsibilities shaped by the nature of the relationships, awareness of which guides Mr. A.'s actions and choices in specific circumstances. Some of these responsibilities are mutually reinforcing. As a parent, he has the responsibility to provide food, shelter, clothing and security to his children. As a citizen of the state of Massachusetts, he is enjoined by law to provide support for his children. As a member of his church, he is enjoined to love and support his children. Conversely, there may be times when these various responsibilities are in conflict. His company may cut back on the maintenance budget for the equipment Mr. A. is in charge of. He knows that if he does not replace certain vital parts of the equipment on a regular schedule, the equipment is in danger of failing, thus disabling other equipment and eventually leading to the failure of the pumping station. He knows that if he complains to his boss that he might get fired, thus jeopardizing his ability to provide for his children. His responsibility to his craft is likewise jeopardized, since he is not able to maintain his machinery at the level he knows is called for. As a citizen of Massachusetts, he has the responsibility to obey the laws of the state, and he realizes that the citizens served by this water system may be harmed by a failure of the system. Thus we see how Mr. A. or any person can be caught up in conflicting responsibilities. We also see that in given circumstances, responsibility varies among the various agents in the situation (the company, the state, the employee, his immediate supervisors, the board of Directors who approve the budget, etc.). Responsibility, therefore, is both exercised within and constrained by the social environment, as French (1984) so convincingly argued. Implicitly, responsibility is always a collective construct; it implies a variety of relationships, all of which condition the quality of responsibility of each of the agents. The role of leadership is to make that collective sense of responsibility explicit, and the source of commitment of all the agents (Barnard, 1938). The role of education is to gradually enable the young to gain developmentally appropriate understandings of their responsibilities as social beings.

Collectivities (corporations, families, neighborhoods, government agencies, churches, voluntary associations, etc.) can be held responsible under the law. When an investment firm, a pharmaceutical company, a law firm, a government agency is convicted in court, the moral fault is usually that some fundamental agreements between professionals, their clients and employees, as well as the people of the community had been violated; that people whose professions were dedicated to service, sought their own benefit in violation of the principles of their profession. Those corporations, firms or agencies were somehow collectively responsible for the harm that both customers and employees suffered.

In a more common example, one can cite the example of a day in the life of any civic community, large or small. The millions of small interactions that take place between people in that civic community are guided by people's sense that they all have agreed to act responsibly. That means that most people will stop at red traffic signals, that grocery store cashiers will return the correct change to customers, that merchants will sell products that are in fact what they claim to be, that automobile drivers will keep a special watch out for children running into the street, that teachers will be fair in grading students' work on tests, that the buses will run more or less according to schedule, that lawyers will take the care to ascertain all the legally relevant facts before advising their clients on a course of action, that pharmacists will fill their customers' prescriptions accurately, that lifeguards at the beach will not fall asleep at their posts, that best friends will stay loyal, that parents will not abandon their infants. In other words, the everyday life of communities depends on the widespread and universal practice of responsibility. Communities are places where the vast majority of its citizens exercise a collective sense of responsibility to themselves, to their fellow citizens, and *to their sense of themselves as a community*. They take responsibility for the consistent actions that will sustain their social relationships, however superficial or close those relationships happen to be. This doesn't mean that there are no mistakes, no misunderstandings, no disagreements. Most of those, however, are cleared up through the parties clarifying what they thought the situation called for, or by the parties agreeing to compromise and get on with other things.

As Turiel (1996) so convincingly argued, however, beneath the surface of this daily enactment of responsibility, one can find deep divisions over the values that are supposed to guide the general assumptions about responsibility. The definitions of responsibilities within the home, for example, continue to place unfair burdens on females. Assumptions about racial or class superiority affect how people in communities nuance responsibilities. In the Jim Crow South, for example, an African American could succeed within the dominant White culture only by adopting a posture of deference that signaled a renunciation of pride in one's racial heritage (Reed, 1996). Okim's analysis of how "typical families" engender unequal attitudes about the responsibilities of women and men for the care of children and of elderly parents, not to mention the daily household work, further illuminates a terrain of contested values and interpretations about responsibilities. The fact that communities seem to function because people behave "the way they are supposed to" does not mean that resentments do not fester due to the perceived injustice of the way relationships of responsibilities are structured and the slights which they seem to permit. Any vestige of these unfair burdens of responsibilities in school settings need to be challenged and corrected. These challenges become part of the curriculum of community.

## CULTIVATING RESPONSIBILITY IN SCHOOLS

In suggesting this theme as constituting a vital part of the center of educational administration, I suggest how the leadership of administrators involves their working with the professional and support staff on this theme.

This work is expressed in the shared development of each teacher's sense of personal and professional responsibilities to all their students, and for the work of stimulating, guiding, and deepening the learning of all their students. Beyond work with individual teachers administrators work at developing a sense of shared responsibility among all the teachers to all the students in the school for their quality learning. Subsequent chapters will go into greater detail about this work. Beyond the work with teachers on *their* responsibilities, there is the further work of designing with the teachers learning opportunities for students to learn a sense of responsibility. These learning opportunities for students will entail their learning their responsibilities to themselves, responsibilities to their circle of friends, responsibilities to other students in the school with whom they have no close relationships as of yet, responsibilities to the work of the school, namely the learning of the academic curriculum, and responsibilities to their school considered as a community. As became clearer in our treatment of the community as curriculum in chapter 5, the learning agenda of the school moves developmentally from interpersonal responsibility to a more collective sense of responsibility for the everyday life of the school. This means helping youngsters take responsibility for themselves and for their relationships. It also means helping them to embrace the notion that they can commit themselves to a collective agreement to take responsibility for the public life of the school. Thus we begin to get a sense of the gradual expansiveness of the curriculum of responsibility corresponding to the psycho-social development of the children.

One person cannot make a school work; however, the student body, joined to the efforts of the adults in the school, can agree to hold themselves responsible for engaging in those actions that will make the school a more satisfying and productive place, and responsible for avoiding those behaviors which will make the school a more threatening, alienating, conflicted, or dehumanized environment. When students grow to appreciate the force of collective responsibility, they begin to understand what collective self-government can mean, and how collective self-government can be sustained by specific types of agreements and processes for negotiating, discussing, exploring, potential courses of action. Again, succeeding chapters will explore how schools can become these kinds of learning environments.

## PSYCHOLOGICAL PERSPECTIVES ON LEARNING RESPONSIBILITY

As has been suggested in earlier chapters, learning is understood as a social activity. That suggests that knowledge is socially constructed. This position does not deny that what we know is in some sense "what is really out there," as opposed to something socially fabricated out of pure fantasy. Neither does it deny the autonomy of the individual knower in constructing his or her unfolding knowledge through the give and take of social exchange. Rather, the theory of the social construction of knowledge denies the dualisms of subject and object, of realism versus idealism (namely that reality is independent of the mind versus that reality is dependent on the mind; Davidson & Youniss, 1995). The theory of the social construction of knowledge also denies the either–or situating of knowledge in empiricism (knowledge obtained through external sense experience) or in rationalism or intuitionalism. Rather, the theory of the social construction of knowledge asserts that knowledge is a shared social construction. Knowledge is part of the reality that is constructed in the context of ongoing and continuing social practices. Knowledge is part of the negotiated reality that defines the complex web of human interrelations (Davidson & Youniss, 1995).

The work of Davidson and Youniss (1995), Youniss and Damon (1991), and Youniss (1981) provide a helpful overview of how more recent research has come to confirm much of what Piaget (1932) proposed about the moral development of the child. Piaget's studies of how children came to understand rules for the game of marbles led him to believe that this process was central to the child's moving toward identification with the larger culture. The child understood that the rules went back many generations in his family, and thus tended to be identified with a permanent aspect of the larger culture. In agreeing to play by the rules, children acknowledged a larger social order. The cultural dimensions of the rules gave the rules a kind of transcendent force. By submitting to the rules, the self of the child gains a larger social identity as he or she performs the culture. The self becomes "more than I" (Davidson & Youniss, 1995, p. 304).

Davidson and Youniss (1995) cited the studies of Corsaro (1985) of children's forming of friendships and learning the rules of the peer culture, Miller and Sperry's studies (1987) of children learning about the rules of adult culture by observing and talking with their parents, and the research of Winegar, Renninger, and Valsiner (1989) on how quickly children accommodate to school rules as ways to participate in school culture. In all three sets of studies, children learn through interaction with peers, parents, and teachers that there are rules that govern how cultures carry on their business. In attempting to reproduce those rules in their actions, children begin to be agents who can reproduce these various cultures with various levels of success and whose identities are thus produced within these cultures.

Beginning with their earliest attempts at friendship, children begin to learn the lessons of reciprocity. Through repeated attempts at interaction with other children, the child comes to learn that it is fair to treat others as they want to be treated. In other words, they learn that if they call the other child an offensive name, they can expect to be similarly affronted; likewise, if they share some of their candy, they can expect to receive some of their friend's candy. Through repeated experiences of interaction with friends, children begin to reflect as they talk to themselves about their experiences, that there tends to be an invariant principle of mutuality and reciprocity if their relationships are going to work consistently. When children disagree with their friends, they have to find ways out of the impasse. They find that they have to talk to one another, to explain why they think their idea is the right one. In the process, they discover that they have to learn to listen carefully to the other person's ideas to see where they differ from and where they are similar to his or her own. In other words, friendships demand not only reciprocity, they demand communication. In making one's ideas clear to a friend, one clarifies one's identity; in listening to the friend, one has a clearer idea of the identity of the friend. The knowledge they develop is intersubjective; that is, it exists at the juncture of the communicative meeting of persons. The objectivity of the knowledge is not the point of the discussion, but rather its validity: does our knowledge mean the same thing to us? (Davidson & Youniss, 1995, pp. 300–301). In all of these interactions, and especially in those involving conflict, the child is learning to be responsible to the friend and to be responsible for doing those things which will sustain the relationship.

Piaget described the child's relationship with adults as one of unilateral authority. The adult transmits advice or commands, principles to be followed. Neither the adult nor the child have similar experiential referents in the communication, so neither one quite knows what sense the other is making. "What the child thinks the adult means is probably more closely associated with the child's version of society than of the adult's" (Davidson & Youniss, 1995, p. 301). This is one reason why adults become so exasperated with children's failure to do what adults have told them to do. How many times have we heard a parent or a teacher say to a child, "How many times have I told you not to do such and such!!!?" For the child what the adult said yesterday was in response to one situation. Today's situation was different. The child's prior understandings did not enable the child to grasp the abstract or universal nature of the command the adult was giving the day before. All he knew was that yesterday he had done something that made this adult unhappy, but not necessarily the reason for the unhappiness. So adults have to continue to repeat the messages, and apply the message to specific situations. Gradually the youngsters get it, but the grasping of the principle has to involve the constructing of the understanding of the principle as making sense from the child's experience and within the prior meanings attached to many experiences. By contrast, the child's learning of a basic sense of responsibility develops more readily from interactions with peers because they are negotiating more or less the same experiential and linguistic landscape.

Davidson and Youniss (1995) concisely summarize their theory of moral development thus:

> The essence of morality . . . is the formation of an identity that goes beyond the self and the capacity . . . to make judgements that go beyond the self. This capacity includes, on the one hand, the obligation to treat others with care, and on the other hand, is the basis for one's moral authority to pass judgements on other's acts. Developmentally, this "going beyond" originates with reference to primary groups like family and peers, and as one's sphere of interaction grows, it expands with reference to increasingly diverse others: persons from different neighborhoods, religions, languages, and even more remote geographical and cultural origins.
>
> Hence, every exposure to new others is a renewed challenge to the conservation of one's norms of reciprocity and respect, demanding the acceptance of a broader class of persons as moral equals, or in other words, requiring a redefinition of the concept of "person" with which one identifies or which constitutes one's moral identity. (p. 306)

One might apply the same kind of moral development to the learning of responsibility. It begins with the experience of negotiating relationships within the family and with peers. Through repeated interactions, the youngster learns the demands of reciprocity, communication and respect—all ingredients of responsibility to others. As one's sphere of interaction expands so too does the learning of new responsibilities. Those responsibilities lead to the progressive growth of more "transcending" kinds of autonomy, where the person learns to replace or transcend egoistic tendencies and impulses in favor of deeper and more inclusive involvement with other people and with broader and deeper social responsibilities. The role of the school is to provide at least some of those kinds of structured learning opportunities that support the ever expansive learning of responsibility. These structured learning opportunities comprise the curriculum of responsibility.


**CONCLUSION**

In this chapter, we have introduced the theme of cultivating responsibility. This theme embraces many of the underlying interests of the two competing schools of thought about a process of education that could be called moral—education for social justice and education for moral character. By situating the cultivation of responsibility at the center of the work of educational administration, we are responding to the needed development of the school's commitment to all children—the taking of responsibility by all the school personnel for the quality education of *all* children in the school, and the closing of the achievement gap (one of the primary goals of education-for-social-justice advocates). The cultivation of responsibility also includes the explicit attention to the teaching of responsibility to youngsters, responsibility to all of their peers in the school, responsibility to the work of learning, responsibility to the school as a community with clearly articulated values. Besides exploring the nature of responsibility as a framework for dealing with moral issues in the school, we have also seen some indicators of how responsibility is coconstructed, and how it is related to one's sense of moral identity. This perspective is consistent with our understanding of learning in the cognitive areas, and suggests ways teacher can design appropriate learning activities.

The following two chapters suggest additional perspectives on what the teaching and learning of responsibility might mean. By exploring the moral nature of learning itself, we recognize mutual responsibilities of both teachers and students toward the activity of learning. Chapter 8 will push our ideas further, as we explore explicit ways to teach and learn responsibility by developing those natural, pre-moral attributes that predispose human beings toward responsibility, and by looking at a multidimensional framework of ethics as that might be applied to learning activities already present in the learning agenda of the school. Chapters in Part II of the book will further spell out the implications of a school community attempting to cultivate responsibility.

## ACTIVITIES

1. List the multiple persons and groups and organizations in your work that you are responsible to. Try to list what you are responsible for in each of these relationships. Try to prioritize those to whom you are responsible, such that, were there a conflict between them, you would know where the more important responsibility lay. Are there major disagreements among the teaching faculty about their responsibilities? If so, what harmful effects, if any, result from these disagreeements?

2. Name five ways in which you try to cultivate responsibility among the students. How consistent are you in these efforts? Do you collaborate with others in the school in these efforts, or does everyone on the teaching faculty do their own thing in this regard? Do the school rules encourage students to develop responsibility, or are they seen as bothersome adult impositions by the students? How might the school improve the taking of responsibility by students?

## REFERENCES

Barnard, C. I. (1938). *The functions of the executive.* Cambridge, MA: Harvard University Press.

Bennett, W. (1994). *The book of virtues.* New York: Simon and Schuster.

Berman, S., & LaFarge, P. (Eds.). (1993). *Promising practices in teaching social responsibility.* Albany, NY: State University of New York Press.

Blomgren, R. (1998). Special education and the quest for human dignity. In H. S. Shapiro & D. E. Purpel (Eds.), *Critical social issues in American education: Transformation in a postmodern world* (pp. 241–259). Mahwah, NJ: Lawrence Erlbaum Associates.

Connell, R. W. (1993). *Schools and social justice.* Philadelphia: Temple University Press.

Corsaro, W. A. (1985). *Friendship and peer culture in the early years.* Norwood, NJ: Ablex.

Davidson, P. & Youniss, J. (1995). Moral development and social construction. In W. M. Kurtines & J. L Gewirtz (Eds.), *Moral development: An introduction* (pp. 289–310). Boston: Allyn and Bacon.

Dobzanski, J. L. (2001). *The "Facing History and Ourselves": Professional development process: Implications for the personal and collective transformation of catholic school teachers.* Unpublished doctoral dissertation. Chestnut Hill, MA: Boston College.

Facing History and Ourselves. (1994). *Facing history and ourselves: Holocaust and human behavior.* Brookline, MA: Author.

Facing History and Ourselves. (1999). *Case studies of Facing History and Ourselves program implementation in four Cleveland area schools.* Brookline, MA: Author.

French, P. (1984). *Collective and corporate responsibility.* New York: Columbia University Press.

Gay, G. (2000). *Culturally responsive teaching: Theory. research and practice.* New York: Teachers College Press.

Goodson, I. F. (1995). *The changing curriculum.* New York: Peter Lang.

Gordon, E. W. (1999). *Education and justice: A view from the back of the bus.* New York: Teachers College Press.

Hodgkinson, H. L. (1998). What should we call people? Race, class and the census for 2000. In H. S. Shapiro & D. E. Purpel (Eds.), *Critical social issues in American education: Transformation in a postmodern world* (pp. 157–168). Mahwah, NJ: Lawrence Erlbaum Associates.

Hunter, J. D. (2000). *The death of character: Moral education in an age without good or evil.* New York: Basic Books.

Johnson, H. C., Jr. (1987). Society, culture and character development. In K. Ryan & G. F. McLean (Eds.), *Character development in schools and beyond* (pp. 59–93). New York: Praeger.

Kozol, J. (1992). *Savage inequalities.* New York: HarperPerennial.

Kreidler, W. (1994). *Conflict resolution in the middle school: A curriculum and teaching guide.* Cambridge, MA: Educators for Social Responsibility.

Land, D., & Legters, N. (2002). The extent and consequences of risk in U.S. Education. In S. Stringfield & D. Land (Eds.), *Educating at-risk students.* One hundred-first Yearbook of the National Society for the Study of Education, Part II (pp. 1–28). Chicago: University of Chicago Press.

Larson, C. L. & Murtadha, K. (2002). Leadership for social justice. In J. Murphy (Ed.), *The educational leadership challenge: Redefining leadership for the 21st century.* One Hundred-first Yearbook of the National Society for the Study of Education, Part I (pp. 134–161). Chicago: University of Chicago Press.

Lickona, T. (1991). *Educating for character: how our schools can teach respect and responsibility.* New York: Bantam.

Lieber, C. M., & Lantieri, L. (1998). *Conflict resolution in the high school: 36 lessons.* Cambridge, MA: Educators for Social Responsibility.

Macedo, D. (1998). English only: The tongue-tying of America. In H. S. Shapiro & D. E. Purpel (Eds.), *Critical social issues in American education: Transformation in a postmodern world* (2nd Ed., pp. 261–272). Mahwah, NJ: Lawrence Erlbaum Associates.

MacIntyre, A. (1984). *After virtue* (2nd Ed.). South Bend, IN: University of Notre Dame Press.

Martin, J. R. (1998). Becoming educated: A journey of alienation or integration? In H. S. Shapiro & D. E. Purpel (Eds.), *Critical social issues in American education: Transformation in a postmodern world* (2nd Ed., pp. 199–212). Mahwah, NJ: Lawrence Erlbaum Associates.

Marty, M. E. (1997). *The one and the many: America's struggle for the common good.* Cambridge, MA: Harvard University Press.

Miller, D. J. & Sperry, L. L. (1987). The socialization of anger and aggression. *Merrill-Palmer Quarterly, 33,* 1–31.

Moran, G. (1996). *A grammar of responsibility.* New York: Crossroads.

Murphy, J. (1999). *The quest for a center: Notes on the state of the profession of educational leadership.* Columbia, MO: The University Council for Educational Administration.

Nieto, S. (1992). *Affirming diversity: The sociopolitical context of multicultural education.* New York: Longmans.

Oldenski, T. (1997). *Liberation theology and critical pedagogy in today's catholic schools: Social justice in action.* New York: Garland Publishing.

O'Keefe, J., & Haney, R. (Eds.). (1998). *Conversations in excellence: Providing for diverse needs of youth and their families.* Washington, DC: National Catholic Education Association.

Okin, S. M. (1989). *Justice, gender, and the family.* New York: Basic Books.

Rawls, J. (1972). *A theory of justice.* Cambridge, MA: Harvard University Press.

Reed, E. S. (1996). Selves, values, customs. In E. S. Reed, E. Turiel, & T. Brown (Eds.), *Values and knowledge* (pp. 1–15). Mahwah, NJ: Lawrence Erlbaum Associates.

Rousseau, J. J. (1979). *Emile: On education* (translation by Allan Bloom). New York: Basic Books.

Ryan, K. & Bohlin, K. E. (1999). *Building character in schools: Practical ways to bring moral instruction to life.* San Francisco: Jossey-Bass.

Shaver, K. G.., & Schutte, D. A. (2001). Toward a broader psychological foundation for responsibility. In A. E. Auhagen & H-W. Bierhoff (Eds.), *Responsibility: The many faces of a social phenomenon* (pp. 35–47). London: Routledge.

Stringfield, S., & Land, D. (Eds.). (2002). *Educating at-risk students.* One hundred-first yearbook of the National Society for the Study of Education, Part II. Chicago: University of Chicago Press.

Swartz, E. (1996). Emancipatory narratives: Rewriting the master script in the school curriculum. In M. Rogers (Ed.), *Multicultural experiences, multicultural theories* (pp. 164–178). New York: McGraw-Hill.

Turiel, E. (1996). Equality and hierarchy: Conflict in values. In E. S. Reed, E. Turiel, & T. Brown (Eds.), *Values and knowledge* (pp. 75–101). Mahwah, NJ: Lawrence Erlbaum Associates.

Tyack, D. B., & Hansot, E. (1982). *Managers of virtue: Public school leadership in America, 1820–1980.* New York: Basic Books.

Villegas, A. M. (1991). *Culturally responsive teaching for the 1990s and beyond.* Washington, DC: American Association of Colleges for Teacher Education.

Weis, L. (1996). Foreword. In B. A. Levensin, D. E. Foley, & D. C. Holland (Eds.), *The cultural production of the educated person: Critical ethnographies of schooling and local practice* (pp. ix–xiv). Albany, NY: State University of New York Press.

Winegar, L. T., Renninger, K. A., & Valsiner, J. (1989). Dependent-independence in adult–child relationships. In D. A. Kramer & M. J. Bopp (Eds.), *Transformation in clinical and developmental psychology* (pp. 157–168). New York: Springer-Verlag.

Youniss, J. (1981). An analysis of moral development through a theory of social construction. *Merrill-Palmer Quarterly, 27,* 385–403.

Youniss, J. & Damon, W. (1991). Social construction in Piaget's theory. In H. Beilin & P. Pufall (Eds.), *Piaget's theory: Prospects and possibilities* (pp. 267–286). Hillsdale, NJ: Lawrence Erlbaum Associates.

# Chapter 7

# Cultivating Responsibility To and For Learning

In this chapter, we explore a view of the academic agenda of the school as requiring a moral excellence namely, being responsible to and for what one learns. From this view, the pursuit of knowledge and understanding involves not only cognitive activity, but moral activity as well. This perspective enables us to appreciate that authentic academic learning involves a moral quest. To appreciate this perspective, however, we need to step outside of the vocabulary of psychology and engage a vocabulary more adaptable to moral philosophy.

## BASIC ASSUMPTION: ISOLATED LEARNING VERSUS RELATIONAL LEARNING[1]

One of the most profound flaws in early modernity was the gradual emergence of an aggressive affirmation of the autonomous individual. This affirmation eventually developed into a philosophical, political, and economic theory. It became firmly entrenched as an ideology of individualism, an unquestioned dogma that the individual, to be fully human, had to assert his independence within family, community, nature, and cosmos. The individual had to stand alone against the cosmic, cultural, and religious landscape; to admit any intrinsic dependence on that landscape was to negate, it was believed, the individual's uniqueness, the particular destiny, the freedom to

---

[1]Much of what follows is taken from R. J. Starratt (1998). Grounding moral educational leadership in the morality of teaching and learning. *Leading and Managing*, 4(4), 245–255.

be the one-of-a-kind person he was entitled to be. (I use the masculine here intentionally.)

That ideology had profound consequences for understanding how such an isolated individual could know the world from which the individual stood decidedly apart. That ideology is reflected in Descartes' struggle to build a logical basis for even knowing that he existed; his *cogito, ergo sum* (I think, therefore I exist) was the act of an isolated individual who had to be the sole explanation of his own knowledge because his standing apart from the world left him no secure bridge or connection to that world. Descartes' radically isolated knower became the starting point for most of the subsequent epistemologies of modernism despite the resistance of the Romantics (Willey, 1966). Somehow the mind of this isolated, separated knower had to be predisposed to know the world objectively, whether through innate ideas or through logical and perceptual mechanisms whose forms naturally conformed to the logical and conceptual forms of objective realities grasped through reason and the methodologies of science. Much of cognitive science today is still wrestling with what is basically the epistemological question inherited from Descartes (Bruner, 1987; Frawley, 1997).

How do we know what we know? If the mind is like a computer that processes information, how does that information become knowledge? If the mind is like a narrator and a reader of stories, how is it that we derive meaning from stories? If, yet again, knowledge is simply equated to whatever we are conscious of, how do we move from the immediacy of consciousness to what we say we know about the laws of gravity or of supply and demand? The new sociology of knowledge, of course, denies the isolation of the knower, placing the knower inside culture, inside a tapestry of already constructed knowledge and language maps, frameworks, threads, logics, and methodologies (McCarthy, 1996). The knower knows by receiving knowledge already constructed for the knower by the community that enfolds the knower. However, to avoid a new version of nominalism—the mistake of equating knowing the names of things with knowing the things in themselves—the new sociology of knowledge still has to deal with how knowledge is constructed in the first place, as well as how the knower who comes to know through the mediation of language and culture knows objective reality (Goodman, 1984).

Cognitive science has been split by similar divisive explanations of knowledge as either information processing by the computerlike brain or as socially constructed. Put rather simplistically, the split is over the question, "Is the world (already) in the mind or is the mind in the world?" Does knowledge of the world come through an association of external stimuli of sensation and perception with already neurologically predisposed processing mechanisms, or does social experience construct the mind as a social construct by which the individual distinguishes between internal experience (my thoughts, which are hidden from outside agents) and external objects and persons? Does social experience provide names for things and languages by which to think about things? On the contrary, is there a universal internal grammar already disposed to organize all my knowledge of the world, the development of such universal grammar triggered by language stimulation in early childhood? Frawley (1997) argued that Vygotsky comes closest to the unification of the social and computational mind by postulating an internalization of sociocultural information by which metaconscious processing (thinking about thinking) is facilitated and becomes internally and developmentally structured. So the world plays a part in the structuring of mind and the mind subsequently (and unconsciously) structures the knowledge of the world. Again, this is a simplified reading of an extraordinarily complex scholarly terrain. Nevertheless, the field of cognitive science seems stuck on Descartes' basic (and misguided) question.

To be fair, we have to acknowledge Descartes was not the first to raise the question about how human beings come to know any aspect of reality. This question has been raised by philosophers who precede Plato and Aristotle and has continued to vex philosophers from the Greeks, Arabs, and Scholastics to the present time. One tradition with a heritage that goes back to Plato and Aristotle and continues on through to the present grounds the act of knowing in a theory of participation. According to this theory, we can know being in its particulars because we participate in being. Without going into the ontology or metaphysics behind the theory of participation, we might for the moment consider that notion of participation as it might be expressed in contemporary science.

More recent philosophers who are familiar with quantum physics and contemporary biology (Bateson, 1979, 1991; Eiseley, 1957, 1978; Lovelock, 1979; Polanyi, 1964, 1974; Prigogine & Stengers, 1984; Seilstad, 1989; Turner, 1991; Whitehead, 1957; Zohar & Marshall, 1994) offer a different epistemology by changing the assumptions about the human individual knower. The individual knower is not isolated from what he or she knows. The human knower already participates in nature. The human mind is embedded in the cosmic field; the energy flowing in that field is flowing in the human mind, in the human brain, and in the history of the culture and its language. That culture, language, mind, and brain are all connected in space and time with everything that ever was, that is now, and that will be. Moreover, through evolutionary history, life was learning how to organize itself. This position (these authors cannot be reduced to a single position; I am creating a fiction for the sake of argument) postulates that there is already in the universe an intelligence within everything that is. The universe, in each of its parts (if it can be said to have parts) and in its unity, reflects an underlying intelligence. It appears to know what it is doing, whether we are talking about astrophysics or subatomic physics, about the evolution of humans and their forms of intelligence as social beings, or about the evolution of culture and civilization and their forms of linguistic, scientific, philosophical, artistic, and religious intelligence.

Humans are not the only beings in the universe with intelligence, not the only ones seeking to know their destiny, and not the only ones using knowledge to adapt to their environment and re-create themselves and their environment. Plants and animals, microbes and bacteria, and cells and their nuclei have developed sophisticated defenses (disguises, antibodies, toxins, mutating processes) against predators and threats in their environments. Although it may take them somewhat longer to solve their problems, given a million years or so, they manage. This is not to say that there are no mistakes along the way. The mammalian immune system sometimes gets a little crazy, commanding white blood cells to attack normal cells, as in some forms of arthritis and hepatitis. Human intelligence took more than a few centuries to correct Ptolemy's interpretation of the universe as Earth-centered. Male intelligence still does not understand female intelligence according to not a few voices in the audience.

If knowledge is not a particular something that an isolated individual somehow steals, coaxes, or conjures from a hostile or indifferent nature, then what is it? To overcome the riddle of knowledge, we must overturn one of the basic assumptions that has led to the riddle in the first place and that is the assumption of the isolated knower, separated from the natural world he or she is trying to know. Dewey, Whitehead, Polanyi, Bateson, and many others suggest that we begin with the assumption that the individual human being is not isolated from nature (and by nature I include human nature in its personal and social forms), but is in relationship to all of nature. Being in relationship to the natural world means being in multiple relationships simultaneously (relationships such as gravity, the food chain, weather patterns, political and cultural institutions, energy exchange, love and fear, aesthetic and economic dependencies, etc.) with that world. Knowledge is a dialogue between the intelligences found in the natural and social worlds and the intelligence of the individual knower. Being in relationship with the natural and social worlds implies mutual involvement and mutual respect. It implies a language or languages by which a dialogue takes place. The knower and the known speak to one another, resist one another, attract one another, threaten one another, seduce one another, and puzzle one another. Because they naturally belong to one another and they exist always and continuously in relationship to one another, there is no question of the knower living independently on some higher plane above the known. They are intertwined, implicated in each other's existence. This holds for relationships of love and relationships of enmity; relationships between humans and songbirds, and humans and the HIV virus; relationships between spouses, and relationships between guards and prison inmates, relationships with weeds in my backyard and with eruptions on the sun's surface. Unless those relationships issue in a dialogue of mutual understanding, which is revealed in their reciprocal activity, there is no knowledge; there are only potential relationships.

## KNOWLEDGE AS INTIMACY: INTIMACY
## AS THE GROUND OF REVERENCE

Knowledge, in other words, can be understood from the standpoint of relationality, from an ontology not of isolated beings, but of beings in a field, the energy of which grounds, creates, and sustains relationality. Looked at this way, we may speak of knowledge as the achievement of a certain mutual intimacy. Using the analogy of human love relationships, we may say that knowing involves mutual self-disclosure. As humans fall in love, they want to tell the other who they are; they want the other to know the inside self who is known by no others. They share secrets, they construct their own coded language, have their own humorous asides, and connect new experiences to special, treasured experiences of the past. Lovers take the being of the beloved inside themselves. They walk around all day carrying the presence of the other in their awareness. There is an amplitude to their daily lives: Present moments carry memories of recent cherished experiences as well as dreams of a shared future. Although separated, they can easily imagine what the other is doing at any given hour of the day. They even see things through the other's eyes, hear through the other's ears, and react to things with the other's sensibility. Whether together or apart, they are like two beings embracing emotionally and spiritually; the dialogue inside is tacitly and continuously taking place.

Intimacy implies nakedness. Nakedness is necessary for the more complete union of the two—not simply physical nakedness, but psychological and spiritual nakedness. Such divestiture of external covering does not happen carelessly or all at once. It requires patience, trust, dialogue, and sharing of stories, fears, dreams, and ambivalences. Even after years in the relationship, the divestiture continues to reveal more of the mystery, more of the hitherto unsuspected complexity. Interestingly enough, the divestiture gradually reveals an appealing paradox: Although divestiture is necessary, it can never be total. The soul, the inner being, is always expressed in language, in symbol, and in form. The Latin word for mask is *persona*. To be a person means to have a face—a face that can conceal as well as a face that can say I care for you. The other is always an other, is always partially concealed, even in the process of revelation, because the face is never able to tell all.

With the fuller disclosure grows the awareness of the beauty as well as the fragility of the other. Beauty holds for a moment and the moment passes. In everything beautiful, there are always traces of imperfection. Sometimes awareness of the imperfection brings out the pathos inside of the beauty. Lovers want to disclose their best selves, their best profile, their best poem, and their most authentic and courageous decisions. But every person has an uncertain hold on their existence. Allowing another to see that uncertainty, to see the imperfection, the mediocrities, the defeats, the talent wasted, the challenges avoided, the self-deceptions, the posturing—and to trust that one will still be loved—extends intimacy to its limits.

Nakedness brings vulnerability. By entrusting oneself to the other, one places oneself in the hands of the other. If there is not a mutual entrusting, if one holds back, then the honesty of the mutual disclosure is tainted. One is vulnerable to betrayal, to the closing off of secrets, to manipulation by the other, and to being used by the other. Unless each remains a *thou* to each other, the other becomes an *it*—an object, a thing to be used, controlled, possessed, and, when inconvenient, discarded. The relationship is no longer mutual; it becomes one-sided, one-dimensional, distorted, distorting, and incapable of mutually fulfilling the parties in the relationship. They have ceased being responsible to and for each other.

If we postulate that knowing is somewhat like loving, that the approach to the object of knowledge requires a profound respect for and sensitivity to its sacredness, that knowing is acknowledging the relationship between the knower and the known, being responsible to and for the known—then we have a different understanding of knowledge. From this perspective, knowing is not only a meeting among intelligences, but also an implicit moral act. In that moral act of knowing, the knower accepts the responsibility of coming to know the known care-fully—that is, full of care for the integrity of the known. That implies avoiding a careless approach to the relationship, to the dialogue, so that the knower knows the known as it truly is or at least as truly as present circumstances allow. It means putting aside one's own sense of superiority or importance, leaving one's own self-centered agenda aside, submitting oneself to the message of the subject, and being willing to be humbled by the integrity of the known. It also means that the knower, when she or he shares their knowledge of the known, represents the known as accurately and sensitively as circumstances allow. That sharing becomes an invitation to another to approach the known with similar reverence and care.

## THE ETHIC OF SCHOLARSHIP

This careful and caring ethic is elaborated in the traditions and rituals that surround the work of scholars. Scholarship is meant to be trusted by the public because the scholar is assumed to be committed to the fullest and clearest understanding of what he or she is studying and to the most honest and undistorted representation of that knowledge as circumstances allow.

Scholars cannot report their findings in dishonest ways, bending their conclusions to fit a preconceived theory to which they have personally committed their reputation. Their job is not to tell the public what it wants to hear, but to let the facts speak for themselves. Insofar as their findings are presented in interpretive frameworks, they should acknowledge the influence of those frameworks on the intelligibility of the findings. Where their speculations go beyond the findings of their research, they should announce them as such. Scholars are obliged to treat their knowledge carefully because they recognize that the search for and disclosure of the knowledge is a moral as well as an intellectual enterprise.

For the scholar, the knowing process involves careful attention the known. It involves listening to the muted and subtle messages being sent by the known. It means bringing the initial interpretation of these messages back to the subject of study, asking repeatedly: Did you mean this or did you mean that? Are my methods of attending to you getting in the way of what you want to say to me? Am I starting from the wrong assumptions when I interpret you this way? Is this what you really mean? Again and again, the scholar checks the evidence, compares the message, and listens with his heart as well as his mind. As Polanyi (1964) suggested, the scholar tries to know the subject so well that he or she develops an intuitive, tacit knowing of the complexity of the subject so that he or she knows without being able to say precisely how until further reflection points to the logic of the conclusion.

Most scholars exhibit a fascination with their field of study and, within it, those special areas of their research. The fascination flows over into affection. They *love studying this stuff.* They love their learning into knowledge and understanding. Some say disparagingly that a scholar is *married to his work.* For scholars, the relationship between themselves and their subject is so gratifying, so thrilling, and so fascinating that it becomes their whole world.

The scholars' love for what they study does not necessarily imply that their relationship with that subject is not frustrating, painful, and disagreeable. The otherness of the subject intrudes on the scholar's plans and timetables. The subject also appears to contradict itself or at least contradict the preliminary conclusions drawn by the scholar. The subject refuses to cooperate with the technology the scholar is using to poke around its insides. The scholar will rant and rave at the subject, accusing the universe of perfidy in allowing this aberration to exist and complaining that the subject is intentionally deceitful. Older couples recognize the theatrics.

## KNOWLEDGE AS A TOOL

Beside the knowledge of the other as it is in itself and in relationship to me, knowledge also reveals the relationships among the properties of various things. We know the properties of types of steel, types of gases, and types of acids. We know that certain gases when heated melt steel; that certain acids corrode steel. We know that steel is stronger than wood; that a steel axe can cut through wood. We know that certain laws protect citizens' rights. We know that termites can eat wood. We understand the relationship among traffic lights, pedestrian walkways, and the flow of traffic. We discover that certain microbes help diffuse an oil spill; that a certain circumference of pipe allows only a certain volume of water to flow through it at any time. Rarely, however, are these isolated, one-to-one relationships. For example, water flows through pipes according to conditions of pressure, as well as conditions of gravity; water does not flow through a pipe going up a hill unless it is pumped or unless the water source is already at a height above the hill. Microbes cannot be introduced into a water system to dispel an oil spill unless the water is sufficiently warm to sustain the life and activity of the microbes. Laws protecting free speech are limited by other laws against libel.

The knowledge that we acquire not only reveals the relationships we have to the world, but also reveals how the world works or how, with some inventiveness, we can make it work. Knowledge not only teaches reverence for the world, it reveals the actual or potential working relationships of the world. Knowledge of these relationships may likewise be the work of the scholar/researcher: research on the food chain in the oceans; research on enzymes that effect a chain of reactions in the human body; research on the brain chemistry of schizophrenics. This kind of sustained inquiry can be fascinating in its own right; it can also have many practical applications. For the moment, I want to focus on knowledge as a tool and on the responsibilities that knowledge imposes.

Knowledge is useful for our work, individually and collectively, in the world. That work involves not only our career, but our work as a family member, a neighbor, a citizen, a homebuilder, a member of multiple organizations, a member of the human race, and an intelligent animal in the natural environment. Often one's work is indeed expressed as one's career: That is where, for many, they make their public contribution to the world. True enough, it is where they earn their livelihood. For most, however, it involves the exertion of one's special talents—whether that is in stacking canned goods in a grocery store, delivering the mail, fixing computers, running banks, designing office buildings, writing poems, teaching children, directing traffic, or delivering babies. That work involves our intelligence, our artistry, and our energy. It also involves a basic sense of responsibility: responsibility not simply to one's employer to give an honest day's work for a day's pay, but a responsibility to the world—however amorphous our definition of that term might be—to make a contribution and respond to some minimal sense of stewardship.

In some traditional societies, that responsibility is expressed in the daily and cyclical observation of the sacred traditions surrounding the preparation and consumption of food, preparations for the hunt, the activities of planting and harvesting, the performance of traditional dances honoring totemic ancestors, and the making of clothing and household implements. Their work is understood as participation in the cyclical rhythms of nature. It carries with it an obligation to perform the work in the prescribed way so as not to upset the harmonies in nature.

Even in the contemporary modern world, humans' work tacitly reveals a subtle, but deeply felt sense of obligation. We are somehow obligated to take responsibility not only for ourselves, but for the world in which we live. We know that we have to live in some kind of basic harmony with each other and our environment if we are to survive at all and to survive in any humanly satisfying kind of life. That harmony does not happen automatically. It is the result of work—not a kind of mindless, flailing-around activity, but a work guided by intelligence, by some knowledge of what is required, what is possible, and some sense of what is desirable. That knowledge is rarely absolute, clear, or reliable, but it is enough to get us started—a basis for further trial-and-error learning, a foundation for moving forward in our response to what we think is needed.

Craftspeople develop a respect for the tools of the craft, for the craft knowledge that is passed down from one generation to the other about the possibilities and limitations of the material of their craft. Those tools and that knowledge enable them to make the products of their craft. They, too, feel a special responsibility in their work. It should reflect the care and respect for their material, bringing out the special qualities of their materials. Occasionally it reflects a creative use of the tools of their craft. It should offer a useful and reliable product to the community; with the more traditional crafts that employ artistry as well, it should please and delight those who use their product, whether it is a shawl, a cabinet, a clay casserole bowl, a set of door hinges, or a set of custom-made stereo speakers. Craftspeople feel a responsibility not only to their customers, but also to their crafts. Shoddy work reflects negatively on the craft community and the ideal of craftsmanship for which it stands.

Professionals are also expected to have mastered the knowledge and tools of their specialization. They are expected to have mastered not only the habits of accepted practice, but also to understand the theoretical aspects of their work. Knowledge of the theory allows them far greater discretion in fashioning responses to the problems of practice. Unlike the craftsperson whose work tends to be carefully circumscribed by tradition and training, the professional is supposed to be broadly versed in the theoretical systems, frameworks, schools of thought, and current research that have historically shaped the field of the professional. To be sure, doctors specialize in specific medical specializations such as heart and lungs, pediatrics, obstetrics, oncology, neurology, and so forth, but they are expected to have a fairly broad understanding of the workings of the human body. So, too, for lawyers and engineers: They may specialize in a narrow aspect of their field, but they have been trained broadly in the history and principles behind law and engineering.

Many professions are involved in providing human services and, therefore, are bounded by explicit ethical principles that govern the way in which they apply their specializations to human subjects. As the economics and technology of professional practice become more complex, explicit laws and regulations have been set in place to require professionals to work within certain boundaries. Those laws reflect the public's awareness of the potential damage that can accrue to a careless or unscrupulous practice of law, medicine, architecture, accounting, banking, engineering, and teaching. The enormous power for serving the common good vested in the knowledge of the professional may also cause enormous damage when it is exercised unprofessionally precisely because of the widespread public trust in the professional. Their exercise of their knowledge carries with it weighty responsibilities. Often it is the idealized image of a professional involved in public service that attracts the young to the profession in the first place. They see it as a high calling, a noble work in which they can find both personal and moral fulfillment.

Unfortunately, there are many examples of unscrupulous people who use their knowledge in exclusively self-serving ways. Almost every day, the media carry reports of people and companies violating the trust of their profession or their craft: insider trading, tax fraud, bribery of public officials, shoddy field testing of medicines, misleading manipulation of experimental research results, cost-cutting procedures that endanger the lives of automobile drivers, violations of health code regulations in food processing plants, insurance companies that refuse to honor the terms of their policies, accounting firms conspiring with clients to "cook the books," violations of construction safety codes, willful violations of workers' workplace safety regulations, and clergy molesting children. The public is outraged precisely because of the betrayal of public trust in the integrity of professionals. Their position of superior knowledge and expertise leads us to place significant aspects of our lives in their hands. Their crimes are more serious than crimes of passion, the fight in the tavern, or the drug-crazed street robber. Professionals violate our trust, our respect for their role as public servants, when they use their profession to break the law and defraud the customer. The unfortunate cynicism toward lawyers and doctors, business executives and politicians, and teachers and clergy is not only a measure of the public's disappointment at their behavior, but also a measure of our continued high expectations of the moral ideal of their professions.

## SCHOOLING AND THE CONSTRUCTION
## OF KNOWLEDGE

When we think now of how knowledge is approached in schools, we find two different kinds of teachers. One teacher assumes that knowledge is objectively out there awaiting a knower, that the student is independent and separated from what he knows, and that learning is simply a matter of appropriating that knowledge either by memorization of its formulation in the textbook or by performing lab experiments that lead to the conclusions prescribed in the textbook. Knowledge is a question of getting the right answers. The right answers are what the experts know and have told us is what we need to know about the matter. The process of explaining what lies behind the right answer is almost always neglected. Covering the syllabus is equated with repeating all the right answers contained in the syllabus. Depending on how many right and wrong answers students come up with in the course of a semester, students receive a grade, indicating how much of the syllabus they have learned or how much they know.

The second teacher is closer to the scholar. One finds with this teacher an enthusiastic fascination with the material being studied. Students sense that the teacher actually *enjoys messing around with this stuff.* The teacher communicates such enthusiasm for the material under study that even normally resistant students go along so as not to hurt her feelings. This teacher invites the students to enter the world of the subject matter, whether that be chemistry, mathematics, or poetry. Entry into that world, however, is not as a tourist; rather, they enter into a world where they are dramatically implicated, where they are in relationship with what they are learning and where they become responsible for and to what they know.

This second kind of teacher views the syllabus as an artificial contrivance, someone's artificial ordering and isolating of a universe of knowledge that in reality is connected to other universes of knowledge, or someone's contrived arrangement of methodological approaches that can easily get in the way of genuine knowledge. This teacher devises learning projects that bring students eye to eye with the complexity of the subject matter, which tease students into dialogue, tell the students as much about themselves as about the subject, and surprise and delight them with fascinating insights into the subject.

Students are constructed by knowledge even as they construct knowledge. Assuming that knowledge is grounded in relationality, knowledge reveals how the knower is in relationship to the known. Learning about chemical compounds not only illuminates the ecology of the immediate environment, but also reveals how their own body works. Learning about the two world wars places them in relationship to their own willingness to die for their country, in relationship to nonviolence as a desirable ethic, in relationship to weapons of mass destruction, in relationship to the actual sufferings of civilian populations, in relationship to the reality of genocide, in relationship to political fanatacism, and in relation to the geopolitics of current history. In such cases, students are taught to take responsibility *for* what they know and be responsible *to* what they know. Learning for right answers is replaced with learning how to live in some kind of harmony with their natural and social worlds. There is no one right answer to that larger agenda. The knowledge that students absorb, however, continues to illuminate their relationship to their natural and social worlds, relationships that continue to become more intelligible, and relationships that make demands on them and demands on their generation.

This second teacher also provides them with experiences in the use of their knowledge to analyze and respond to problems in the real world. Through computer simulations, for example, a mathematics teacher might set students to work on an engineering problem, an investment strategy, or a census-taking issue. Using case studies and computer simulations, a biology teacher may present students with problems from the world of public health, environmental protection, food processing technologies, and genetic research. A foreign language teacher may encourage students to communicate via the Internet with students in countries using that language, not simply to create friendships, but also to explore mutually beneficial trade relationships, cultural exchanges, and similar environmental issues. A social studies teacher may have students construct family histories using stories from relatives still alive, letters from deceased relatives, old newspaper stories, and family picture albums. They may not only trace their genealogies, but may also attempt to understand the human and civil rights issues their forebears faced, the technologies available to them for various survival tasks, and their cultural enjoyments and artifacts.

In other words, the second teacher teaches the students how to use their knowledge and how to apply what they know to real people and real situations. In the process, the teacher teaches them how to honor the tools of generating knowledge and applying knowledge, how to report their findings with integrity, how to avoid going beyond the evidence, and to announce speculation when it is being employed. Furthermore, the application of their knowledge is used to explore ways in which to improve the situation under study. How might the public health department better monitor the processing of food or the levels of bacteria in the water supply? How might companies change their policies toward whistle blowers to encourage early detection of serious production problems? How might human rights abuses in developing countries be more effectively treated in international law?

This second teacher looks for ways in the local community for students to put their knowledge at the service of people or agencies to use. In this way, students experience how it feels to use their knowledge as a service to others rather than simply as a means to getting a grade on a test. In this way, students learn that their talents were given to them primarily to serve the community and only secondarily to be used for their own advantage. The practice of using and applying their knowledge is accompanied by continuous admonitions (brief homilies whose repetitions sticks in the memory) such as: Knowledge brings responsibility; If we do not use our knowledge to improve people's lives, then what good is it?; Respect the integrity of what you know and how you came to know it; Respect the craft of language and rhetoric; Respect the audience that receives your knowledge reports by providing them with illustrative examples and precise language, and occasional humor for when they get drowsy.

The major sermon to the students is this: You do not have the moral option to choose not to learn. Choosing not to learn is choosing not to know what you will need to know in order to make a contribution to the world. Your chosen ignorance may be the occasion of an accident, the loss of life, the failure of an important project, the frustration of a community's dream, or the disappointment of people who were counting on you to perform. An organization or community's achievement of excellence is dependent not only on the quality of its most talented members, but on the intelligent cooperation of its ordinary members like you. The shoddy or incompetent work of anyone diminishes the achievement of the whole. As a civilization, we have achieved whatever level of greatness, excellence, and good order because countless people like you knew what to do when it counted most. They were prepared. That is why learning what you learn in school is not only a privilege, but a duty to yourselves, your community, and your future children and grandchildren.

These practices and admonitions are fundamental ways to build up both good intellectual habits as well as habits of responsibility in the appreciation and use of knowledge. Learning communities need these second types of teachers if their efforts to improve the intellectual rigor of the curriculum are to bear fruit. The first kind of teacher takes new curriculum standards and encourages the same unreflective, alienating kind of learning that currently obtains in schools. Authentic learning has to be reverential. All learning places us in relationship to an immense beauty, a marvelous history, and a heroic destiny. Learning is also about our responsibilities to a world filled with marvelous possibilities and complex problems. Today's young people have to appreciate how they are nurtured by their natural environment, their human community, and the values, ideals, and achievements of their culture. They also have to discover how they can use their knowledge to make a difference. The moral implications of knowledge—both for the healthy constructing of ourselves and the reverential reconstructing of our world—are of equal importance to the mastery of the knowledge. I suggest that neither aspect of knowledge—its intellectual or moral content—can be properly engaged without the other.

## WHAT ARE THE IMPLICATIONS FOR EDUCATIONAL LEADERSHIP?

If educators were to dwell inside this understanding of learning as intrinsically moral, they would work every day to create an environment in their schools in which that kind of learning would flourish. Their leadership would be informed by the morality of the core work of the school. Cultivating that kind of learning is to honor the moral excellence of learning.

Alfred North Whitehead (1932) provided the foundational text for this understanding of the moral excellence of learning:

> The essence of education is that it be religious. Pray, what is religious education? A religious education is an education which inculcates duty and reverence. Duty arises from our potential control over the course of events. Where attainable knowledge could have changed the issue, ignorance has the guilt of vice. And the foundation of reverence is this perception, that the present holds within itself the complete sum of existence, backwards and forwards, that whole amplitude of time, which is eternity. (p. 23)

## ACTIVITIES

1. Ask a student or two in your school whether they can think of anything they learned in school during the past week that could be useful to any one or any group of people in their local community.
2. Prepare a faculty discussion on the moral nature of learning. How would you organize some of the key ideas that you wanted the faculty to take away from the discussion? What kind of activities might you suggest for them to try out in their classrooms?
3. If you were to organize one or two student assemblies on their responsibilities to and for their learning, how would you go about it?
4. What are some objections you might hear from the school board if they were to hear that you were talking about learning as a moral activity? How would you answer them?

## REFERENCES

Bateson, G. (1979). *Mind and nature: A necessary unity.* New York: E. P. Dutton.
Bateson, G. (1991). *A sacred unity: Further steps to an ecology of mind.* New York: HarperCollins.

Bruner, J. (1987). The transactional self. In J. Bruner & H. Haste (Eds.), *Making sense: The child's construction of the world* (pp. 81–96). New York: Methuen.

Eiseley, L. (1957). *The immense journey.* New York: Vantage.

Eiseley, L. (1978). *The star thrower.* New York: Times Books.

Frawley, W. (1997). *Vygotsky and cognitive science: Language and the unification of the social and computational mind.* Cambridge, MA: Harvard University Press.

Goodman, N. (1984). *Of minds and other matters.* Cambridge, MA: Harvard University Press.

Lovelock, J. (1979). *Gaia: A new look at life on earth.* Oxford: Oxford University Press.

McCarthy, E. D. (1996). *Knowledge as culture: The new sociology of knowledge.* London: Routledge.

Polanyi, M. (1964). *Science, faith, and society.* Chicago: University of Chicago Press.

Polanyi, M. (1974). *Scientific thought and social reality.* New York: International Universities Press.

Prigogine, I., & Stengers, I. (1984). *Order out of chaos: Man's new dialogue with nature.* New York: Bantam.

Seilstad, G. A. (1989). *At the heart of the web: The inevitable genesis of intelligent life.* New York: Harcourt Brace.

Turner, F. (1991). *The rebirth of value: Meditations on beauty, ecology, religion and education.* Albany, NY: State University of New York Press.

Whitehead, A. N. (1957). *Process and reality: An essay in cosmology.* New York: Free Press.

Willey, B. (1966). *Nineteenth century studies: Coleridge to Matthew Arnold.* New York: Harper Torchbooks.

Zohar, D., & Marshall, I. (1994). *The quantum society.* London: HarperCollins.

# Chapter 8

# Cultivating a Responsible Community

## FOUNDATIONAL HUMAN QUALITIES FOR MORAL LIVING

A moral way of being is a way of being human. Hence, one's morality flows from one's humanity. Three qualities of a fully human person are *autonomy*, *connectedness*, and *transcendence*. These are the foundational human qualities for a moral life; it would be impossible to be moral without developing these qualities.[1]

---

[1]Rather than distracting the reader with a blizzard of references for each of the particulars in the text, I list here some of the main sources for this material. First, hovering over this whole chapter is the figure of John Dewey. As I reread his writings, I keep stumbling across pieces of his work that have influenced my thinking, although I have forgotten the precise source of the influence. Beyond Dewey, the work of John MacMurray, the Scottish ethician, has been crucial for understanding the complementary demands of autonomy and relationship; see his *Persons in relation*, London: Faber & Faber, 1961. The more recent work of Charles Taylor echoes much of MacMurray's themes; see *The ethics of authenticity*. Cambridge, MA: Harvard University Press, 1991. Others who influenced the theme of connectedness have been Robert Bellah and his colleagues R. Madsen, W. Sullivan, A. Swidler, and S. Tipton, in their two books, *Habits of the heart*, Berkeley, CA: University of California Press, 1985; and *The good society*, New York: Alfred A. Knopf, 1991. Other influences have been David Bohm, *Wholeness and the implicate order*, London: Routledge & Kegan Paul, 1980; Gregory Bateson, *Steps to an ecology of mind*, New York: Ballantine, 1972; Elise Boulding, *Building a global civic culture*, New York: Teachers College Press, 1988; Donald Oliver, *Education, modernity and fractured meaning*, Albany, NY: State University of New York Press, 1989; and Danah Zohar and Ian Marshall, *The quantum society*, London: Hamingo/HarperCollins, 1994. For the theme of transcendence, I have been influenced by John Gardner's *Excellence*, New York: Harper & Row, 1961; Joseph Campbell in his commentary on his work, *Hero with a thousand faces*, as found in P. Cousineau (Ed.), *The hero's journey: Joseph Campbell on his life and work*, San Francisco: Harper & Row, 1990; and C. Pearson's *The hero within: Six archetypes we live by*, New York: Harper & Row, 1989.

Being autonomous means owning oneself, being one's own person. It does not mean acting in isolation from one's culture, one's socialization into that culture, or from the specific social context in which one finds oneself. Being autonomous means that, once these cultural and contextual influences are taken into account, one takes responsibility for what one does. The choices an autonomous person makes belong to him or her; they carry a personal signature and are clearly distinct from choices due to mindless routine, fear of reprisal, or unquestioning obedience to external authorities. Ironically, an autonomous person cannot express his or her autonomy except in relationship to another person, to a culture of meanings and traditions, as a male or female in this historical social moment. As we have seen autonomy is developed in reciprocity. This leads us to the next foundational quality.

Being connected means being in a relationship with someone or something and accepting the responsibilities implicit in the relationship. Every human being is involved in a network of relationships and with obligations and privileges that attend to these relationships. Human life implies social living, and social living implies a moral code by which the contingencies of social living are conducted. To be sure, culture determines how these moral codes are expressed and negotiated. Specific contexts (the family kitchen, the bleachers at the local ballpark, a poker game at the OK Saloon, the coffee table at one's workplace, a town meeting to discuss a new shopping mall development) also provide clues for moral expectations. Nevertheless, there appear to be certain universal demands in relationships and communal living that define us as human beings. Every culture has categories that define inhuman treatment of other people.

Being connected, moreover, means being connected to a tradition—a cultural heritage that provides the language and worldview for defining oneself and the human and natural worlds. There is a sense in which that connection to a cultural heritage brings moral obligations to honor the heroes of that tradition, those who have played a part in the ongoing regeneration of human ideals and visions of greatness by which the people of that tradition have been able to stretch beyond self-centered concerns for the preservation and renewal of the community.

Being connected also means being connected to nature and the natural universe. The recognition that humans are members of an eco-community brings a sense of responsibility toward the environment. Recognizing that we are beneficiaries of a bounteous nature brings a sense of obligation to preserve the integrity of the air, soil, water, and various forms of life.

Finally, an essential quality to living a fully human life is the quality of what I call *transcendence*. Transcendence is what leads us to turn our life toward someone or toward something greater than or beyond ourselves. One form of transcendence is reaching for a form of excellence, whether in athletics, creative arts, scholarship, professional expertise, founding of an organization, or a craft. Another form of transcendence involves turning toward some kind of ideal embodied in collective action, such as an association concerned about the environment, child care, political freedom, legal protection, or preservation of historical sites.

Every culture has some way to express the heroic impulse in humans. That heroic impulse, however modest and understated, underlies most expressions of altruism in society. Humans apparently need something heroic to validate their own identity, either through their individual striving or through identification with something heroic in their associations, culture, religion, or national origins.

When transcendence is joined with the qualities of autonomy and connectedness, we begin to see how the three qualities complement and feed each other in the building of a rich and integral human life.[2] Autonomy makes sense only in relation to other autonomous persons, when the uniqueness and wealth of each person can be mutually appreciated and celebrated. Connectedness means that one is connected to someone or something other than oneself. Hence, it requires an empathetic embrace of what is different from the autonomous actor to make and sustain the connection. Community enables the autonomous individual to belong to something larger; it gives the individual roots in both the past and present. However, the community is not automatically self-sustaining. It is sustained by autonomous individuals who transcend self-interest to promote the common good, who join with other individuals to re-create the community. This transcending activity includes, for example, offering satisfying and mutually fulfilling services for one another, services of protection and support, care and help, joint action on a common project, celebration of a common heritage, honoring a community tradition by connecting one's own story to the larger story of the community. This give and take of life in the community simultaneously depends on and feeds the heroic imagination of individuals, whose actions in turn give new life to the community.

Although we speak of these three foundational qualities of a moral life somewhat abstractly, we do not want to think of them as a list of virtues we set out to acquire. These qualities are never achieved as an acquisition. They are always to be found in the action of a specific person in this moment, in these circumstances, with these people, and hence are never perfectly or fully expressed. They are achieved only in the doing and in the doing constantly repeated.

If these qualities are foundational in developing a responsible person, then schools should be concerned to nurture those qualities and discour-

---

[2]The material in the following paragraphs is adapted from R. J. Starratt (1994). *Building an ethical school,* London: Falmer.

age the development of their opposites. Hence, teachers need to reflect on how they can use the everyday activities of youngsters in their classrooms and other areas around the school to nurture these qualities. Of course, youngsters develop in recognizable patterns, so what might be appropriate for a 10-year-old may not be appropriate for a 16-year-old. How one nurtures the sense of transcendence in kindergarten would differ from an approach taken in seventh grade. Yet the three qualities can be supported in every grade in ways suitable for the children.

It would be a mistake, however, to expect all children to manifest these qualities in the same way. Sex, race, culture, and class all nuance the child's expression of autonomy, connectedness, and transcendence. Class-bound and ethnocentric teachers will have difficulty with such varied expressions. Sensitive teachers will observe the different expressions and listen to youngsters explain their behavior. Over time, such teachers will be able to promote these qualities within an appropriate range of plurality and diversity.

In any event, a major agenda of administrators cultivating a responsible community is to encourage teachers throughout the school to design explicit learning activities that involve the development of these foundational qualities. This agenda provides the basis for the next level of ethical education. At this juncture, however, we should realize that the promotion of these foundational qualities should not disturb those parents and teachers who worry about religion inserting itself into the curriculum of the public school. Although one would hope these qualities would not be perceived as antithetical to religion, it would be difficult to point to any religious institution or church as claiming these qualities as their exclusive doctrinal property. Rather, they belong to the human race.

## FRAMEWORKS FOR DEVELOPING EXPLICIT MORAL UNDERSTANDING

The next step in developing a curriculum of responsibility is concerned with frameworks for explicit moral understanding. These frameworks attempt to explain what constitutes certain actions as ethical and other actions as unethical. In the field of ethics, we can find a variety of frameworks that provide a rationale for moral interpretation.[3] Some stress an ethic of justice as an overall framework; others stress an ethic of care; still others criticize those ethics as politically and culturally naive, preferring an ethic grounded in critique. I suggest that we consider a large framework that embraces all three schools of thought in a multidimensional framework. That is, each of these schools of thought provides direction for an important part

---

[3]Much of the material dealing with these three ethics is adapted from Starratt (1994).

of a curriculum of responsibility, but no one of them taken alone is sufficient. When combined, they complement each other to provide a richer understanding of the complex ethical challenges facing contemporary society.

What follows is not an attempt to develop a full-blown ethical theory. We
discuss core ethical values, going somewhat into the arguments that support them, but without delving into the comprehensive philosophical blueprint that undergirds them. Each theme is developed consecutively. While
attempting to remain faithful to the theory or body of theory from which
the theme was selected, the exposition is guided by the demands of the educating context. Underneath these three ethics, of course, are the irreduc-
ible assumptions and cultural beliefs about what is valuable in human life,
in which every theory is grounded.

## THE ETHIC OF CRITIQUE

Because the historical moment appears to be one of transition and transformation, as we move into a global market, a global information age, a global
awareness of ecological catastrophe, and a global awareness of vulnerability
to terrorist violence, it seems best to begin with the ethic of critique. The
ethic of critique developed here draws its force from critical theory—that
body of thought deriving from the Frankfurt school of philosophers and
others sympathetic to their perspectives (Adorno, 1973; Apple, 1982; Bates,
1994; Freire, 1970; Giroux, 1988; Habermas, 1973; Young, 1990). These
thinkers explore social life as intrinsically problematic because it exhibits
the struggle between competing interests and wants among various groups
and individuals in society. Whether considering social relationships, social
customs, laws, social institutions grounded in structured power relationships, or language, these thinkers ask questions such as: "Who benefits by
these arrangements?" "Which group dominates this social arrangement?"
"Who defines the way things are structured here?" "Who defines what is valued and disvalued in this situation?" The point of this critical stance is to
uncover which group has the advantage over the others, how things got to
be the way they are, and to expose how situations are structured and language used so as to maintain the legitimacy of social arrangements. By uncovering inherent injustice or dehumanization imbedded in the language
and structures of society, critical analysts invite others to redress such injustice. Hence, their basic stance is ethical because they are dealing with questions of social justice and human dignity, and the morality of social and political resistance.

Examples of issues confronted by critical ethics include sexist language
and bias in the workplace, in legal structures, and in the very language used
to define social life; racial, sexual, and class bias in educational arrange-

ments; the preservation of financially powerful groups' hegemony over the media and the political process; and the rationalization and legitimation of institutions such as prisons, orphanages, armies, and nuclear industries. The point the critical ethician stresses is that no social arrangement is neutral. Every social arrangement, no matter how it presents itself as natural, necessary, or simply "the way things are," is an artificial construct. It is usually structured to benefit some segments of society at the expense of others. Even the institution of marriage is structured in many cultures in favor of males and places the unmarried woman in a less privileged social status. The ethical challenge is to make these social arrangements more responsive to the human and social rights of all citizens. The critical ethic seeks to enable those affected by social arrangements to publicly withhold participation—to have a voice in evaluating the consequences of and altering social arrangements in the interests of fuller participation and justice for individuals.

This ethical perspective provides a framework for enabling the school community to move from a kind of naiveté about the way things are to an awareness that the social and political arenas reflect arrangements of power, privilege, interest, and influence, often legitimized by an assumed rationality, and by law, and custom. The theme of critique, for example, forces educators to confront the moral issues involved when schools disproportionately benefit some groups in society and fail others (Connell, 1993). Furthermore, as a bureaucratic organization, the school exhibits structural properties that can easily promote a misuse of power and authority among its members.

From a critical perspective, no organizational arrangements in schools have to be that way; they are all open to rearrangement in the interest of greater fairness to their members. Where unjust arrangements reflect school board or state policy, they can be appealed and restructured, as evidenced in laws now governing the education of children with special needs and the equal access of young women to participate in school athletics. The structural issues involved in the management of education, such as the process of teacher evaluation, homogeneous tracking systems, the process of grading on a curve, the process of calculating class rank, the absence of important topics in textbooks, the lack of adequate due process for students, the labeling criteria for naming some children gifted and others disabled, and the daily interruptions of the instructional process by uniform time allotments for class periods—all these and others imply ethical burdens because they contain unjustifiable assumptions and impose a disproportionate advantage to some at the expense of others.

The ethic of critique, based as it is on assumptions about the social nature of human beings and the human purposes to be served by social organization, calls the school community to embrace a sense of social responsibility not simply to the individuals in the school or school system or the education profession, but to the society of whom and for whom the school is an agent. In other words, schools were established to serve a high moral purpose—to prepare the young to take their responsible place in and for the community. Besides the legal and professional obligations, yet intertwined with them, the moral obligation of educators is to see that the school serves society the way it was intended.

## THE ETHIC OF JUSTICE

One of the shortcomings of the ethic of critique is that it rarely offers a blueprint for reconstructing the social order it is criticizing. The problem for the school community is one of governance. How does the school community govern itself while carrying out educating activities? The ethic of critique illuminates unethical practices in governing and managing organizations and implies in its critique some ethical values such as equality, the common good, human and civil rights, democratic participation, and the like. An ethic of justice provides a more explicit response to the question of self—governance, although that response may itself be flawed. We govern ourselves by observing justice. That is, we treat each other according to some standard of justice that is applied uniformly to all our relationships. The theory of justice we employ to ground those standards requires a grounding in anthropology and epistemology. Socrates explored this grounding in The Republic; his search was to be continued by a long line of philosophers up to the present day (Sullivan, 1986).

Currently, there are two general schools of thought concerning the ethic of justice. One school can trace its roots to Thomas Hobbes in the 17th century and can find a contemporary expression in the work of Nozick (1974). In this school, the primary human reality is the individual independent of social relationships: The individual is conceived as logically prior to society. Individuals are driven by their passions and interests, especially by fear of harm and desire for comfort. According to this theory, individuals enter into social relations to advance their own advantage. Individual will and preference are the primary sources of value. Social relationships are essentially artificial and governed by self-interest. The maintenance of social life requires a social contract in which individuals agree to surrender some of their freedom in return for the state's protection from the otherwise unbridled self-seeking of others. In this school of thought, human reason is the instrument by which the individual can analyze in a more or less scientific fashion what is to his or her advantage and calculate the obligations to social justice called for by the social contract.

The second school of thought on the ethic of justice finds its roots in Aristotle, Rousseau, Hegel, Marx, Mead, and Dewey. They placed society as the prior reality within which individuality develops. Furthermore, it is through experience, through living in society, that one learns the lessons of morality. Participation in the life of the community teaches individuals how to think about their own behavior in relationship to those immediately present and in terms of the larger common good of the community. In this school, freedom "is ultimately the ability to realize a responsible self-hood, which is necessarily a cooperative project" (Sullivan, 1986, p. 22). Ethics is grounded in practice within the community. The protection of human dignity depends on the moral quality of social relationships, and this is a public and political concern. Citizenship is a shared responsibility among persons committed to mutual care.

From this perspective, a communal understanding of the requirements of justice flows from both tradition and the present effort of the community to manage its affairs in the midst of competing claims of the common good and individual rights. That understanding is never complete; it is always limited by the inadequacy of tradition to respond to changing circumstances and by the impossibility of settling conflicting claims conclusively and completely. Yet the choices are always made with sensitivity to the bonds that tie individuals to their communities.

Lawrence Kohlberg, whom some associate with a Rawlsian framework, also believed that moral reasoning and choices were best made in a communitarian setting. Kohlberg (1987) carried this belief into the formation of *just community* schools.

Hence, it can be argued that an ethic of justice, especially when focused on issues of governance in a school setting, can encompass in practice the two understandings of justice—namely, justice understood as individual choices to act justly and justice understood as the community's choice to direct or govern its actions justly. In a school setting, both are required. In practice, individual choices are made with some awareness of what the community's choices are (school policies), and school community choices are made with some awareness of the kinds of individual choices that are made every day in school.

It does not take much imagination to perceive the close relationship of the ethic of critique to the ethic of justice. To promote a just social order in the school, the school community must carry out an ongoing critique of those structural features of the school that work against human beings.

## THE ETHIC OF CARE

One of the limitations of an ethic of justice is the inability of the theory to determine claims in conflict. What is just for one person might not be considered just by another person. Hence, discussions of what is just in any given situation tend to become mired down in minimalist considerations. (What minimal conditions must be met to fulfill the claims of justice?) For an ethic of justice to serve its more generous purpose, it must be complemented or fulfilled in an ethic of love. Although earlier discussions of the incompleteness of the ethic of justice took place in a theological context (Neibuhr, 1935), more recent discussions have grounded the ethic of love and caring in a philosophy of the person (Buber, 1970; MacMurray, 1961). Scholars such as Gilligan (1977) and Noddings (1984) have promoted these ethical directions from a vantage point of psychology, especially women's moral development, in the current literature on the ethic of caring.

Such an ethic focuses on the demands of relationships, not from a contractual or legalistic standpoint, but from a standpoint of absolute regard. This ethic places the awareness of human persons in relationship as occupying a position for each other of absolute value; neither one can be used as a means to an end by the other; each person enjoys an intrinsic dignity and worth and, given the chance, will reveal genuinely lovable qualities. An ethic of caring requires fidelity to persons, a willingness to acknowledge their right to be who they are, an openness to encountering them in their authentic individuality. An ethic of caring implies a loyalty to the relationship. Such an ethic does not demand relationships of intimacy. Rather, it postulates a level of caring that honors the dignity of each person and desires to see that person enjoy a fully human life. Furthermore, it recognizes that it is in relationships that the specifically human is grounded. Isolated individuals functioning only for themselves are but half persons. One becomes whole when one is in relationship with another and with many others.

A school community committed to an ethic of caring is grounded in the belief that the integrity of human relationships should be held sacred, and that the school as an organization should hold the good of human beings within it as sacred. This ethic reaches beyond concerns with efficiency, which can easily lead to using human beings as merely the means to some larger purpose of productivity, such as an increase in the district's average scores on standardized tests or the lowering of per-pupil costs.

Educators can promote an ethic of caring by attending to the cultural tone of the school. Often the use of language in official communiques tells the story. Formal, abstract language is the language of bureaucracy, impersonality, distance; humor, familiar imagery and metaphor, and personalized messages are the language of caring. Some schools clearly promote a feeling of family and celebrate friendship, loyalty, and service. Laughter in the halls, frequent greetings of each other by name, symbols of congratulations for successful projects, frequent displays of student work, hallways containing pictures of groups of youngsters engaged in school activities, and cartoons poking fun at teachers and administrators—these are all signs of a school environment that values people for who they are.

## A LARGER ETHICAL FRAMEWORK

One can argue for the necessary interpenetration of each ethic by the others if one is to argue for a fully developed moral person and moral community. Even a superficial familiarity with these ethics suggests that each implies something of the other. The ethic of critique assumes a point of view about social justice and human rights and about the way communities should govern themselves. The ethic of justice assumes an ability to perceive injustice in the social order as well as some minimal level of caring about relationships in that social order. The ethic of caring does not ignore the demands of community governance issues, but claims that caring is the ideal fulfillment of all social relationships, although most relationships among members of a community function according to a more remote form of caring.

Moreover, each ethic needs the strong convictions embedded in the other. The ethic of justice needs the profound commitment to the dignity of the individual person; the ethic of caring needs the larger attention to social order and fairness if it is to avoid an entirely idiosyncratic involvement in social policy; the ethic of critique requires an ethic of caring if it is to avoid the cynical ravings of the habitual malcontent; the ethic of justice requires the profound social analysis of the ethic of critique to move beyond the naive fine tuning of social arrangements in a social system with inequities built into the very structures by which justice is supposed to be measured.

These considerations point to the importance of employing a multidimensional ethical framework in any effort to cultivate a responsible community (see Fig. 8.1).

## CULTIVATING A RESPONSIBLE COMMUNITY

One way administrators can cultivate a responsible community is to encourage individual teachers to nurture the foundational qualities of autonomy, connectedness, and transcendence in their classrooms, as well as communicate the large ethical framework of justice, critique, and care (Starratt, 1994). Relying on the imagination and professional talent of the teachers, the administrator can simply suggest that they bring these perspectives into play in their individual classrooms. However, the administrator's responsibilities go beyond working with individual teachers. Administrators should bring a large vision of a responsible community to engage the whole school community in a conversation about how they might more intentionally and programmatically create a moral learning environment.

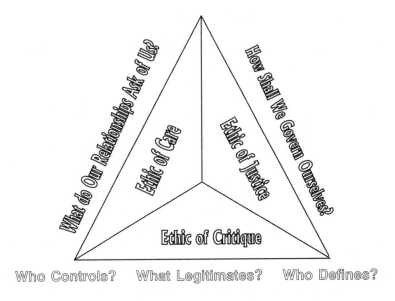

FIG. 8.1.   A multidimensional ethical framework.

Most schools shy away from a proactive approach to nurturing morality. There is a wariness of self-righteous posturing and of appearing to espouse a religious kind of preachiness. There is concern about respecting the freedom and conscience of the students, to avoid superimposing a moral creed that might conflict with the values held at home. However, never to engage youngsters in discussions about moral issues is to communicate, by default, the message that moral issues are irrelevant to the public life of the community and that the lessons learned in schools exist in some improbable, fictional moral vacuum. It can be argued that one of the major lessons of an educating process is the importance of the *discussion* (not the imposition) of moral values as they are embedded in the circumstances of everyday life (Buber, 1965). Indeed, this is the position we take here: A responsible community is one that struggles with the ethical ambiguities and tensions in contemporary life, which engages its members with the burden of the effort to live morally in community (Sullivan, 1995; Wolfe, 1995).

## INITIAL STEPS

As with any undertaking this important, administrators need to pause at the outset and try to gain clarity about what they are trying to accomplish. Conversations with colleagues, and perhaps with consultants who have worked in this area, will help to clarify those essential goals one wants to set before the community, or even those essential characteristics of a moral community one wishes to nurture in the learning process. This initial step may also involve reading and building up a small library of references that others may dip into once the conversations begin.

Another concern of major importance is the trust levels that exist in the school. If the teaching faculty is not trusting enough to engage in conversations about matters that they may not be articulate about or about matters where legitimate differences need to be respected, then the effort to build a moral community has to start right there by attending to the lack of trust and the reasons why they are not more trusting. Such an apparently simple foundation may take 2 or 3 years to develop; without it, however, the enterprise cannot move forward. Finally, the members of the teaching faculty need to have some confidence in their ability to develop a responsible community. Some initial seminars or workshops can settle many of their anxieties because, collectively, they already possess the abilities to carry out the enterprise.

In most schools, administrators find a relative absence of formal and programmatic attention to moral education. And thus it is necessary to start from the beginning, or almost the beginning. In every school, one can find numerous examples where the members of the school community do, in fact, teach or at least discuss moral values (Jackson, Boostrom, & Hansen, 1993). Hence, the effort to build a responsible community should start there, with explicitly stating the many responsibility lessons the school already teaches. Although it is easy to focus on the prohibitions in the school's rules and student handbook, the conversation should concentrate on the positive responsibilities the school is trying to teach by enforcing those rules.

I have elsewhere (Starratt, 1994) outlined a detailed process of using the foundational qualities (autonomy, connectedness, transcendence) and the ethical frameworks (justice, care, critique) to create a coordinated series of learning opportunities throughout all the K–12 school years that would enable students to analyze and understand the landscape of moral life. The process begins with a steering committee of parents, teachers, administrators, and students guiding the learning community to create a map of existing learning opportunities for the foundational qualities which various teachers in the school might already, though rather haphazardly, engage in. The process then suggests that members of the school community examine which of these existing learning opportunities they wish to programmatically and intentionally build into the learning agenda of the school's curriculum of responsibility for all students. Building on that analysis of what already exists in the school, the process goes on to develop maps of "what might be"—those further learning opportunities that seem called for in a more thorough-going curriculum of responsibility.

Then the steering committee guides the school community through a similar process of discussing the ethical frameworks, creating maps of what sporadic learning opportunities already exist in the school, and then mapping a fuller curriculum of learning opportunities that includes desirable additions to what already exists. At the end of both of these mapping efforts (building opportunities for all students to learn the foundational qualities and building opportunities for all students to learn the ethical frameworks), the school community will have completed the planning of the first two segments of the curriculum of responsibility. Figures 8.2 through 8.7 provide abstract visuals of what the mapping of such a curriculum would look like. Implementation of these two steps is outlined in greater detail in an earlier work (Starratt, 1994).

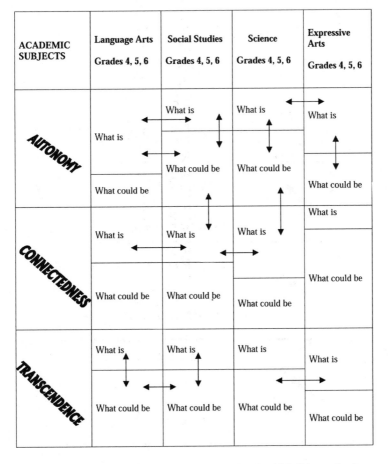

FIG. 8.2. Summary map of "What Is" and "What Could Be" in academics.

FIG. 8.3.   Mapping What Is and What Could Be: Institutional Supports.

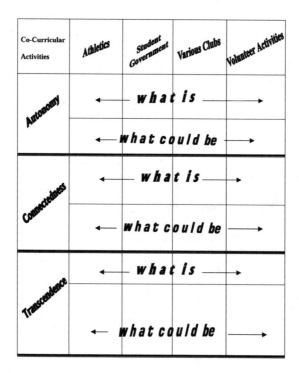

FIG. 8.4.   Mapping "What Is" and "What Could Be": Co-curriculars.

| Academics | Language Arts | Science & Technology | Social Studies | Expressive Arts |
|---|---|---|---|---|
| **Ethic of Care** | What Is | What Is | What Is | What Is |
|  | What Could Be | What Could Be | What Could Be | What Could Be |
| **Ethic of Justice** | What Is | What Is | What Is | What Is |
|  | What Could Be | What Could Be | What Could Be | What Could Be |
| **Ethic of Critique** | What Is | What Is | What Is | What Is |
|  | What Could Be | What Could Be | What Could Be | What Could be |

FIG. 8.5.   Map of "What Is" and "What Could Be": Grades 10–12.

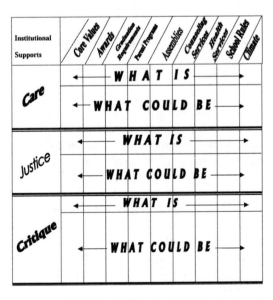

FIG. 8.6.   Mapping "What Is and "What Could Be": Institutional supports.

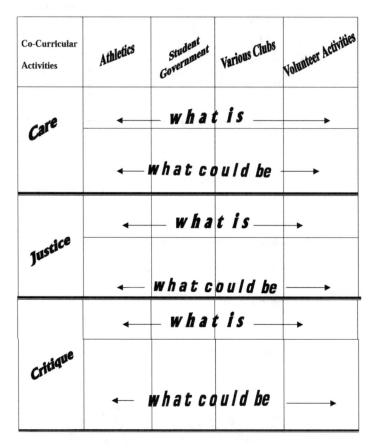

FIG. 8.7.   Mapping "What Is and "What Could Be": Co-curriculars.

This process would comprise the second step in the development of the curriculum of responsibility, namely a developmentally appropriate series of learning opportunities, using material already to be found in the existing academic curriculum, in the school's co-curriculars, and the institutional support systems such as the guidance and discipline system. The arrows in the figures are meant to suggest the explicit linking of curriculum areas. This process of working through the foundational qualities and the ethical frameworks and their application to existing learning opportunities in the school would take about 5 years or more. While that work was moving forward, the school could begin to develop the third step of the curriculum of responsibility, which is to develop a method of analyzing responsibility situations.

**Analysis of Responsibility Situations**

This third step in developing the responsibility curriculum is focused on bringing individual students and groups of students to consider what their responsibilities might be in specific situations. In developing this step, I am adapting the work of Auhagen (2001) who in the course of studying people's experience of responsibility in everyday life, developed a unit of analysis which she termed a *responsibility situation*. A responsibility situation involves responsibility for something, towards someone, and in relation to a specific instance. (We hear echoes of the analysis in chap. 6.) That responsibility situation could be described and analyzed according to several variables which I have adapted from Auhagen (2001) as the following:

1. Cognitive understandings or interpretations of the responsibility situation:
    a. *Causation:* Was the situation caused primarily by the actor, or by others?
    b. *Kind of situation:* Is the situation private, public, professional/work or family related; routine or exceptional?
    c. *Importance of the situation:* To the agent? To others in the situation?
    d. *Degrees of freedom involved in the situation:* Does the responsibility involve actions that are obliged under law, or under psychological coercion, or part of one's duties, or simply voluntary?
    e. *Scope/latitude of action in the situation:* What are the external supports or constraints; what internal capability does the actor possess?
    f. *Evaluation of results/consequences:* Anticipatory evaluation of probable consequences of actions; after the fact evaluation of what happened.
2. Moral understandings of the responsibility situation:
    a. *Felt inner need* to respond?
    b. *What moral principles* are being called into play?
    c. *Are there conflicting moral principles* involved?
    d. *What specific moral response* is called for?
3. Social understandings of the responsibility situation:
    a. Is the situation *within a family, a neighborhood, a public institution?*
    b. Are there *friends or enemies or neutrals* involved?
    c. What are your *ties to the people* involved?
    d. Is your *reputation or standing in the community* at stake?

   e. Are there *serious conflicts of interpretation* grounded in race, sex, class, culture, or generational standing involved in the situation?

Using these facets of responsibility situations as a means of shared analysis, teachers and students can approach material in the existing academic curriculum which lends itself to this kind of reflection. Students can be asked to go through the facets that apply to the situation and articulate what is at stake. The exercise can conclude with the student having to state what he or she would do in that situation and why. Coaches and faculty advisors and assistant principals and counselors can work with individual or groups of students to look at actual responsibility situations in the co-curricular activities, and in the various institutional support programs. Examples of these can be articulated and placed in a loose leaf folder for imitation and adaptation. Every year, new examples can be added, and less appropriate or ineffective examples can be discarded. Although this part of the curriculum of responsibility might not have exactly the same learning activities to be engaged by all students in a given school year, all students would be exposed to a sufficient number of these learning activities, so that the school could point to a common effort to engage students in these important questions.

## CONCLUSION

In the interests of brevity, I may have made the process sound simple and easy. In one sense, the overall plan is simple. However, working out basic understandings and their potential applications in the classroom, the playing fields and the school cafeteria; negotiating and resolving disagreements and massaging differing sensitivities; and the general energy drain on people already overworked—this work will require patience and a long-range view of the change process (Shipengrover & Conway, 1996). This is clearly a multiyear project. Furthermore, the emergence of a more responsible community is inescapably slow and imperfect. However, the slow development and occasional lapses actually constitute precisely the "stuff" that moral communities have to deal with. That is what moral communities do—reach out for ideals that are always out in front of them, confront their own and others' shortcomings, and heal the rifts that inevitably occur among the members.

   Responsibility in any aspect of living and learning is always something only partially achieved. The responsible community is a community that knows it is on a journey, a journey that is never complete; the virtue is in the striving much more than in the definitive achievement. The point is that there is a sense of direction for the journey, a journey toward the fulfillment of their own humanity.

## ACTIVITIES

1. In teams of three, discuss the foundational qualities of autonomy, connectedness, and transcendence as they relate to your own sense of a moral life. Give examples from your own life where those qualities came into play in your own moral growth. Are there other foundational human qualities that you think should be added to these three?

2. In teams of three, design three learning activities that you think would nurture each of the three foundational qualities. Share these activities with two other teams, who will share theirs with your team. Each person in this nine-person group should choose one of the nine learning activities and try to adapt it for use in his or her own educating context during the coming week. Each person can then report back the following week on the results of the experiment.

3. Of the three ethical frameworks, perhaps the most difficult one to deal with is the ethic of critique. As a way of exploring that framework, ask yourself the questions asked in the chapter and relate them to your work environment. "Which group dominates the social arrangements around here?" "Who defines what is valued and disvalued in situations around here?" "Does my school disproportionately benefit some groups in society and fail other groups?" "Are the practices of teacher evaluation, homogeneous tracking systems, grading on a curve, calculating class rank, the labeling criteria of gifted and handicapped, the absence of topics in the curriculum inherently unfair to some?" After you have written your reflections in your journal, share them with the members of your study group.

4. Repeat the steps of Activity 2 for the three ethical frameworks.

5. Rate your own work environment on a scale of 1 to 10 for its intentional promotion of a responsible community. What are the major obstacles to it becoming better? If you were the leader of your organization, what would you do to overcome these obstacles?

## REFERENCES

Adorno, T. W. (1973). *Negative dialectics.* New York: Seabury.

Apple, M. (1982). *Education and power.* Boston: Routledge & Kegan Paul.

Auhagen, A. E. (2001). Responsibility in everyday life. In A. E. Auhagen & H. W. Bierhoff (Eds.), *Responsibility: The many faces of a social phenomenon* (pp. 61–77). London: Routledge.

Bates, R. (1994). Corporate culture, schooling, and educational administration. *Educational Administration Quarterly, 23*(4), 91–115.

Buber, M. (1965). The education of character. In R. G. Smith (Trans.), *Between man and man* (pp. 104–116). New York: Collier.

Buber, M. (1970). *I and thou.* New York: Scribner's.

Comer, J. P. (1988). Educating poor minority children. *Scientific American, 259*(5), 42–48.

Connell, R. W. (1993). *Schools and social justice.* Philadelphia: Temple University Press.

Epstein, J. L. (1985). Home and school connections in schools of the future: Implications of research on parent involvement. *Peabody Journal of Education, 63*(13), 18-41.

Freire, P. (1970). *Pedagogy of the oppressed.* New York: Continuum.

Gilligan, C. (1977). *In a different voice: Women's conceptions of self and morality.* Cambridge MA: Harvard University Press.

Giroux, H. (1988). *Schooling and the struggle for public life.* Minneapolis: University of Minnesota Press.

Habermas, J. (1973). *Legitimation crisis.* Boston: Beacon.

Jackson, P., Boostrom, R., & Hansen, D. (1993). *The moral life of schools.* San Francisco: Jossey-Bass.

Kohlberg, L. (1987). The just community approach to moral education in theory and practice. In M. Berkowitz & F. Osler (Eds.), *Moral education: Theory and application* (pp. 27–87). Hillsdale, NJ: Lawrence Erlbaum Associates.

MacMurray, J. (1961). *Persons in relation.* London: Faber.

Neibuhr, R. (1935). *An interpretation of Christian ethics.* New York: Harper & Brothers.

Noddings, N. (1984). *Caring: A feminine approach to ethics and moral education.* Berkeley, CA: University of California Press.

Nozick, R. (1974). *Anarchy, state, and utopia.* New York: Basic Books.

Shipengrover, J. A., & Conway, J. A. (1996). *Expecting excellence: Creating order out of chaos in a school district.* Thousand Oaks, CA: Corwin.

Starratt, R. J. (1994). *Building an ethical school.* London: Falmer.

Sullivan, W. M. (1986). *Reconstructing public philosophy.* Berkeley, CA: University of California Press.

Sullivan, W. M. (1995). Reinstitutionalizaing virtue in civil society. In M. A. Glendon & D. Blankenhorn (Eds.), *Seedbeds of virtue* (pp. 185–200). Lanham, MD: Madison Books.

Wolfe, A. (1995). Social and natural ecologies: Similarities and differences. In M. A. Glendon & D. Blankenhorn (Eds.), *Seedbeds of virtue* (pp. 163–183). Lanham, MD: Madison Books.

Young, R. (1990). *A critical theory of education.* New York: Teachers College Press.

# BRINGING THE VISION
# TO REALITY

# Chapter 9

# Cultivating a Perspective
# on Learning

In the first part of the book, we developed the foundational themes of cultivating meaning, community, and responsibility as the primary focus for educational leadership. In the second part of the book, we draw out some of the implications of these foundational themes for the way schools conduct themselves, and for the work of administrators in leading schools committed to cultivating meaning, community, and responsibility. In this chapter, we focus on applying those themes to the fundamental work of the school—namely, student learning. By gaining a clearer idea of what constitutes the student's work, we gain a clearer perspective on the teacher's work, and thereby a clearer idea of how administrator's work supports the teachers' and students' work. Many administrators have forgotten how complex the process of learning can be and how carefully teachers have to plan and design a variety of learning activities that stimulate and guide this process. By and large, books on educational administration do not review the complex processes of learning and teaching, assuming that their readers are already familiar with those understandings or that that material is treated somewhere else in the university preparation of administrators. Curriculum courses, teaching methods courses, and learning theory courses, however, are usually conducted for teachers, not administrators. This chapter provides a model of learning and teaching that administrators might employ in their all-important work with teachers on improving the depth and quality of learning for all students. The model does not cover all the microaspects of teaching. Rather, it provides a large conceptual map that administrators can use in their conversations with teachers for cultivating meaning, community, and responsibility.

## THE STUDENT AS WORKER

Schools are currently organized under the assumption that teachers are the primary workers. Through their instructional strategies—their work—it is assumed that they produce learning in the students—learning that can be replicated by the student on standardized tests. Behind this view of teachers' work in schools lies the assumption that knowledge is *out there* somewhere waiting to be packaged by a curriculum designer and textbook writer and then explained, treated, and passed along by the teacher. The techniques of teaching—the teacher's *bag of tricks*—consist in the shaping of the lesson material so that students will *get it*—be able to repeat the definition, use the words of the vocabulary lesson in a proper sentence, apply the mathematical formula to a series of simple problems that resemble the model problem, memorize the textbook explanation of the mercantile system, describe the eating and hunting customs of native peoples of the Arctic, and so forth. In this arrangement, the student is thought of as a passive recipient of nuggets of information being delivered by the teacher.

To be sure, there has to be some activity on the part of students, just as there has to be some activity on the part of anyone being fed (chewing, swallowing, etc.). Yet the teacher is the one who selects what is to be learned, how it is to be learned, how the learning is to be evaluated, and according to what measurable standards of mastery it will be judged. Even where the teacher is urged to help students relate the present learnings to prior learning or personal experiences, the focus is on a motivational strategy, not an epistemological value. The point is not for students to construct or produce something that is personally and singularly their own, but to see their own experience as simply an example of the abstract textbook learning defined in the curriculum. Testing and grading convey this message: The personal life of the student does not count; the replication of a predetermined piece of material is what counts. It is as though students are expected to leave their own lives at the schoolhouse door; they—or at least their minds—belong to the school during the school day. It is what the school determines is to be learned that matters, nothing else.

If we make the student the worker, then this form of schooling has to change. The student now enters more actively into the learning process. Learning is the active engagement of the student, including all the sensitivities, points of view, talents, and imagination that he or she possesses, with the material under study, whether it is a short story, an algebraic operation, a question in biology, a comparison of the technique of Matisse with that of Pissarro, or his or her own poem about the season of spring. In the process of learning, and as a result of their active engagement with the material, students are asked to produce something that expresses their learning.

It may be helpful to highlight what has already been developed about the nature of learning. Learning is not exclusively or primarily a matter of passive intake of information. Arguments continue in the field of cognitive science about the relative importance in the activity of knowing attached to the built-in neural wiring of the learner's mind as opposed to the active construction of knowledge and meaning by the learner (Frawley, 1997). It seems clear that the claims of both groups of cognitive psychologists need to be taken into account. Learning involves a conditioned processing of intake data acted on by different parts of the brain, but it also involves an active effort of the individual who chooses to pursue inquires further to explore various relationships within multiple frameworks of intelligibility. The educational policy community seems committed to the view that students can and must make their brains work harder, can and must enter much more actively and intentionally into the construction of knowledge. School renewal policy is based on this premise. The spirit of the arguments of the first part of the book also endorses this perspective. In summary, we have proposed that:

- learning involves an active construction of knowledge and understanding in a sociocultural context;
- learning is a reflexive shaping of the self;
- learning is intrinsically social;
- learning involves a striving for and development of personal and social excellence;
- learning is an intrinsically moral activity; and
- personal learning has to become public learning and applied learning on the way to generating academic understanding.

## PERSONAL, PUBLIC, APPLIED, AND ACADEMIC MEANINGS: A MODEL OF LEARNING

In the work of learning, students need to generate four kinds of meaning: personal, public, applied, and academic. For learning to be anchored in the life world of the student, it has to be personal. The student should always be able to say in a variety of ways,

> This is what my work in school today or this week means to me; it talks to me about this aspect of nature or of human nature, which I find in myself or in my circumstances; I can see examples of this in my own family, circle of friends, in my neighborhood or larger civic and natural community. What I learned helps me to understand myself better, to reposition myself in relation to nature, to social practices, to the cultural or political world I inhabit. What

I learned teaches me a moral lesson about what I should do in similar circumstances, or what I need to watch out for, or avoid, or try out.

Obviously, younger students cannot present their personal appropriation of the material under study in such abstract terms; in their concrete narratives, however, their teachers can discern how the material is affecting them. The personal meanings each student derives from the learning activities are diverse, representing the cultural background, interests, motivations, self-image, and socialization of each youngster. Nevertheless, it is important for students to voice them—to weigh their importance and value in the construction of themselves as the person they want to be and to become.

The student then has to bring those personal meanings to the table of public discourse to see how those personal meanings relate to the personal meanings that other learners bring to the table. As students share the personal meanings they derived from the material under study, they can enter conversations about the similarities and differences among their personal meanings and explore common knowledge and understandings from their joint learning. They can construct provisional definitions of things on which they agree. They also need to relate their common understandings to the wider public. How are these matters talked about and understood in the wider public? Here the teacher can act as a Socratic facilitator, asking questions that stretch their understanding of the public views of the topics under discussion. This also can be a stimulus for the students to converse with their parents and members of their extended family about how they understand the material they have been studying. Although time constraints limit the extent of these explorations of public understandings, as they become a habitual part of the ongoing learning process, students gain an appreciation of the connections that their work of learning has to the larger public world. They become increasingly facile in placing their classroom understandings within larger public contexts.

As an extension of students' discussions of the public meanings of what they are learning, they should be required to generate at least two potential or actual applications of what they have learned to life in the home or larger community. They should pose questions such as the following: "What would this knowledge be useful for?" "What problem or issue in our home or community could be addressed by this knowledge or understanding?" "How would this be used in two or three occupations?" "Suppose a team of us from the class were called in by the Mayor to help the community solve this particular problem. How would what we just learned help us address the problem?" As students work to apply their knowledge to a new situation, the new situation requires understanding it from different perspectives, seeing the knowledge put to use, now in one context, now in another. Often the context requires them to modify their understanding or create analogies with more familiar contexts. As more than a few scholars have noted, our knowledge in the abstract may remain rather simplistic or one dimensional; when we have to do something with it, we understand it differently and can call on that understanding for use in other contexts (Newman, Secada, & Wehlage, 1995).

When the learning has generated personal, public, and applied meanings, we are in a better position to appreciate the academic meanings behind or within the learning activities. Academic meanings refer to those abstract principles, definitions, constant relationships, logical arguments, methodological principles, or large cognitive patterns or frameworks that lend an underlying intelligibility to the academic discipline, whether we are talking about the discipline of chemistry, history, geography, or poetry. The Harvard project, *Teaching for Understanding* (Wiske, 1998), has mapped the terrain of academic meaning quite clearly and provided rubrics for assessing various levels of academic mastery. Teachers, however, need to recognize that students are often unprepared to absorb the alphabet soup of academic meanings. Teachers who jump right into the academic meanings of the topic under study presume that students have the same readiness and interest as the academic scholar. All too often, students are required to grapple with new words, definitions, and formulas without any context in which to place them. Unless the learner has had an opportunity to muddle around with the material, look at its connection to his or her own life or the life of the public community, or test it out in various experiments and applications, the academic meanings become simply things to be memorized for tests and exams, but easily forgotten after classes are dismissed.

The model of learning presented here insists that for every significant unit of the curriculum, students should be required as part of the assessment process to articulate the personal, public, applied, and academic meanings they generated during that unit. If students are to enter into the learning process as a way of actively constructing themselves, if they are to develop a sensitivity to a plurality of points of view as well as work within that plurality for some pragmatic agreements on what will constitute some necessary public activity needed by the community, if they are to develop a sense of the usefulness of their learning in their present and future lives, then the weekly requirement that they generate personal, public, applied, *and* academic meanings from their learning activities will develop the kind of necessary foundation for these habits of mind and heart. As students complete the product or performance of their understanding of the curricular material, they should engage in a reflective assessment exercise. This reflective assessment exercise is different from and precedes the summative assessment exercises that involve using agreed-on rubrics to assess the quality of the performance or product (cf. Figs. 9.1 and 9.2). This latter exercise

FRAMING  STUDENT  WORK

| Creating | Purpose/rationale for this unit |
| Readiness | |
| For | Expected Outcomes for this Unit: |
| the | • Science Project Demonstration |
| Work | • Musical Performance |
| | • Historical Research Report |
| | • Policy Debate |
| | • Composition of a Story in Writing or Film |
| | Rubrics for Assessment of Learning Outcomes |
| Doing<br><br>the<br><br>Work | Learning Activities: analyzing a political or economic issue, narrating a human drama, designing an experiment, comparing the work of two artists, debating two interpretations of a historical event, composing a letter in Spanish to a person in Argentina, explaining a chemical effect on brain cells, composing a response to drought in the sub-Sahara, testing water contamination in a nearby river, writing an op-ed piece on low-income housing, and so on.<br><br>Learning Outcomes: Expressions of<br>• Personal Meanings<br>• Public Meanings<br>• Applied Meanings<br>• Academic Meanings |
| Assessing<br><br>the<br><br>Work | Review of Rubrics for Assessing Personal, Public, Applied, and Academic Learning<br>Student Reflective Assessment of Personal, Public, Applied, and Academic Learnings<br>Teacher, Peer, and Public Assessment of Personal, Public, Applied, and Academic Learnings<br>Reflection on Feedback from Assessment for Future Learning (anticipatory scaffolding for new learning activities) |

FIG. 9.1.   Framing student work.

involves not only the student assessing his or her own work in the light of the rubrics, but also peer assessment of the various products and performances of the class in the light of the rubrics, the teacher's assessment of each student's product or performance in the light of the rubrics, and, from time to time, the public (parents and/or community experts) assessment of students' products and performances.

Figures 9.1 and 9.2 attempt to visually represent the desired components involved in student learning. They comprise a model of student learning that can inform discussions administrators have with teachers about the way they design the antecedents and feedback elements of students' work. Both diagrams involve a form of backward mapping. More and more scholars of learning are tending to stress that the design of student work has to begin at the end (Newman et al., 1995; Perkins, 1998; Wiggins & McTighe, 1998). A performance view of understanding requires that teachers think about what kind of performances will reveal an understanding of the material under study and what qualities of the performance will reveal deeper under-

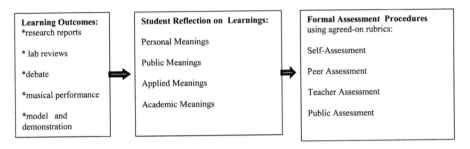

FIG. 9.2.    Reflection on and assessment of students' learning.

standings than others. That is why we began with the importance of having the student engage in reflective assessment on the personal, public, applied, and academic meanings generated by the learning activities. All too often, teachers begin their instructional planning by designing what appear to be interesting learning activities (coloring maps, making costumes, reading a story, doing mathematical word problems) before clarifying for themselves what it is they want the students to learn by engaging in these activities. What are the large ideas they want the students to grasp? What is the lesson they should all take away from the activity? What kinds of things should students be able to do at the end of these activities to authenticate that they have a rich understanding of the material? What products or performances would be legitimate expressions of the students' understandings of the material?

More recently, teachers are being asked to relate learning activities in the classroom to curriculum standards adopted by the district. Before designing the activity, they should look at the standards and think about the *many* activities that can be used to generate ideas and skills contained in the standards and then choose the activities that best and most richly respond to the standards. I would take the design and planning work back even farther. I would have the teachers ask themselves to provide a clear purpose or rationale for taking up the curriculum unit they are planning to engage. Without going off on an abstract or philosophical explanation, the teacher should be able to briefly explain why this curriculum unit they are about to take up is considered important within the academic area; what relationship this material has to real issues in the contemporary world; how this material could be useful to them. With this brief explanation of purpose, the teacher can then introduce the material and point to the kind of product or performance that is expected of the students as a result of their engaging the material. Depending on the material under consideration, the teacher may propose several exemplary types of products (a documentary film with accompanying commentary; the staging of a debate; a scholarly research report; an op-ed piece for the local newspaper; a series of illustrative drawings that sequence the procedures under study, a power-point presentation, a story using imaginary creatures to dramatize the understanding, etc.).

As indicated in Fig. 9.1, these steps help create a readiness on the part of the student to take up the work. Presenting and explaining rubrics for assessing the quality of expected student products or performances comprise an additional part of the readiness stage. Teachers should provide examples of student performances that reflect the assessment rubrics (e.g., a research report on a topic in the science curriculum that provides abundant evidence for the conclusions of the report, clearly indicates how the research methods were employed, qualifies the findings by pointing out inherent limitations to the research, etc.; or a scrapbook biography of a grandparent, including photographs of three important times in the grandparent's life, illustrations of various technologies employed in the grandparent's home, stories about the grandparent's education, an account of two or three significant national or international events that the grandparent remembers from earlier years, and an account of the grandparent's major joys, struggles, and life lessons). Students would also see examples of student work that failed to meet one or more of the rubrics or met them only partway. Exposure to the rubrics at the start of the lesson allows them to see the criteria for how they will be graded on their own work.

As students are about to engage the material in a variety of learning activities, the teacher can provide one more important element in creating readiness for learning. This is referred to as *scaffolding*. The teacher asks the students to recall earlier learning activities and the skills and perspectives they engaged. The teacher asks them whether the present learning challenge reminds them of any they encountered in the past. When students volunteer that this lesson looks something like what they studied last month, the teacher can draw out of the students the ways they tackled that earlier learning, what worked and what did not work then, and how they might apply both the key concepts and inquiry skills from what they learned earlier to the study of the present material. By spending a little time at the beginning of a new learning unit, the teacher helps the students get focused, develop potential strategies to tackle the material, and see similarities to earlier inquiry procedures. In this way, the teacher brings prior learnings into active play in the new work.

At this point, the students should be quite ready to engage the material through a variety of learning activities. This may involve reading and note taking from two or three historical sources; conducting a science experiment employing careful measurement and mathematical computation; analyzing maps for significant geographical information; comparing and contrasting the editorial positions of two regional newspapers on political, economic, and ecological issues; reading a short story and writing a different ending that remains consistent with the initial characters' personalities;

creating a still-life watercolor; writing a letter to the editor of the regional newspaper about a hotly contested issue in the community, after having carefully assessed the merits of the three major perspectives on the issue; researching the nature symbols in textiles used for Japanese kimonos for the comparative cultures course; researching the mathematics used in navigation on the high seas; or analyzing, comparing, and contrasting the design of cities with a view toward writing a recommendation to the local urban planning commission for improvements in the transportation system.

These examples illustrate how the learning activities are closely tied to producing or performing a product of some kind. Although the product requires considerable antecedent exploration and analysis of the material at hand, and strategizing how to construct or perform the product, a significant part of the learning is involved in the creation of the product itself. Students do not understand what they know until they have actively created something with that knowledge. Thus, in Fig. 9.2, the learning activities and learning outcomes overlap, indicating that one is still learning while producing the outcome, and that producing the outcome is a learning activity in its own right. In their coaching role, teachers encourage students to refer back to the assessment rubrics before composing the final version of their product or performance. This additional review of the assessment rubrics enters into the learning process as well, and can cement a clearer understanding of the methodological requirements or inquiry skills the lesson intends to reinforce.

A major mistake educators make is to disassociate learning from assessment. An enormous amount of learning can take place by careful attention to assessment. That is why in Figs. 9.1 and 9.2 so much appears to be made of assessment. The reflective assessment already referred to should follow the performance of the learning. This enables students to further clarify what the learning meant to them personally, discuss with peers the common public meanings to be derived from the learning activity, imagine the various applications the new learning might have to several different situations, and place the new learning within frameworks of intelligibility that are reflective of the academic disciplines (e.g., "That's how gasses are supposed to react"; "That is what we should have expected from a colonial power in the 19th century"; "That is just another example of the slope-intercept formula"; "That conforms to the methodology of a controlled laboratory experiment"; "That is simply a variant in Elizabethan rhyming"; "That nature symbolism in Japanese textiles is another example of the Japanese borrowing from the earlier Chinese culture and creating their own local variations"). The value of this kind of reflective assessment seems so obvious, yet it is so often neglected.

The recent emphasis on teaching to state curriculum standards and preparing youngsters for high-stakes tests has reinforced the use of assessment rubrics by more and more teachers. Again, the opportunity for important learning is present in the summative assessment exercises. These summative exercises should involve personal assessment, peer assessment, teacher assessment, and, on occasion, public assessment. In this step of the learning process, students should be asked to judge their own work according to the criteria contained in the rubrics provided at the beginning of the unit. Their assigning a grade to their work should require justification by clear references to the performance criteria of the rubrics. This kind of self-assessment indicates whether the student has grasped the understandings of the unit implied in the rubrics. It also helps students see where they can improve in future learning assignments.

The whole class should be shown the products of two students—one superior and one average, according to the rubrics—(without identifying to whom they belong) so they might practice evaluating performances according to the criteria contained in the rubrics for that unit. In the interests of time, each student might then be asked to evaluate two or three peer products according to the rubrics. This exercise provides students with further experience with the rubrics and helps them see the reasoning behind them. It also provides the student whose work is anonymously being assessed by some of his or her peers additional feedback. From them, he may learn that assessments may vary depending on how one interprets the criteria in the rubrics and how one analyzes the performance or product. When this feedback is joined to the feedback of the teacher, the student should get a clear understanding of the quality of learning expected from the unit. If on occasion someone from the community (usually fairly knowledgeable in the matter) is asked to comment on the quality of the student's product or performance, it helps the student recognize the further significance of the learnings achieved in that unit. One final learning exercise should bring the student work in this unit full circle. The student should be asked to reflect on what he or she learned through the assessment exercises that will be useful in responding to future learning opportunities. These reflections (e.g., "I need to review how that slope-intercept formula really works"; "I need to be more aware of how one culture borrows from another, but how in the translation, those cultural borrowings are always changed"; "I need to cite more examples when making generalizations"; "I have to be more careful about incomplete sentences") provide some anticipatory scaffolding for future learning activities. They also develop a habit of reflection on ways to improve one's work.

The Model of Student Learning (Fig. 9.3) attempts to place this student's work in a larger context. The work of learning is strongly influenced by what the student brings to the work at hand. That includes the various qualities in the student's make-up: the emerging self-image; what particular interests capture the student's attention (athletics, politics, music, science

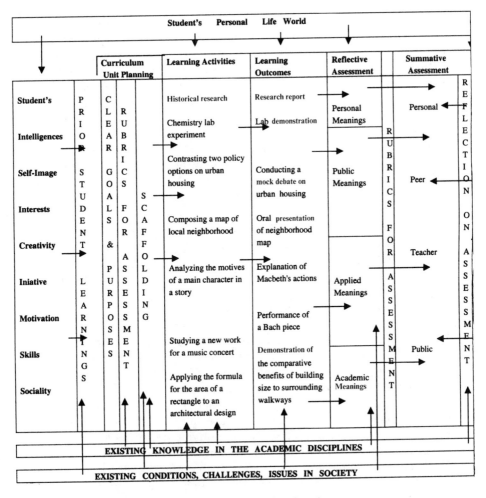

FIG. 9.3. A model of student learning.

fiction); what level of initiative the student tends to bring to school work; what motivates the student to work hard, to persevere; what learning skills the student brings to the work; how well the student works with others; and how creative a student is in brainstorming various strategies for tackling a learning challenge.

Besides the student's make-up, there is the student's personal life world that exercises a continuing influence on the quality of learning. If a student experiences confusion, ambiguity, unpredictability, humiliation, and rejection in his or her life world, that will negatively influence the student's ability and motivation to engage the learning activities. A student coming from a working-class family situated in a working-class neighborhood brings different experiences, perspectives, and attitudes to school than those of his or her peers who come from affluent families in affluent neighborhoods. Youngsters who have frequently changed residences bring a different set of life-world experiences than those who continue to live in the same home where they were born. The life world of the youngsters is strongly influenced by the family's race, religion, culture, and class; that life world nurtures various interpretations of cultivating meaning, community, and responsibility, some of which conflict with the interpretations within the school or classroom. Therefore, the learning of the student is continuously influenced, for better or worse, by all those influences in the life world. Insofar as the learning can be connected directly or indirectly to that life world, it engages the student at a deeper level.

Another major influence on the student's learning are the existing conditions, challenges, and issues in society at large. Included here, of course, would be issues within the youth culture of that society—issues that get reflected in music, dress, lifestyle, language, and popular heroes. Insofar as the work of learning can have some direct or indirect relationship to the larger youth culture, it engages the student more deeply. Many teachers are decidedly uncomfortable, however, with what they perceive to be the values portrayed in the youth culture. Nevertheless, school learning occasionally has to engage that culture, look beneath the sometimes silly surface expressions of that culture to the deeper yearnings, dreams, and human struggles seeking a voice, and build bridges between what is being learned in school and what is being explored in the youth culture.

Beyond the youth culture, the larger society is struggling with multiple issues and challenges to which the school learning should be connected. Not only should students be taken seriously enough to be invited to study these issues and challenges, but they must be convinced that these struggles and challenges are theirs—the stuff that will affect their adult lives as well.

A third major influence on student learning is the existing knowledge, understandings, and challenges in the various academic disciplines. These academic disciplines exert a huge influence through their dominance of university studies that in turn strongly influence the curricula of K–12 school systems. Furthermore, the academic disciplines strongly determine the subject matter and materials in textbooks. As advances in the academic disciplines progress, the subject matter in textbooks changes. As we have seen, however, textbooks tend to present a simplistic view of knowledge and the process of knowing, and often contain points of view biased in favor of the dominant class, race, sex, and nation. Nevertheless, under the pressures of state curriculum frameworks, teachers in the present context of school renewal are struggling to keep themselves up to date with developments in the academic disciplines that provide the subject matter of what students are to learn.

## A MODEL OF TEACHING

Figure 9.3 presents in visual form the logic driving student learning and the syntax of influences on that learning. Teachers need to continually attend to these influences as they plan for and design student work, bringing these influences into play in the scaffolding of the students' work. Thus, teachers should remind students of what they learned in their previous curriculum units, how the new material continues building on that previous learning, how the new material relates to their life world, interests, challenges facing society, the searching of the youth culture, and the conceptual frameworks and methodologies of the academic disciplines they have been learning. This scaffolding is different for each unit, each class, and each teacher. It is, however, an essential part of the craft of teaching and calls on the imagination, invention, and organizational talents of teachers to bring all these considerations to bear on making the learning in this new unit exciting, interesting, and potentially useful.

    Figure 9.4 attempts to diagram the teacher's backward mapping of the work of teaching. Keeping in mind the curriculum standards that are to guide student achievement, the teacher prepares a clear statement of the

## Teacher's Work

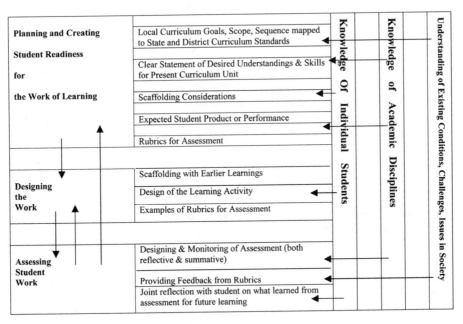

FIG. 9.4. Mapping teachers' work.

purpose and rationale behind this new learning unit. That purpose and rationale is related both to the academic discipline as it is embedded in the year's curriculum as well as to the existing conditions, challenges, and issues in present society. The teacher explains what are the large, desired, and expected understandings that result from their engaging the material in this unit and indicates the one or several ways that understanding can be represented in a product or performance. The teacher then explains the rubrics for assessment of that product or performance, indicating the criteria to be met for a high grade and, when ignored, for a low or failing grade. The teacher then engages in scaffolding the new material to be studied, drawing attention to similarities in earlier learnings that assist them in engaging the new material. As the students engage in the learning activity and prepare to translate their learning into authentic performances or products, the teacher engages in coaching, Socratic questioning, encouraging, suggesting a second look at the evidence, and so forth, all the while recognizing that the student has to produce the learning rather than repeat information delivered by the teacher. Another crucial aspect of the teacher's work is to monitor the assessment exercises carefully, recognizing that they contribute mightily to the student's deep understanding of the material of the unit.

## A LESSON FROM ROCKS

Some illustrations might clarify the teacher's monitoring of the assessment process. As students are completing their product or performance, teachers might ask them how their learning affected their understandings of themselves. They may have just finished an interdisciplinary unit on rocks. That unit began with a story about the rabbit's encounter with the lonely rock. In discussing the story, they were encouraged to reflect on what it feels like to be lonely, on the importance of friends to play with, on the need to be sensitive listeners when someone confides how they feel to us. They also reflected on how they take rocks for granted, how each rock has a history much longer than their own, that each rock has a unique composition of minerals. They were encouraged to look more closely at various rocks in their neighborhood environment and note the unique features of each rock. They were asked to choose a pet rock, give it a name, and talk to it about stuff going on in their lives. These encounters with rocks were enriched by the work they did in science class where they analyzed the minerals in their rock, classifying them and measuring them at least in rough proportions, and learning about how and when the rock was formed geologically. In art class, they drew several sketches of their rock seen from different sides and different lighting. Further nuancing of those learnings occurred in their social studies classes where they studied the rock and sand gardens in Japanese culture, and how, within that culture, such gardens are considered an art form. Additionally, the father of one of the students, a stone mason, showed a slide lecture to the class on various types and shapes of rocks used in various types of construction, from garden walls to fireplaces to foundations for homes and to exteriors of whole buildings. Besides the practical properties of various rocks, the stonemason also spoke about the aesthetics of color, shapes, position, and balance in working with rocks, and how different types of rocks have different personalities.

In this example, students are developing a set of personal meanings about rocks, as well as gaining scientific, aesthetic, and craft understandings about rocks. They are also learning to look more closely at nature to understand more about evolutionary and cosmic time, and to consider the many human uses natural objects can be put to, both functionally and aesthetically. Students might perform their knowledge about rocks in a variety of media and a variety of presentations. These presentations contain both personal and public meanings. When their fellow students present their performance of their knowledge, then students hear their peers express their personal appropriation of the unit on rocks and thereby learn how various interpretations of the material help to enrich and complement their own understanding. The teacher also asks the students to converse about the public meanings about rocks. This would include the obvious scientific facts about rocks, especially to be found in the science of geology, but it would also include public knowledge about the aesthetic properties of rocks (marble, sandstone, gemstones, slate, granite, etc.), the various crafts associated with rocks, famous rocks around the world (Uluru, Gibraltar, Shiprock, etc.), famous sculptors of rock, and so forth. The teacher can also structure several exercises that require students to apply their knowledge to solving a problem (e.g., in designing a sea wall out of rocks, creating a poem about rocks, or creating a company that sold a variety of rock [not rock 'n roll] products). Finally, the teacher can coach students into generating academic meaning from all these exercises (scientific categories and temporal frameworks in geology and paleontology, aesthetic principles in rock gardens and sculptures, principles of measurement involved in classifying rocks, the physics of mass and gravity to be found in handling rocks).

After students have completed the reflective assessment in their journals, they should engage in exercises of summative assessment. In these exercises, students should be asked to evaluate how well their own work and that of other students has measured up to the assessment rubrics for the assignment. The first summative assessment exercise, the personal assessment, is crucial because the student has to engage the intelligibility of the rubrics and his or her own work according to standards of performance. Beyond the students' personal assessment of their own work (as produced individually or by a team), students should also be required to do a summative assessment of other students' or one team of students' work. Again, this requires the students to attend to the intelligibility of the assessment rubrics now applied to another project. The exercise should further reinforce their understandings of the substance, methodology, and applicability of the materials under study, and lead to a more articulate grasp of the standards embedded in the various academic disciplines. Peer assessments should not be entered into the final grades of the students being assessed. Grading is the sole prerogative of the teacher.

When those assessments are completed, the teacher provides his or her own summative assessment of all this work. Although the assessment is summative—that is, it leads to a judgment of whether this block of work measures up to the performance rubrics for that work—the teacher may engage in formative assessment as well, pointing out to students aspects of their work that need further refinement as they approach the next learning unit. In subsequent classes dealing with that next learning unit, the teacher can repeat those points from the prior summative assessment, urging the students to avoid making the same mistakes this time, helping them to see, in the presentation of the assessment rubrics for that next learning unit, how to carry on their work more effectively.

Finally, these summative assessment exercises should, at least occasionally, be complemented by parental commentary and by having appropriate people from the community offer feedback on students' work in some kind of open forum, either at the school or in a community agency. In this way, students can gain an appreciation of how their work in school is seen as related to the life of the larger community.

## ADMINISTRATORS' WORK

At this point, we have a clearer idea of the work of administrators in the cultivation of meaning, community, and responsibility. This work consists of conversations with external and internal constituencies and, in the light of these conversations, follow-up work on the restructuring of various institutional components of the school. It should be noted, however, that prior to these conversations, the preliminary work of exploring and clarifying the central focus of the school on cultivating meaning, community, and responsibility has to occur. In the light of these clarifications, a new look at the teaching–learning process is also necessary. I am not implying that administrators should have a blueprint etched in stone that they can then impose on all internal and external constituencies. Rather, administrators should develop clear ideas about a blueprint that provide a starting point for conversations. That blueprint is adapted by additional local concerns, filled out by the pregnant ideas of others, and constrained (at least for the present) by political, fiscal, and other entrenched positions in the community. Even where the local environment is weakly disposed to look beyond anything other than the familiar (however dysfunctional) routine, the preliminary work of clarifying a well thought-out and defensible educational blueprint provides administrators a starting point for changing the system over time. It also provides administrators a well-articulated platform for influence within the educational policy community, as well as within the larger civic leadership community, both of which have tended to view the educational agenda both superficially and simplistically.

In Fig. 9.5, we can see the work of administrators sketched on a large canvas. Obviously, the conversations on that canvas do not include the many microdetails of administrative work. Those microdetails, however, should be enacted in the service of the central conversations with those constituencies.

## CONVERSATIONS WITH EXTERNAL CONSTITUENCIES

Administrators' work involves conversations with parents, civic leaders, and various cultural communities and organizations within the larger civic community. In other words, administrators should use their position within a visible public institution as a kind of bully pulpit—a dialogical bully pulpit to be sure—to state their position about the central focus of the school on cultivating meaning, community, and responsibility. Presentations and conversations vary in complexity depending on the audience. Administrators need to craft multiple versions of their message for a variety of audiences. For not a few administrators, it may mean sharpening their command of rhetorical argument and, initially, even going through several rehearsals with critical friends to ensure both clarity and brevity. Even the best preachers can put the most sympathetic congregations to sleep after 5 minutes. Besides oral presentations to various audiences, newsletters, and op-ed pieces in the regional newspapers, position papers and other forms of the written media can also carry the conversation forward. Conversations with various parent groups are essential so that the focus of the school curriculum can be echoed in a variety of ways in the home. These conversations should also seek to involve parents as volunteers in communicating with other parents so that the message gets communicated in vocabularies and examples that parents can identify with.

An important part of the dialogue is to relate the cultivation of meaning, community, and responsibility to the agenda of school renewal. Illustrating how the emphasis on authentic student performance of their understandings relates to various curriculum standards helps the external constituencies grasp the needed connection with the mandates of local and state edu-

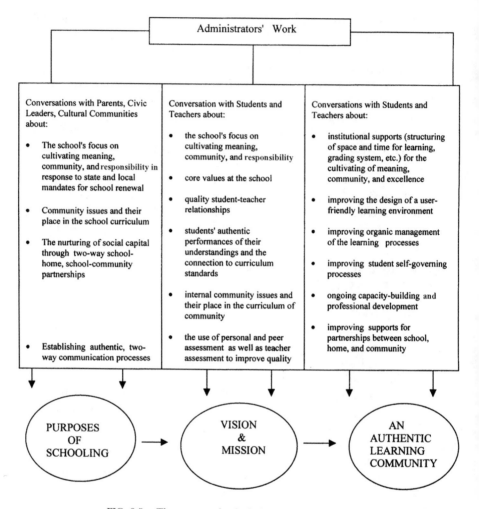

FIG. 9.5.    The core work of administrative leadership.

cational authorities. These conversations should also involve discussions about various forms of testing and the sometimes simplistic and inflammatory judgments expressed in the media about test scores. Questions about the types of knowledge and understanding tests are looking for, issues about opportunities to learn, funding of professional development for teachers to develop appropriate instructional materials for newly imposed curriculum standards, issues around the testing of recently arrived immigrant children with limited proficiency in English, assumptions about the significance of testing children with severe disabilities, discussions about within-school and within-class variance in students' readiness for the curriculum, and the resulting statistical distortions that occur in grouping student test scores—all of these complexities should be raised and aired so that the public better understands how to interpret reports of aggregate student scores on state and national tests.

Administrators need to dialogue with their external constituencies to stay familiar with long-standing and emerging community issues. Various community groups may want the school to teach (or demand that the school *not* teach) perspectives on a host of topics, from AIDS education and its corresponding relationship to sex education and health education, driver safety, drug and alcohol education, religious education, character education, gay and lesbian studies, ecology education, civil rights and active antiracism, multicultural education, global issues, vocational education, cooking, and a variety of other issues. Administrators can all too often adopt a cynical or patronizing attitude toward some or all of these groups, failing to recognize that these groups have constitutionally guaranteed rights to voice their opinions, and that as public servants they have a responsibility to listen attentively and sympathetically. As public servants, they also have a role to play in calling to the attention of these groups the conflicting demands and perspectives of other groups, and to legal decisions already made in the adjudication of these conflicting demands (e.g., legislation concerning children with special needs or bilingual/bicultural children, local school board rulings on program cuts or reductions). As educators, they should also have worked out reasoned *educational* positions in response to these various demands so that the dialogue can remain focused on the educational implications of various demands, as well as on various institutional constraints on schools.

Another valuable outcome of these conversations with external constituencies concerns the inclusion of specific local issues in classroom applications of the curriculum. For example, state investigators may have recently required the community to monitor more closely the pollution of a river flowing through its area to determine whether three local industries were observing industrial waste disposal requirements. That issue could be included in one or more science and social studies classes where students were required to apply scientific, political, and economic understandings learned in class to respond to this issue. They might work with one or more representatives of the local agencies responsible for monitoring water quality in the river, as well as representatives from the companies involved. In another example, the community might be facing a debate on whether to build mixed-income housing with a small adjoining park on an open parcel of land or turn it over to a developer to build a golf course surrounded by expensive homes. Students might be asked to apply what they knew about the principles of urban planning to this debate and offer a reasoned argument for one or the other position. In another example, the local library may have received a generous grant from a local millionaire who was interested in documenting the history of the community. His grant would enable the library to compose and publish the biographies of 100 of their most senior citizens. This might provide a wonderful opportunity for a significant number of high school students whose participation would thereby enable them to apply their understandings of historical research and connect the writing of the biography with a major writing project. Each student might work in collaboration with one or more adults in the community who were assigned to interview a particular senior citizen in the community. In another example, students might be asked to report on all the computer applications used in the work setting of one of their parents. Such a project might involve students meeting with the person responsible for computer technology in that parent's work environment, as well as having the parent explain the company's computer technology from the parent's perspective.

These examples point to a few of the many ways schools may engage in learning partnerships with the community. These learning partnerships develop the social and cultural capital of the school. By that I mean that students come to see that their learning in school is supported by their parents and by groups in the community. These partnerships enable the students to appreciate that their school learnings can be connected to important issues in the community, can open them to new cultural learnings, and can enable them to explore possible career opportunities. Administrators who remain in an ongoing series of conversations with various groups in the community can initially explore potential learning opportunities with these groups and bring those ideas back to the school for consideration by the teachers.

## CONVERSATIONS WITH INTERNAL CONSTITUENCIES

Administrators can bring the focus on cultivating meaning, community, and responsibility to conversations with teachers, students, and support staff. Initially, administrators need to propose these ideas within the framework of state and locally mandated school renewal. As seen in Part I of this book, the focus on cultivating meaning, community, and responsibility provides multiple avenues for approaching school renewal and connecting school learnings to the state and local curriculum standards while providing a larger, more fully developed learning environment within which attention to curriculum standards constitute one essential focus. Each local school setting should be unique, with its own history, internal chemistry, and relationship to the larger community. This means that administrators should craft their presentation of the cultivation of meaning, community, and responsibility to fit the local school. The school may already enjoy a tradition of a rich and highly professional learning environment, a supportive and participative parent community and school board, and a well-integrated student body. The initial conversations with that teaching faculty and student body about cultivating meaning, community, and responsibility would be quite different from the initial conversations with the internal constituencies of a school with a history of poor relations with the teachers' union, a culture of teacher isolation and autonomy, a curriculum with no schoolwide sense of scope and sequence, and a student body polarized by race, athletics, and college-bound versus job-bound students. Different schools require not only different conversations, but also different strategies for approaching various groups within the school. What is common to all schools, however, is the necessity of continuing to focus on school renewal. That provides the initial opening for administrators to address the importance of quality learning for all students. From those initial conversations, administrators gather clues about directions to take to enlarge the conversation to the larger focus on cultivating meaning, community, and responsibility.

However those conversations develop, they must include discussions about the students' authentic performance of their understandings and the connections of those products and performances to the state and local curriculum standards. As an integral part of these conversations, administrators bring teachers to ongoing discussions about assessment rubrics for those products and performances. The continuing dialogue among teachers about assessment rubrics constitutes one of the most crucial influences on a school's progress toward authentic learning.

As those conversations develop, administrators can introduce considerations about the place of internal community issues among the student body as well as issues in the larger community within the formal curriculum. In other words, the learning of being and becoming a community is presented as something of equal importance to the learning of the academic curriculum. Indeed, the learning of one curriculum is seen as implying a great deal of learning of the other curriculum. Furthermore, the enriching of the academic learning depends on the variety of applications the students are encouraged to make to real problems and issues within the home, neighborhood, and larger civic community. Administrators can encourage teacher groups to brainstorm a variety of applications of classroom learnings to real issues in the larger community. From their conversations with parents and various groups within the larger community, administrators can offer additional potential applications of classroom learning to issues and problems within the community.

Other conversations with the teaching faculty should take up the connection between various forms of assessment and the enrichment of student learning. Sometimes these conversations should come first as a lead in to the larger considerations about school renewal and cultivating meaning, community, and responsibility depending on the readiness of the teachers to take one perspective or the other. In either case, administrators need to raise issues around assessment to review how the teachers engage and monitor a variety of assessment procedures and activities.

## CONVERSATIONS ABOUT INSTITUTIONAL ARRANGEMENTS

As those two sets of conversations with the external and internal constituencies unfold, administrators also need to look at the present institutional arrangements at the school in the light of the focus on cultivating meaning, community, and responsibility. These arrangements include the daily, weekly and semester schedules; allocation of instructional spaces; time available for teachers to work together in planning and strategizing new classroom protocols and for visiting each other's classes; decision-making procedures; relationships with central office authorities; budget preparation and budget administration procedures; student assessment systems and grade reporting systems; presence and functioning of any kind of student government; parental partnership arrangements; student discipline policies; any co-curricular organizations and how they function to create or divide the community; the school's reward and award systems; student counseling and health arrangements; institutional communication patterns and media employed; student and faculty committees; and so forth. Along with the administrators' assessment of how well these institutional arrangements support a focus on cultivating meaning, community, and responsibility, students and teachers should be invited to engage in similar assessments and offer suggestions on how those institutional arrangements can be improved in a system design of a user-friendly learning environment. Parents should be invited to converse with teachers on ways to enhance the school–home partnerships that nurture enriched student learning.

What is sought is the development of an organic management of the learning process in the pursuit of meaning, community, and responsibility. By that is meant the creation of a learning community in which all decisions are related to the support and encouragement of quality learning for each and every student, in which decisions are made by those closest to the activity of learning, or by those most directly affected by the decision. Attention to these institutional arrangements is taken up in subsequent chapters.

## RECAPITULATION

In this chapter, we have seen the development of a model of student learning that points to a model of teaching. Elaboration of these two models, at least in a summary fashion, points to the essential work of administrators.

As this work becomes clarified, it becomes evident how much a redirection of administrative work is called for in this era of school renewal. This clarification of the essential work of administrators does not eradicate their concern about the *administration* of the daily life of the school, nor about the necessary administrative coordination with the central office of the local school district or authority. Rather, it places that administrative work within a larger framework, *in the service* of that work of the school community, rather than in the service of some kind of abstract organizational efficiency. In one sense, it partakes of some characteristics of mass administration, in the sense that it belongs to a local, state, and federal system of school administration. Nevertheless, educational administrative work has as its essential purpose the fostering of a learning community engaged in cultivating meaning, community, and responsibility. That essential purpose overrides and integrates all other administrative work.

## ACTIVITIES

1. Talk with three outstanding teachers at your school. Ask them whether they have students reflect on personal meanings they might derive from the learning activity. Do these teachers prepare students for this kind of personal reflection when they introduce the curriculum unit to the class by suggesting possible connections to their lived experience? Discuss Figs. 9.1 through 9.4 with them.

2. Ask the same teachers whether and how they use explicit rubrics for assessing student learning.

3. Do any teachers in your school require students to keep a portfolio of their work? If so, how are portfolios used?

4. Name all the examples that indicate your school's commitment to the principle of student active performance of their learning. Share your list with three other teachers in the school to see whether they can add to it.

5. Are teachers required, in the teacher supervision/evaluation process at the school, to present examples of student work?

6. What ideas from this chapter might you easily put in practice in your own work? What ideas for schoolwide practice?

## REFERENCES

Frawley, W. (1997). *Vygotsky and cognitive science: Language and the unification of the social and computational mind.* Cambridge, MA: Harvard University Press.

Newman, F., Secada, W. G., & Wehlage, G. G. (1995). *A guide to authentic instruction and assessment: Vision, standards and scoring.* Madison, WI: Wisconsin Center for Educational Research.

Perkins, D. (1998). What is understanding? In M. S. Wiske (Ed.), *Teaching for understanding* (pp. 39–57). San Francisco: Jossey-Bass.

Wiggins, G., & McTighe, J. (1998). *Understanding by design.* Alexandria, VA: Association for Supervision and Curriculum Development.

Wiske, M. S. (Ed.). (1998). *Teaching for understanding.* San Francisco: Jossey-Bass.

# Chapter 10

# Empowerment

In chapter 5, we realized that community need not be opposed to individuality (although it is opposed to individualism as an ideology). As a matter of fact, mature communities cannot reach their potential unless they are made up of members with a strong sense of individuality. In this chapter, we explore this theme further. The thesis is that cultivating community requires cultivating empowerment.

We begin with the premise that good communities are made up of good individuals, strong communities of strong individuals, innovative communities of innovative individuals, caring communities of caring individuals, and self-governing communities of self-governing individuals. We assume that schools as communities are made up of both adults and students. Hence, what applies to teachers in our discussion also applies to students, with, of course, appropriate allowance for their earlier stages of human development. When we speak of cultivating strong, inventive, caring, and self-governing communities, therefore, we are speaking of growing strong, inventive, caring, and self-governing students as well as teachers.

To get a clearer fix on what empowering teachers and students means and how we might attempt a process of empowerment, we need to clean up some misunderstandings, make some distinctions, and get beneath the surface definitions of empowerment and its root word, *power*. Then we focus on three sources of power: the power to be oneself, the power of connected activity, and the power contained in ideas, dreams, and visions.

## EMPOWERMENT IN SCHOOL REFORM

*Empowerment* is a term frequently used in discussions of school reform, especially discussions that focus on increasing the professionalism of teachers. The term, however, carries a variety of interpretations, not all of them benign. For some of the more assertive teacher union leaders, empowerment means more power in the hands of the teachers to control school policies and practices. In some extreme cases, the union would replace administrators with committees of teachers, leaving administrators with little more than the work of clerks and secretaries. For others, empowerment means the involvement of teachers in major decisions in the school. In this latter interpretation, teachers and administrators would work as peers and colleagues to arrive at appropriate decisions regarding school affairs. In many parts of the United States, Canada, Australia, and elsewhere, the move toward school-based management has been linked to shared decision making.

Empowerment as a strategic tool of school reform, however, is not the panacea that many initially expected. Those who would place teachers in charge of schools have discovered that the principals and other administrators do not simply fall over and surrender their positions. Administrators have used their collective political power to resist any such wholesale takeover of the schools by teachers. In addition, many teachers have resisted such a move on the grounds that they do not want the responsibility of running the school, saying that they simply want to teach with minimum interference from administrators.

Those who want empowerment through shared decision making are finding that many teacher colleagues resist such initiatives for at least two reasons. First, they are suspicious that the authorities simply want to give them more work to do without any increase in pay. Second, many teachers resent the enormous amount of time required to make shared decision making work. Many meetings are spent simply on procedural and legalistic matters. Even when substantive curriculum matters are taken up, the process of curriculum redesign is tedious and lengthy. Teachers complain of being distracted from their main work—teaching children in classrooms.

Lurking in the background of most attempts at these types of empowerment is the issue of trust. Everyone seems to assume a hidden agenda. Everyone fears being manipulated. Again and again one hears cynical interpretations of the *real game.*

The previous interpretations of empowerment, however, are too narrow and too absorbed in the politics and technical procedures of participation within a bureaucratic organization. We need to recognize that there are various forms of empowerment people can experience: bureaucratic, professional, moral, and existential. In its bureaucratic form—the form of empowerment referred to earlier—empowerment is concerned with shared decision making and teamwork. In its professional form, empowerment means growth in professional performance, competence, and efficacy. In its moral form, empowerment is revealed in a growth in autonomy, in ownership of one's choices. In its existential form, empowerment is concerned with the power to be this unique person with these talents, this heritage, and these awesome possibilities.

I suggest that these forms of empowerment can and should be integrated. That is to say, professional empowerment should be linked to bureaucratic empowerment so that the shared activity or shared decision making would not simply be a kind of contrived collegiality or merely a human relations exercise to help people feel good about themselves. Thus, to the exercise of shared decision making, teachers would bring the growing sense of competence in the profession of teaching and a specific focus on improving student achievement (Sykes, 1999). The actual sharing in decisions would also challenge and enlarge the professional competence of the participating teachers because their views would be stretched by the potentially competing or differing views of the others in the decision-making group (Marks & Louis, 1997). Similarly, to the combined forms of bureaucratic and professional empowerment a teacher would bring a growing sense of moral empowerment—namely, that one would bring a greater sense of responsibility to the work of professional shared decision making. The game would shift from one of seeking the upper hand in the decision-making process or shared activity, or of seeking personal or group advantages in the decision-making process, regardless of the needs of others—to a greater sense of responsibility that the decision-making process or shared activity actually served the students and their learning agenda first and foremost. Coupling moral empowerment to bureaucratic and professional empowerment brings a greater integrity to the decision making—a sense that the group has moral obligations to keep the best interests of children uppermost. Finally, to these three forms of empowerment, one can join the most basic form of empowerment: the power to be me, to express my authentic humanity in this shared decision making or shared activity. Thus, one's performance in the shared activity is an expression of one's true self and is a way one lives out who one is (Palmer, 1998). The remainder of this chapter spells out what this integration of the various forms of empowerment might look like in a school setting.

## WHAT IS POWER?

For many people, power has negative overtones. It is associated with force, coercion, threat, and sometimes violence. Power is often viewed as something only a few people have: The powerful are thought to control or unduly influence the affairs of the community. From that vantage point, empowering people implies that those who hold power over others give them some of their power. Yet the reality is that no one has power over another unless that person is allowed to have that power. If everyone refuses to comply with those in power, they have no power. We saw that happen in the disintegration of the communist states in Eastern Europe. Even the power of persuasion implies that the listener assents to the reasonableness of the other person's argument. The power of the judge to impose a prison sentence is based on an assumed prior agreement of people to live according to the law.

## THE POWER TO BE ONESELF

Besides power as meaning power over someone or something, we can conceive of power as something each person possesses—a power to be and a power to do. The most interesting power each of us possesses is the power to be ourselves. No one else has the power to be me: Only I can be me. Often we fail to use that power and instead try to live up to an idea that others have of us or to some collective image of what the truly modern, sophisticated, cosmopolitan, urbane woman or man should be.

We are all socialized, to one degree or another, to displace what we want to be or do in order to conform to social norms of propriety and tradition. "*Good* boys" don't do that! "*Good* girls" would never dream of doing that! "At Mangrove School, we simply don't *do* things like that." We grow up maintaining our fragile sense of self-esteem by continually weighing what others think of us. Often this leads to a suppression of ever being or doing what our spontaneous wishes suggest out of fear of disapproval.

What *growing up* means, however, is that we learn how to be ourselves and still live, more or less, within the acceptable bounds of social propriety and tradition (Kegan, 1994). Maturity means taking responsibility for ourselves, being the person we want to be, and loving the person we are. It means deciding to resist the fads and trends of popular culture when they start to twist what we value. When our own sense of integrity is at stake, we risk the disapproval of others. In other words, each of us has the power to say yes and no. To be sure, that power is heavily circumscribed by the cultural meanings, values, and associations that lead me to censure certain choices; it is further circumscribed by my physical attributes. I cannot be a bird (although some acquaintances may think I am a rare one, indeed) or the Golden Gate Bridge. Nevertheless, the power to be me is a power I never lose. Although we may turn it over to other people, it always belongs to us, and we can take it back whenever we choose. That is the power of freedom, the freedom, especially, to be myself, to sing my own song, dance my own dance, speak my own poetry—the freedom to be true to my best self, to be that unique and unrepeatable being, the likes of which has never been nor ever will be after I am gone.

The paradox about this power is that, although it is mine, I can only exercise it in relationship to my community. Some mistakenly think that the power to be an individual is a power *against* the community—a power that necessarily defies the community. Yet that attitude leads to a kind of narcissistic, selfish isolation. That form of self-centeredness is actually self-destructive. I can be myself only in relation to others, to other selves whom I value as they value me. I can only express myself in relation to the world, to another person, to a particular circumstance that at that moment is part of my definition (such as my home, my workplace, my neighborhood, my garden). I express myself by responding to persons and events in my immediate surroundings, and that expression is an expression of either giving or taking, an expression of gratitude or greed, an expression of celebration or complaint, or an affirmation or a denial of life. So far as my expression of myself is giving, thankful, celebratory, and affirming, I myself receive life, I grow, and I am nurtured. So far as my expression of myself is taking, hoarding, complaining, and denying, I hurt myself and those around me. The self I express in negativity is an expression of self-destruction.

It is important, however, to add at this point that some people are so overwhelmed by their circumstances that even the power to be themselves is drastically circumscribed. A sexually abused child can be emotionally crippled in her or his power to be her or himself. A *crack child* is hampered from saying yes or no by internal demons that physicians and psychologists have yet to identify. A teenage Appalachian mother who has dropped out of school and scrapes by on welfare is fighting huge obstacles in trying to make a life for herself and her child. For an angry, unemployed, African-American 20-year-old male, the power to be himself may find expression in ways that the dominant, White culture censures. The larger culture does not want those on the psychological, economic, or cultural fringe to express themselves, and it has at its disposal numerous ways to censure such expression—from the pink slip to the search warrant, to exclusion from clubs and restaurants, from neighborhoods and bank loans. Even in constrained circumstances, however, that power is never totally smothered. Without denying the injustice and tragedy of wasted human potential, one can find in any outcast community of humans a diversity of characters whose self-expression remains fiercely and humorously, quaintly and outrageously unique, as is reflected in the work of the sociologist, Douglas Harper, who portrayed the men of the hobo camps and skid row in the tramp world (Harper, 1982).

Hence, the power to be myself is a remarkable power. It is an enormously creative power, a power to create myself, so to speak, while adding to the life around me; or it is an enormously destructive power, a power to destroy myself (even though that takes place by barely perceptible, miniscule choices) while smothering and depressing life around me. That is why some people choose not to exercise that power at all: They sense the existential risk involved. Better to leave the choices in the hands of others.

## EMPOWERMENT AS A PROCESS
## AND AS AN ACHIEVEMENT

When we speak of empowerment, we should distinguish between the process of empowerment and the achievement of empowerment. Just as with the word *liberation*, there are two meanings: One deals with the activities in which one engages to liberate oneself while one is not yet liberated; the other meaning signifies that one has reached the state of liberation. Empowerment in a school context is a relational process, in which administrators and teachers engage in a mutual process of bringing to the surface what the power to be and the power to do *means* in this particular school, what positive qualities are attached to the exercise of that power, and what limitations are imposed by the circumstances of the communal effort at schooling. Empowerment is not the process of administrators giving power to teachers. Rather it is a process that involves mutual respect, dialogue, and invitation. It implies recognition that each person enjoys talents, competencies, and potentials that can be exercised in responsible and creative ways within the school setting for the benefit of children and youth. In this sense, we can see the blending of the moral and professional process of empowerment that also acknowledges the power of each teacher to be a unique voice and source of life.

Empowerment is also an achievement—an arriving at a state of autonomy and responsibility in the exercise of one's power to be and teach using all the talents and wisdom at one's disposal (Palmer, 1998). As an achievement it is always relative because we never exhaust the possibilities of our power to teach. Empowerment as a policy is a commitment that the school environment will continually nurture teachers' growth in their ability to promote the growth of students, both through their own responsible modeling of what it means to be an authentic person and through their professional engagement with the students and the learning material.

## EMPOWERMENT ON AN INDIVIDUAL BASIS

Empowerment has to happen with each individual teacher. Each teacher must be invited to be authentically her or himself. Sometimes that invitation can be direct, as when a principal asks: "What would you like to explore in your work as a teacher?" or "What do you need to do better that you already do well?" Sometimes the invitation is indirect, as when teachers are asked for suggestions for next year's staff development days. Sometimes the invitation is simply an attentive ear when a teacher needs to discuss a problematic situation at the school.

Empowerment, of course, does not mean a flabby acceptance of anything a teacher does. We are not interested in empowering teachers to be mean. Individuals have selfish as well as altruistic motives. Empowerment is not intended to encourage selfishness. Rather, it means encouraging the best that is in each person. It may also mean, at times, the indirect or direct discouragement of the worst that is there. However, I do not need to encourage administrators in the responsibilities to correct teachers. For some reason, administrators seem to learn that skill quickly and with great sophistication. Rather, administrators need to focus their attention much more on empowering the best that is in teachers, rather than on controlling their flaws. Accentuating the positive possibilities for people tends to diminish their negative possibilities.

Empowerment has to be individualized. Although all teachers may be invited to develop new skills, such as using computers in classroom instruction or developing debate formats within classrooms, each teacher should be expected to bring his or her own creative insight and intuition to the exercise of those generic skills. If empowerment means the development of a talent—say, the talent to orchestrate a productive class discussion—then the teacher needs time and encouragement to practice that talent and the administrative support to improve, refine, and enlarge it. The power in that teaching talent is the power to tease out students' insights, understandings, and acceptance of differences—the power to stimulate and nourish the new life of expanding minds. Assisting teachers to expand their talents leads necessarily to the spread of those talents in the learnings of the students.

Empowerment as a school policy means recognizing the power that both teachers and students have to be themselves and to express themselves through their talents. It means inviting them to exercise that power with joy, laughter, and compassion: joy because the exercise of their talent brings profound satisfaction, laughter because in the exercise of our individuality we often catch ourselves acting absurdly or foolishly, and compassion because the exercise of individuality can sometimes lead to mistakes, excesses, or misunderstandings. The expectation that forgiveness is an everyday necessity is a precondition for any communal exercise of our power to be ourselves.

That leads to a consideration of a fundamental requirement for any effort at empowerment, and that is the requirement of trust. If a teacher is to feel free enough to try more spontaneous activities, he or she must trust that there is room for mistakes, that differences are tolerated, and that unique insights are honored. Most teachers have been socialized into relatively limited protocols of teaching. They have not been encouraged to go beyond the textbook and curriculum guide to think for themselves and to design creative student learning activities. They have to know that they are trusted to try out new possibilities in a responsible and effective manner. If they expect immediate criticism of deviations from standard operating procedures, they will not risk trying something new.

Administrators are often not aware of how critical this sense of trust is. Simply telling teachers to have trust does not work. Trust is something built over time through the personal relationship an administrator is able to establish with each teacher, through always telling the truth, encouraging the sharing of ideas and criticisms, and acting on teacher suggestions. Only when trust has been established can teachers believe that administrators' talk about increased teacher autonomy and creativity is genuine.

## EMPOWERMENT ON A COMMUNITY BASIS

Empowerment on an individual basis, however, is only a small part of the empowerment agenda. Empowerment must be felt and exercised by the whole staff. When individual teachers who feel empowered work together with other empowered teachers to respond to schoolwide needs, empowerment is raised to a new strength. An empowered staff comes to believe that it has within its ranks enough talent and insight to respond to most school problems and to create from their own talent an outstanding school. By discussing ideas, sharing experiments, and pooling resources, an empowered staff can generate extraordinary energy and enthusiasm. That should be the ultimate goal of any policy of empowerment. When an administrator has nurtured that kind of empowerment, the whole staff becomes involved in the exercise of leadership. The united efforts of the staff in sharing their individual visions of the school can result in an overarching vision for the school; mutual problem solving and organizational evaluations can lead to structural redesign and institutional transformation. That in turn leads the staff to a greater sense of empowerment, confidence in their own creative talents, and even greater willingness to pursue the dream of creating an exciting and satisfying school.

From this vantage point, one can view empowerment as a genuine exercise of self-governance and moral fulfillment. Cultivating community means encouraging a community to take charge of its destiny and, in so doing, achieve the satisfaction of creating something wonderful. Every teacher worthy of the title dreams of a school environment in which youngsters find learning an exciting and awe-filled experience. That is the ideal we all hold.

Empowering teachers to work collectively toward that goal is what cultivating a learning community is all about.

## THE POWER OF CONNECTED ACTIVITY

It follows easily from the previous discussion that the empowerment of individuals takes place within an empowering community. We can engage in a process of growth, self-discovery, and self-expression in a community of persons who care for us, respect us and all the ways we are different, and appreciate and embrace our talents as sources of enriching the community. A second important focus in the empowerment process, therefore, is building a supportive and collaborative community. This means building a community culture that supports differences of opinion, differences in teaching protocols, and differences of cultural expressions.

The process of building community encourages creativity and initiative and discourages the *tall poppy syndrome*. The tall poppy syndrome is manifested in a group that cannot tolerate someone in the group excelling at anything. The group cuts down to size anyone whose head sticks up above the commonly approved height of the group. The group assumes that anyone who achieves beyond the group's norms is showing off, trying to impress the authorities, and is thus putting their own performance in a bad light and is a threat to the group's solidarity. When this syndrome is present in a school culture, administrators need imagination to invent a variety of initiatives for many people in the faculty so that the whole group may, as much as possible, move away from their routine ways of behaving. By cheerleading the various members of the group who are attempting new responses in their teaching, the administrator can promote an acceptance that in any given circumstance anyone can stand out in leadership activity without thereby implying as assertion of superiority.

Another way to build a supportive community is to create team projects (Leithwood, Jantzi, & Steinbach, 1999; Senge et al., 2000). Putting two to five teachers together on a project often produces a team that can find a diversity of talents among themselves, all of which are needed to achieve the project's goals. A new networking of individual talents takes place—a connecting of abilities that enables talent to play off and utilize other talent. The results are usually a new awareness and appreciation of the talents of others, and a new sense of bonding that supports the expression of those talents. In turn, the individual teacher gains a new appreciation of his or her own talents and can find new outlets for their expression within the team. This kind of teamwork is perhaps best exercised in house teams, where a team of teachers have major responsibility for the education of a limited number of students over a 2- or 3-year period.

Whatever the arrangements, the experience of teamwork, in which teachers are engaged in meaningful projects that relate directly to improved learning for their youngsters, is electric (Sergiovanni, 1994; Smith, 1993). Through the work of the team, each individual experiences a new sense of autonomy, of being in a place where he or she can make decisions with the team that will improve the learning of the children. Because a house team usually has the discretion to rearrange its use of time, space, groupings, and sequence of curriculum units, there is the empowering sense of genuinely participating in something whose significance transcends the work of teaching in an isolated classroom. There is an opportunity to explore new relationships among teaching strategies and curriculum topics, new field trips and field projects, and new learning activities. There is a feeling that one's own ideas and the ideas of the team are the creative stuff of their work, rather than a passive following of chapter sequences in a textbook or topics in a syllabus.

## THE POWER OF LARGE IDEAS, IDEALS, AND VISION

Finally, I want to argue for the empowering force of ideas, ideals, and visions. Under the press of legislated school reform, the professional empowerment of teachers has tended to become quite narrowly focused on mapping their instruction to the curriculum standards in the school reform guidelines. To be sure, many teachers may need to upgrade their content knowledge of the curriculum they are called on to teach and develop a wider repertoire of teaching strategies to reach underachieving students. Gradually, however, teachers are going to master the necessary competencies to teach to the standards. The danger in this narrow focus is that teachers can lose sight of the necessary connecting of the school curriculum to the world of the child's everyday life, to the world of cultural politics, to current social history.

This lack of involvement in the world of ideas stems in part from our culture's concentration on technical rationality at the expense of substantive rationality. By this distinction, I mean the difference between, on the one hand, a rationality that concentrates on how things work, on breaking things down into simpler component parts, on inventing new technologies, on procedures and organizational arrangements, on quantitative analyses of relationships, and, on the other hand, a rationality that seeks the larger gestalt, the deeper, complex relationship of parts to larger wholes that in turn are parts to larger wholes, the multiple relationships that define the significance of moments, places, stories, symbols, and works of art. Technical rationality seeks to answer the questions of how: how to do, how to fix, how to design, how to sell, how to build, how to negotiate. Substantive rationality seeks to answer questions of what and why: What is it we really want? What is it we seek to do, attempt to say, seek to find? Why are we doing this? Why should we choose this rather than that? What does this mean? Why should I believe you? Substantive rationality seeks meaning. Technical rationality seeks efficiency, economy, and procedural logic. Substantive rationality tends to focus on purposes, values, and ends. Technical rationality tends to focus on means, procedures, quantitative relationships, technical invention, and virtuosity.

Proposing that teachers develop a greater sense of empowerment by increasing their professionalism implies that teachers develop greater technical virtuosity, a more flexible repertoire of teaching protocols, and more technical mastery of the academic disciplines. Indeed, teachers who grow in this kind of professionalism experience empowerment.

In addition to administrators supporting and nurturing this enhanced professionalism, there is the work of engaging teachers in the exploration of powerful ideas—ideas that are capable of mobilizing the energies of teachers with a greater sense of purpose and value (Duckworth, 1996; Meier, 1995). We can see this kind of power at work in alternative schools (Wood, 1992). As teachers organized their school around one, two, or three themes, they found that they had discovered a new logic and meaning to their everyday work with students. The meaning of what they were doing took on a new significance. Fired by the excitement of the newly discovered significance of what they were doing with youngsters, they found within themselves resources of creativity, intuitive insight, and sheer physical energy that had gone untapped in their more traditional roles in more traditional schools. As they explored the generative themes that grounded their school's identity and attempted to translate those themes into learning units, they often had to confront the socioeconomic realities facing their students with a new understanding. They had to make new connections to the world outside the school. They had to see the consequences of their ideas and relate their thinking more explicitly to the students and their parents.

One might say that these teachers created a dream or vision of what their schools could become. These dreams and visions brought them to new levels of activity, well beyond the passive conformity to the bureaucratic arrangements of traditional schools. They overcame the enervating resentment toward school policies and practices formulated long ago on the factory metaphor of schooling (Callahan, 1962). When teachers are captured by exciting possibilities, by a new vision for their schools, they are empowered with a deep sense of meaning and a new energy to work for its realization. Administrators who work with teachers to create authentic learning communities are offering teachers a chance to regain their own sense of mission as teachers. That sense of mission gives them a renewed sense of the power and significance of their work.

## WHAT ABOUT STUDENTS?

All that we have said about the empowering of teachers also applies to the empowering of students. The empowering work with teachers should be directed toward translating *their* sense of empowerment into their work with students. Students should feel empowered by their teachers. The sources of this empowerment can be found in encouragement to be themselves and to express their talents, in the support that a community of students and teachers can give to the inventive exploration of the connections between learning and the project of creating themselves, and in the source of ideas and dreams for the creation of themselves as a community of strong, inventive, caring, and self-governing individuals. The empowering work for teachers can play itself out in their empowering work with students. In the process, administrators can find the community beginning to co-create itself. The work of the administrator is to get the process rolling and support its unfolding.

## STRUCTURAL IMPLICATIONS OF EMPOWERMENT

This kind of empowerment does not take place simply by wishing for it. Besides the personal involvement of administrators with individual teachers, and of teachers with individual students, there have to be structural arrangements in place that nurture and support the process of empowerment. Empowerment themes must be tied to the process of curriculum development and embedded in the curriculum itself. The design and implementation of teacher professional development and accountability have to be placed largely in the hands of teachers. A variety of reward and recognition schemes needs to be in place so that a variety of different talents and initiatives can be honored. Other structural arrangements might include a weekly and monthly schedule that allows for a wide variety and frequency of small-group staff workshops and seminars, perhaps a design studio with computers and visual media with which to design new curricular units, and perhaps retreat opportunities where teachers can explore the appropriate integration of their life stories with their teaching. Similar opportunities must also be created for students.

Schools and school systems are notoriously impoverished environments. Some administrators expect teachers and students to be empowered because they circulate a photocopy of a speech about it. Empowering teachers and students, however, requires schools to enrich their environments with opportunities for empowerment, to make the place of work so exciting and full of ideas and stimulating discussions of new possibilities that it would be impossible not to grow. Administrators sometimes blame teachers for becoming stale after their first few years of teaching. They blame the students for lack of motivation and responsibility. That is to blame the victims of a disempowering environment that smothers enthusiasm in routine and that punishes inventiveness by subtle demands for conformity and uniformity.

This kind of leadership is what we are all called to. It is an ideal, but unless we see the ideal, there is nothing on which to build a vision. Administrators always need practical administrative techniques, but they need much more the dream of what it is possible for the school community to create together. The payoff, of course, is for the youngsters in the school. The drama of their lives will be enriched because of what teachers do. More new songs will be sung, more new inventions will be tried, more compassion will flow between people, the community will feel greater confidence in its ability to govern itself, and students might even find themselves called to create a more benign society.

## RECAPITULATION

We began this chapter with a description of what might be termed *bureaucratic empowerment*. We saw that bureaucratic empowerment by itself can be an organizational arrangement with little or no significance for improving the quality learning for all students in the school. As bureaucratic empowerment becomes linked with professional, moral, and existential empowerment, we can see how this integration of the forms of empowerment can energize the transformation of teaching and learning, especially when that empowerment is embedded in a large vision of what the school can become.

But no one ingredient or process can carry the whole burden of the transformation of schooling. Empowerment is important, but it must be linked to other dynamics. The following chapters fill out those essential elements of administrative and leadership work.

## ACTIVITIES

1. In your journal, cite three instances in the past month when you clearly exercised your power to be yourself. What was going on at these times? Then cite three instances in the past month when your power to be yourself was diminished, thwarted, or threatened. What was happening at these times? Do you experience the power to be yourself often or rarely in your present work? What are you doing to become more empowered?

2. Ask yourself whether teachers and students in your school are empowered in the way we speak of it in this chapter. Give several examples of peo-

ple who are. Explain why this kind of empowerment is absent in some people in your school. With specific teachers and students in mind, suggest various kinds of specific empowering things you could do with them.

3. At the policy level, ask yourself how teacher and student empowerment might be nurtured in your school. Write five specific policy proposals. Discuss them with administrators in your school system and report back to your study group on their reactions.

4. Identify as many disempowering practices and aspects of your school's culture as you can. For each instance, design a counterpractice that would increase empowerment. Discuss the results of these findings with your classmates, and then come up with a class proposal for creating more empowering experiences for teachers and students.

## REFERENCES

Callahan, R. (1962). *Education and the cult of efficiency.* Chicago: University of Chicago Press.

Duckworth, E. R. (1996). *"The having of wonderful ideas" and other essays on teaching and learning.* New York: Teachers College Press.

Harper, D. (1982). *Good Company.* Chicago: University of Chicago Press.

Kegan, R. (1994). *In over our heads: The mental demands of modern life.* Cambridge, MA: Harvard University Press.

Leithwood, K., Jantzi, D., & Steinbach, R. (1999). *Changing leadership for changing times.* Philadelphia: Open University Press.

Marks, H., & Louis, K. S. (1997). Does teacher empowerment affect the classroom? The implications of teacher empowerment for instructional practice and student academic performance. *Educational Evaluation and Policy Analysis, 19,* 245–275.

Meier, D. (1995). *The power of their ideas: Lessons for America from a small school in Harlem.* Boston: Beacon.

Palmer, P. J. (1998). *The courage to teach: Exploring the inner landscape of a teacher's life.* San Francisco: Jossey-Bass.

Senge, P., Cambron-McCabe, N., Lucas, T., Smith, B., Dutton, J., & Kleiner, A. (2000). *Schools that learn.* New York: Currency/Doubleday.

Sergiovanni, T. (1994). *Building community in schools.* San Francisco: Jossey-Bass.

Smith, G. (Ed.). (1993). *Public schools that work: Creating community.* New York: Routledge.

Sykes, G. (1999). The "New Professionalism" in education. An appraisal. In J. Murphy & K. S. Louis (Eds.), *Handbook of research in educational administration* (2nd ed., pp. 227–249). San Francisco: Jossey-Bass.

Wood, G. H. (1992). *Schools that work: America's most innovative public education programs.* New York: Plume.

# Chapter 11

# Organic Management
# for Student Learning

In chapter 10, we spoke about a process of empowering people. We spoke of the energy of the community to govern itself when the individual members of the community feel empowered to be themselves, when their work is connected to the work of others in the community, and when they feel energized by core ideas and values of the community. In this chapter, we consider more structural ways of building a learning community. Assuming that the primary work of a learning community is continuous learning—revealed in the construction of meaning, community, and responsibility—we want to put in place administrative structures that facilitate that primary work of the community while enhancing the ability of the community to govern itself around that central focus. In other words, the self-governance of the community should be exercised in and through its work. We first look at the need for a culture of commitment to this common purpose. We then turn explicitly to organic management and its focus on the primary work of the school, student learning. Two aspects of organic management—the principle of subsidiarity and the dynamic of job enrichment—further develop our understanding.

## BUILDING A CULTURE OF COMMITMENT

Rowan (1990) offered a helpful distinction between two ways to administer a school: through control or through commitment. Administration by control implies the imposition, by a hierarchical structure of authority, of a means–end rationality that not only assumes uniform agreement on goals, but also uniform methodologies to achieve these goals. Administration by control represents a simplistic application of the factory metaphor to schooling (Patterson, Purky, & Parker, 1986). The activities of teaching and learning are not easily captured in a reductionistic formula of inputs, outputs, and feedback loops. The objectives of schooling are not easily boiled down to three or five uniform and highly specific outcomes. They are numerous, and they are open to numerous performances by both teachers and students. The process of teacher evaluation and supervision is fraught with simplistic assumptions about what constitutes effective or good teaching (Sergiovanni & Starratt, 2002; Stoldowsky, 1984). Similarly, assessment of student learnings by standardized testing is of limited usefulness because it encourages a simplistic understanding of learning and promotes an equally simplistic practice of teaching when all the efforts of the teacher are focused on preparation for these tests (Kidder, 1989; Lopate, 1975; Louis, Toole, & Hargreaves, 1999; McNeil, 1988; Shepard, 1989). The flaws in the assumptions of administration by control are numerous. The counterproductive effects on practice are serious (Blasé, 1990; Fullan, 1997; Wise, 1988).

Rowan (1990) suggested that there may be a more effective strategy for administering a school, which he called *administration through commitment.* In schools that run by commitment rather than control, there is an entirely different dynamic at work. In these schools, there is still a concern with schoolwide goals as well as learning outcomes. However, the assumptions and beliefs behind administration by commitment are quite different. Within the teaching faculty, there is a much greater awareness of diversity and difference among the student body. Teachers assume the need for flexibility in teaching protocols, pacing, and the performance of the learning that will be accepted as indicators of mastery. There is a belief that one can teach many things simultaneously, that on any given day students may be more disposed to learn than on others; that cultural pluralism in the classroom requires sensitivity to a variety of meanings generated by classroom activities; and that along with academic learning there are many social lessons to be learned, such as learning to respect racial, ethnic, and sexual differences; learning how to negotiate disagreements; learning how to control antisocial impulses; learning how to listen to and appreciate another point of view and enrich one's understanding with those other perspectives. Note the repetition of "listen and respond to" in the core theme of responsibility.

Schools administered by commitment make no attempt to monitor each teacher's classroom according to a predetermined, one best way to teach. Rather, administrators communicate the expectation that teachers, carefully reading the talents and interests of their students, are responding to both the curricular objectives and the complex chemistry of the human beings in their classes. Because there are multiple talents and levels of expertise among teachers, administrators encourage continuous collaboration among teachers to explore and design a variety of learning activities to assist their students' appropriation of the curriculum material and their creation of meaning through those activities (Elmore, 2000). Administrators do not control what goes on in the classroom. Instead they encourage teachers to take responsibility for all students learning well in classes that create exciting learning possibilities for every child. Administrators cultivate the teachers' collective commitment to develop a rich and diverse menu of interesting and fulfilling learning activities that respond to the complex diversity in the classroom, while leading students toward mastery of the state and district curriculum.

How does a school nurture this kind of commitment? There is a growing awareness in the research literature that a school's culture can be enormously influential on the quality and degree of teachers' commitment. By concentrating on building a culture of shared purposes, a sense of mission, and a sense that in their work teachers are making a significant contribution to the lives of their children, administrators and teachers develop a deep motivation to make the school experience successful for youngsters (Elmore, 2000; Fullan, 1993; Leithwood, Jantzi, & Steinbach, 1999; Sergiovanni & Starratt, 2002).

In a culture of commitment, one finds a kind of shared covenant—an unspoken rule that the school will not work unless everyone is fully involved. There is a feeling of being responsible to each other, a sense of the bonds of loyalty and common ideals, a sharing of common beliefs about teaching and learning, about how children grow, about the social purposes of schools, and about what it means to be a full human being.

In such cultures, teaching is a reflective activity. It is the work of the professional who continually tests theories and intuitions about what will work in this circumstance by attending closely to the immediate results. This kind of reflective teacher is always looking at the student, at what is going on, engaging the student in a dialogue so the teacher has a sense of what is happening inside the student's head and heart. That is difficult to do with 20 or 30 children in a class or with 120 children in the course of a school day. Good teachers find ways to keep close to the work that students are doing. Even a brief review and comment lets the students know the teacher cares about their work.

In cultures of commitment, it is not so much the administrators who hold teachers accountable, but rather the teachers who hold themselves responsible to create genuine learning opportunities for their students. Their sense of responsibility is passed on to the students. Teachers work on motivating the students to take responsibility for their individual and collective learning.

## ORGANIC MANAGEMENT

One builds such a culture of commitment by a process of organic management. By *organic management,* I mean that the administrator continually tries to focus on the core or central work of the school and brings others' attention to that central work. Other forms of management, such as the bureaucratic management of traditional schools, begins with an organizational arrangement. The school day is divided into seven or eight periods of 40- to 45-minute segments. The school day ends at 2:30 p.m. School bus schedules are arranged so that most of the students are expected to go home at 2:30 p.m. regardless of whether they have finished their work at school for that day. Teachers are assigned textbooks and specific classes; they are expected to fill out report cards formatted the same for everyone. The curriculum is parceled out in 40- to 45-minute periods. In other words, the core work of the school—student learning—is arranged to fit an organizational structure that is already in place even if that organizational structure impedes the core work of the school.

The core work of the school is the work of learning. That is the work that students do. The work of students is not to produce a uniform product as workers on an assembly line do. The work of students is the creation of knowledge appropriated from the culture and academic resources available in the school and in the community in the form of books, films, computer data banks, electronic switchboards, and communication networks. That work also involves applying knowledge to the interpretation of personal experience and to the interpretation of community issues and problems. It also involves invention and creative expression in which the student takes his or her learning and makes something new out of it—poem, song, political statement, computer application, design, interpretation, or suggestion for recycling plastics. It also involves social learning, the appreciation of other, possibly quite different points of view, learning how to disagree, learning teamwork, and discovering how one's ideas are enriched and complemented by the ideas of others.

By always keeping in mind that the students' work is the core task of the school, the administrator employing organic management engages the staff and students in exploring ways to make that work more felicitous, productive, and effective. The administrator and staff periodically have to take the present organizational arrangements and imaginatively throw them all away. Assuming no schedule, no classroom, and no weekly and monthly calendar in place, they ask how they can better organize their resources of space, time, money, and personnel so as to improve the core work of the school—namely, student learning. The work of learning should dictate how the day is scheduled and how teachers work with students (Wood, 2001). Perhaps some of that work can be done more effectively outside the school building at some location in the community at large. Some of the work may best be done individually, some in teams of students. Some of the work may require intensive teacher involvement at the beginning and minimal involvement as the project matures. Some work may involve sophisticated computer hookups to major data networks that can only be done within the school. However, some may be done with a computer at home. Some work is best achieved in apprenticelike relationships with resource people in the community; some may involve participating in meetings of various public and volunteer agencies in the community.

The point of organic management is to keep teachers and students focused on the core task of the school: the promotion and enhancement of student learning. Organic management of schools continually evaluates how that work is managed so that institutional arrangements do not get in the way (Wood, 2001).

## THE PRINCIPLE OF SUBSIDIARITY

An important part of organic management is the principle of subsidiarity. According to this principle, the authority to make discretionary decisions concerning the work is placed as close to the work as possible. This means that operational decisions about the work are not made at the superintendent's level or even at the principal's level. They are made where teaching and learning take place. The persons closest to the task are given the authority and responsibility for carrying out the task. Subsidiarity unites authority with responsibility. If students have the responsibility to produce the learning, then as much authority as possible should be placed in their hands to decide the details of its production. The teacher, as the next closest to the task, should likewise have the authority to negotiate the production of learning with the student.

This does not mean that superintendents and principals should have no say in what goes on. Clearly, their voices need to join with the voices of the teachers as discussions are held about the schoolwide and districtwide goals of the school. As educators with overall responsibility for a K–12 system or for a whole school in the system, they have a broad perspective on the large goals of schooling. There are necessary support systems (assessment results, interpretive guides for using assessment information, provisions for authentic remediation for underachieving students, supports for parental involvement in their children's learning, etc.). Furthermore, there are occasions when essential decisions have to be made in the face of divided opinions on a particular matter when no consensus is available. Administrators, while listening to both sides of the argument, nonetheless have to make the decision. The state also has a voice in setting general graduation requirements, as well as determining legal constraints on school systems to prevent illegal activities and to provide special services to children with special needs. This is all taken for granted.

Nevertheless, the essential work is done at the student level through the coaching and instruction of teachers. This work cannot be micromanaged from a distance because the number of variables needed to be taken into account in the production of learning only can be dealt with at the micro-level, not at the system or state level. If learning involves the production and performance of meaning, then ultimately the meaning has to be the student's. The culture provides the ingredients for constructing meaning; the state and local school board set the curriculum to be covered; the teacher, as the closest other person to the student's production and performance of learning, strongly influences what and how that learning comes to be through the teacher's interpretation of the cultural ingredients and curriculum material; but the student is the one who, by her or his autonomous activity, *does* the learning.

## FOUR REQUIREMENTS FOR SUBSIDIARITY

The principle of subsidiarity as the centerpiece strategy of organic management requires four elements if it is to work. Subsidiarity requires (a) trust, (b) knowledge of what the task is, (c) capacity to carry out the task, and (d) a sense of the whole. If any one of those elements is missing, the strategy does not work. Teachers and students may know what the task is, but lack the trust of the school board and, hence, lack the discretionary authority to effect the work. Teachers may know that the student has to be actively involved in the production and performance of meaning, but they have been socialized into a way of teaching that blocks such active involvement by the student. A sense of the whole must influence decisions about the parts (Senge, 1990). Students may want to study only science and math and have no interest in the rest of the curriculum; teachers may want to work only with bright students. In either case, we have people who do not want to work with the larger whole, which is necessary if subsidiarity in decision making is to contribute to the common life of the school. Let us explore what these four requirements mean.

### Trust

One of the difficulties that newly appointed administrators have is dealing with their authority and their sense of accountability to their superiors. In popular understanding, administrators are supposed to be in charge. They are supposed to make things happen. When things go wrong, administrators are blamed. Yet most administrators know, at least at a subconscious level, that they cannot control all the details of a school, even a small school. Apprehension over what the public or school board might think of them if something were to go wrong, however, can lead them to suppress this knowledge that they cannot control things (even while that same knowledge subconsciously fuels their apprehension) and to establish tight reins of control (Cusick, 1992; Elmore, 2000). No decisions are made unless cleared with the principal; no expenditures of funds are allowed unless first cleared by the principal; no letters to parents are sent home unless first cleared through the principal; no deviation from the assigned curriculum is allowed unless the principal explicitly grants an exception. Mandate follows on mandate. New rules are constructed to account for yet another unforeseen situation. Not only does the administrator end up continuously frustrated by her inability to anticipate every mess (messes are a daily, ontologically guaranteed certainty in schools), but teachers and students resent her attempts to control every facet of school life. This resentment, in turn, leads to noncompliance or, at best, minimal compliance with all the control strategies. Messes are invented just to see the principal turn apoplectic. Of course, complaints filter up to the principal's superiors, who in turn send queries back down to the principal that, to this now half-crazed unfortunate, are interpreted as complaints about his inability to *control* things at the school.

The beginning principal has to learn, often the hard way, that one cannot control every facet of school life and, furthermore, that one should not attempt to control any facet of school life. Rather, the administrator's job is to get people to take responsibility for their own work. This does not mean that, once everyone has agreed to take responsibility for their own work, messes disappear. People still make mistakes, still misunderstand each other, and still descend to selfish concerns. If they have agreed to take responsibility for their work, however, the administrator can ask them to take responsibility for cleaning up their own messes.

The lesson to be learned here is that when people know that you rely on them, they do the job more energetically than you would have imagined possible. Perfection eludes us all. There are problems, bruised egos, petty jealousies, and plain childishness from time to time. In a climate of trust and mutual responsibility, however, these things can be worked through. Furthermore, when individual teachers feel trusted, they more easily develop a sense of team—a sense that together they can collaborate on the resolution of nagging problems. In a climate of trust, individual teachers and groups of teachers can approach administrators with their concerns. They can indicate that they need some help in working out a problem. They can openly address schoolwide issues that are negatively affecting student learning. In other words, one administers by encouraging the self-governance of which we spoke of in the last chapter.

People more readily take charge of their work when they perceive that they are trusted to do so, when they understand that they are expected to do so. A parent holds the spoon and feeds an infant. As the child grows older, the parent expects the child to feed him or herself. When adults are trusted to do a good job, the quality performance of that job becomes habitual. No one has to give them permission to do the job. Doing a good job is simply the way one works (DePree, 1989; McGregor, 1960).

If teachers have formerly not been trusted to do a good job, then it takes some time to convince them that you really trust them. There are disappointments along the way as some betray your trust by cutting corners. Some teachers accuse the trusting principal of naivete, wimpishness, and indecisiveness. Principals are told by superiors to *come down hard* on certain teachers. Nonetheless, persistence in trusting is the answer. Most people can be motivated to do a decent job by trust.

### Knowledge of the Task

Trust alone does not guarantee that teachers manage their work well. They need to understand what the task is for which they are responsible. One of the difficulties of teaching is that the tasks for which teachers are responsible are multiform. Many of these tasks are not spelled out in the teachers' contract. Many of the tasks are never covered in preservice courses in teacher education. For example, what does one do when a youngster throws up all over his desk? Of course one must protect oneself and the other children from possible contamination by viruses or bacteria and get the child to the school nurse. But should one provide prior instruction to the children about the procedures to be followed in this situation, or is it better to make light of it and not create unnecessary anxieties? What if the ill child has, not chicken pox, but AIDS? How does a teacher break up a fight in the school yard? How does a teacher speak to a child whose lack of social sensitivity leads to her ostracism by the other children? How does a teacher help a child develop study habits when her home life is totally chaotic? How does a teacher respond to an assertive parent who is convinced that his second-grade child is a budding Fulbright scholar when all indications are that the child has rather average academic talents? These concerns may not be treated in the formulas for effective instruction in the teacher education textbooks, yet teachers are expected to deal with all these contingencies as a professional. Induction and mentoring programs for beginning teachers are supposed to cover much of this, but often teachers are left to flounder. Of course, they are blamed when they make a mistake, although they have never been informed of school policies for dealing with specific situations.

Administrators need to work with the teachers, both individually and in groups, to encourage them to identify their major tasks. Teachers initially may identify these tasks by highly particularized examples, such as teaching students how to work out equations with fractions, use the subjunctive voice, or learn the names of the major rivers in the United States. Teachers need to be asked why these learning tasks are included and others are not. They need to talk about the larger purposes and values that ground particular learnings. Through these conversations, they can be led to a clearer definition of the task that encompasses the many small things they do. They may come to understand that they are attempting to develop in their students habits of life-long learning, habits of learning how to learn, habits of applying their learning to real-life problems and issues, habits of using their learning to define themselves, habits of continually refashioning themselves in relationship to their physical, social, and human worlds, habits of collaboration in negotiating cross cultural misunderstandings, and habits of developing political skills. These larger definitions of the task of teaching enable the teacher to bring a larger sense of purpose and mission to the daily work with the students.

## Capability to Accomplish the Task

In the course of these conversations, administrators and teachers need to discuss what they need in order to do the work more effectively. In the present context of standards-based school renewal, many teachers need guidance in mapping their instruction to the curriculum standards. In some instances, the majority of teachers in a specific school need extensive, in-house professional development, working in teams to align their instruction with the standards. In other circumstances, the discussion may lead to the realization that the teacher needs to know a lot more about child development or learning disabilities. In other instances, they may come to the conclusion that there are certain academic areas where the teacher is weak—say physical science or history. In other instances, the teacher may come to realize that he or she simply does not understand the cultural backgrounds of the children. This may be due to differences between the race, ethnicity, or class of the teacher and students. The teacher may need workshops in multicultural sensitivity or a course in the history of the children's culture. This academic enlargement of the teacher's cultural horizons may need to be supplemented with more direct conversations with the parents of the children so they may work out ways of collaborating together in the children's education. In any case, administrators have to adhere to the principle that holding teachers accountable for high levels of learning by all their students means that administrators must hold themselves accountable to cultivate increased teacher capacity so they can do what they are supposed to do.

## A Sense of the Whole

The principle of subsidiarity also requires a sense of being part of a larger whole. If teachers and students are to have the authority to make discretionary decisions about their learning, they have to make those decisions with the realization that they have responsibilities—not simply to do this specific task, but to the working of the larger community and its variety of tasks. Besides mastery of those curriculum standards mandated by the district and state, students and teachers need to hold themselves accountable to living up to the school's core values as well as the important social and moral learnings involved in the daily work of constructing community (Oakes et al., 2000).

A sense of the whole also applies to the use of resources, including the resources of time and space for learning. Students may be encouraged to take the necessary time to complete a project, but this project may be only one of many projects. If the student is a member of a team that is working on another project, the team has some claim on that student's time as well. Teachers may want to provide an abundance of colored construction paper to their children, but they have to leave enough in the supply closet for the other classes to have their fair share. In other words, the discretion to make decisions necessary to carry out the work is not a license to disregard the needs of everyone else in the school.

Ground rules and explicit agreements about the use of space, time, and resources are a necessary component of organic management. However, they should be worked through by the people most involved with the work, rather than dictated from a remote administrative office. At the beginning of every school year, teachers and students need to review these agreements. More than likely, meetings need to be called from time to time to work out imbalances in the way resources are shared in the various learning tasks. The work of the administrator is to cultivate and monitor the self-governance of the teachers and students around the learning agenda and facilitate and arbitrate when the parties cannot work out their disagreements on their own.

The brief examples mentioned earlier are intended to illuminate the requirements of trust, knowledge of the task, capacity to accomplish the task, and a sense of the whole. We can see at this point that all four requirements feed on one another. Organic management requires an ongoing learning of the task, developing greater strength and versatility to tackle the various dimensions of the task. As greater concentration on learning tasks develops, teachers and students have to balance the demands of those tasks with the whole curriculum and the limited resources at their disposal. As they honor the demands of the whole, teachers and administrators develop greater trust in their ability to address the practicalities of the learning tasks.

It is also evident that one of the major investments of an administrator's time is in conversation with teachers, including both informal and formal conversations about their work. Regular conversations ensure clear lines of communication, both vertically and horizontally. Through regular conversations, problems are identified and possible responses tested; conflicts between teachers and students, teachers and parents, teachers and other teachers, and teachers and administrators can be raised and addressed before they reach the boiling point. The commitment is to making the school work for youngsters for their enhanced learning. Hence, the conversations should continually raise and encourage the common commitment to this work and the awareness of each person's responsibility to engage in that work.

As teachers and administrators discuss the nature of the task—the promotion of the student's enhanced understanding of herself in relationship to the physical, social, and human worlds and her involvement in those worlds—it should become evident that teachers need to work more in teams. In other words, the work of the school is a multifaceted and complex one—a task that is larger than the ability of one teacher to achieve. Teachers working in teams can accomplish significant units of the task or indeed the whole task (Elmore, 2000; Oakes et al., 2000; Senge et al., 2000). In teams their talents and areas of expertise complement one another; collectively they can make a qualitatively richer response to the work of students' learning.

In some instances, this may mean a team of teachers working with a group of, say, 100 students over the course of 3 or 4 years. In contrast to the tendency toward specialization, where the work of teachers is narrow, repetitive, and separated from the sense of the larger task, teachers working in teams can work on a variety of facets of the large task with a sense of how their work fits together. This, of course, enhances the students' sense of the connectedness of their learning to the large unities of the physical, social, and human worlds. When teachers work in teams, the authority and responsibility for the work is clearly located as close to the work as possible. The work is managed organically because the decisions made flow from the intrinsic demands of the present contingencies of the work of learning, rather than from an artificially constructed administrative structure built on the assumption of uniformity of learning, learners, daily readiness for learning, cultural backgrounds, and learning performances.

Whether talking with individual teachers or teams of teachers, the administrator is concerned with another sense of the whole: the larger school curriculum. Teachers who work with a particular grade level need to keep in mind how the work at that level fits within the overall curriculum. Usually their work is so focused on the immediate learning tasks that they seldom refer to the larger curriculum framework. Thus, teams of teachers from different grade levels also need to coordinate their efforts so they can see their work as contributing to the larger work of the school curriculum. Administrators can often provide daily opportunities for teachers to make those connections while on their rounds.

## JOB ENRICHMENT

Besides the principle of subsidiarity, the theory and research of job enrichment provide further insight into the dynamics of organic management. The work of Hackman and Oldham (1976) is especially informative. Although their studies involved workers in the industrial and corporate worlds, the dynamics they describe apply as well to the dynamics of organic management we have proposed for schools. Hackman and Oldham found that workers were motivated to perform high-quality work that they could be proud of when a consistent set of job dimensions were in place. These dimensions led to an internal experience of the job that was highly satisfying and meaningful. These internal experiences of the job, in turn, led to high-quality performance of the work. Their findings are summarized in Table 11.1.

Hackman and Oldham found that five core dimensions on the job made all the difference between work considered highly satisfying and work that was not. Three of those dimensions had to do with the task or work itself: skill variety, task identity, and task significance. Workers prefer variety in their work, rather than a fixed routine of the same tasks. They enjoy using a variety of skills on the job, rather than narrowly specialized, single skills. Task identity refers to the clarity of understanding what the work entails. Workers need to know that the task has a core and that it has boundaries.

TABLE 11.1
The Dynamics of Job Enrichment

| Core Job Dimensions | → | Critical Psychological States | → | Personal & Work Outcomes |
|---|---|---|---|---|
| • Skill Variety | | Experienced | | High internal motivation; high-quality work |
| • Task Identity | | Meaningfulness | | |
| • Task Significance | | of the work | | |
| • Autonomy | | Experienced responsibility for results | | High satisfaction and pride |
| • Feedback | | Knowledge of actual actual results | | High satisfaction and enthusiasm |

They do not want to be held responsible for work not assigned to them. They want to know clearly what it is they are expected to do. They want to have a clear understanding of the substance of the work. Task significance refers to the value attached to the work. What does the work mean in relation to a larger framework of value?

The variety of skills a teacher needs in her work with students qualifies the work of teaching as potentially highly satisfying. Conversations between the principal and teachers by which they identify the meaning of what they are doing is an example of an attempt at task identity. The teachers' sense of task significance can become quite ephemeral. Teachers get little feedback from parents or administrators that their work with students is valuable, that it has significance in the ongoing life of the community. Many beginning teachers start out with a sense of mission, but the traditional culture of bureaucratic schools quickly drains it away, replacing it with a pragmatic or cynical political perspective of survival. Exposure to the daily routine of the teachers' room is enough to defeat most ideals. "Ideals?! God forbid we should get caught with such a social disease! Ideals, you say! Better for you to guard against the stupidity of superiors and the incorrigibility of children and simply get on with the next five pages of the textbook, thank you. Enough about ideals, already. We don't need any more do-goodniks around here."

To combat these attitudes, principals need to continually remind their teachers of the value of their work. Although it may sound like motherhood and apple pie, principals who believe in the social and humanistic value of education need to employ inspiring imagery in their attempts to remind teachers of the nobility and sacredness of their work. What could be more sacred than nurturing the values and idealism of the country's next generation of leaders? What could be more noble than nurturing the imagination and intelligence of the next generation of artists, musicians, builders, astronomers, police officers, architects, farmers, doctors, judges, geophysicists, and poets? What could be more worthwhile than expanding the humanity of the new generation of parents and citizens? What could be more exciting than exploring the boundaries of knowledge with young minds? What could be more sacred than participating in the reflexive and inventive process of the universe in its continuing creation of itself? The work is so sacred it is scary. Perhaps that is why teachers cover it over with the ritual of routine. Ordinary people could never do such extraordinary things. Ideals . . . God forbid.

The two other job dimensions that Hackman and Oldham highlighted are autonomy on the job and feedback of results. Obviously, autonomy does not mean total latitude to do whatever you want in your work. It does mean that the worker has enough discretion to respond to situations that are beyond the routine guidelines for getting the job done. It also means discretion to pursue an insight about how the work could be improved. Where the work goes beyond the assembly-line production of uniform widgets, where the work involves selling, marketing, or designing, or negotiating an organizational conflict between two competing groups, the worker has the autonomy to channel the work in a way that makes sense to him or her. If the decision turns out to be inappropriate, the worker learns from that and stores that learning in the bin labeled *Avoid in the future*.

Although teachers enjoy a fair amount of autonomy, it is not an autonomy granted to a mature professional. It is an autonomy granted by indifference, expediency, and administrative conspiracy. It is an autonomy embedded in a culture of isolation and an organizational structure of loose coupling of the core work of the school with vague and conflicting goals (Elmore, 2000, Lortie, 1975; Murphy, 1999). Many administrators are indifferent to the specific ways teachers nurture learning. If most of the children are getting passing grades, the assumption is that the teacher is doing a good job. There is no effort to explore with the teacher how student learning could be qualitatively enhanced by the introduction of new approaches. *Good enough* is a judgment often made with little understanding of whether that means the teacher has done a spectacular job with youngsters of limited talents or a mediocre job with students of high talents. Given the way school systems interpret the task of instructional supervision, the lack of stimulating collaboration with teachers is neglected from a sense of expediency; there is only so much time available for a once or twice a semester observation. In the previous section on subsidiarity, we have seen the antidote to this dysfunctional form of teacher autonomy.

Feedback or knowledge of results is important to job satisfaction and enrichment because it enables the worker to gain confirmation that he or she is doing a good job or needs to attend to some things to improve the work. Feedback complements autonomy. The more autonomy one has to use inventive discretion in one's work, the more one needs some way of getting feedback about the results of the work. Unfortunately, for many teachers, the only official feedback they receive is the collective results of their children on standardized tests.

When teachers are working collaboratively with other teachers on a continuous basis to improve the quality of learning for all of their students, they share ideas and practices. This working in teams often provides feedback on what works well with students. Also teachers involved in a more careful assessment process with their students derive a clearer sense of what students are, in fact, learning well or learning poorly, thus providing information for further work on learning activity design.

Furthermore, with the results from state and district tests increasingly available in intelligible statistical formats, teachers can study how their classes have achieved. Principals, cluster leaders, department chairs, grade-level coordinators, and other administrators should also be conversing with each teacher about the test results of the students. Such feedback helps teachers and administrators identify students who are floundering and probe possible sources of the difficulty and address them. These conversations about test results offer administrators an excellent opportunity to engage teachers in conversations about their work and explore responses to evident problems uncovered by the test data.

The nature of *what* is assessed, moreover, needs to be examined. Few teachers receive feedback on their efforts to teach youngsters to appreciate the opinions of others or resolve their disputes in nonviolent ways. Normally, the only time teachers receive feedback on these efforts is when something unpleasant happens between students and teachers are blamed for not attending to it. If the building up of community is important to the school, teachers should receive feedback on the results of these efforts as well. Knowledge of results of standardized tests is good, as far as it goes, but there are many more student learnings in the curriculum of community and the curriculum of responsibility that teachers attend to, the results of which are hardly ever assessed.

We have not applied Hackman and Oldham's model of job enrichment to student work. However, a quick review of their categories reveals how applicable they are to student learning. Their model provides a framework for teacher and student self-assessment, classroom action-research, as well as conversations among teachers and between teachers and principals. The model provides a basis for analyzing the learning agenda of the school for its students. Such an analysis further assists teachers and administrators in providing a focus for their organic management of the core work of the school—learning.

## SUMMARY

This chapter explored how one can cultivate meaning, community, and responsibility through a process of organic management. *Organic management* means management by commitment rather than by control, and therefore implies attention to the development of a culture of commitment. We saw that organic management begins by identifying the core work of the school—the active learning of students and the facilitating work of teachers in promoting this active learning. With a clear sense of the core work of the school, organic management involves designing all administrative procedures and structures to enhance and facilitate this core work. We then explored the principle of subsidiarity as providing the strategic orientation to aligning administrative procedures with the core work of the school, by placing the authority to do the work as close as possible to those who have the responsibility to do the work: teachers and students. The requirements of trust, knowledge of the task, capacity to do the task, and a sense of the whole were seen as essential to subsidiarity. Finally, Hackman and Oldham's job enrichment theory shed further light on the dynamics of organic management. As in earlier chapters, we have not developed a list of how-tos. That is the work that lies before us as we take the general ideas of organic management and study how our own school workplace can be restructured and recultured.

## ACTIVITIES

1. Study your workplace. Is the school governed by control or by commitment? If by control, what are the undesirable and desirable results of this in terms of morale, professionalism, inventiveness, and productivity of the staff and students? If by commitment, what are the values that explicitly or implicitly ground that commitment, and how are they sustained? In either case, make three policy recommendations that would improve the way your school governs itself.

2. In your workplace, what is the definition of the core work of the organization? How does this core work relate to the organizational structures and administrative procedures that channel and direct the work? What needs to be done about the situation if anything? Do you have any policy recommendations?

3. Use the job enrichment schema in Table 11.1 to analyze the level of enrichment that people experience in your workplace. What policy recommendations would you make to improve work enrichment?

4. Discuss your results with others in the class and come up with some systemwide policy recommendations that would encourage organic management in all the schools of the district. Develop short- and long-term plans for implementing these policy recommendations.

## REFERENCES

Blase, J. (1990). Some negative effects of principals' control-oriented and protective political behavior. *American Educational Research Journal, 27,* 727–753.

Cusick, P. A. (1992). *The educational system: Its nature and logic.* New York: McGraw-Hill.

DePree, M. (1989). *Leadership is an art.* New York: Doubleday.

Elmore, R. (2000). *Building a new structure for school leadership.* Washington, DC: The Albert Shanker Institute.

Fullan, M. (1993). *Change forces.* London: Falmer.

Fullan, M. (1997). *What's worth fighting for in the principalship.* New York: Teachers College Press.

Hackman, J. R., & Oldham, C. (1976). Motivation through design of work: Test of a theory. *Organizational Behavior and Human Performance, 16*(2), 250–279.

Kidder, T. (1989). *Among schoolchildren.* New York: Avon.

Leithwood, K., Jantzi, D., & Steinbach, R. (1999). *Changing leadership for changing times.* Philadelphia: Open University Press.

Lopate, P. (1975). *Being with children.* New York: Poseiden.

Lortie, D. (1975). *Schoolteacher: A sociological study.* Chicago: University of Chicago Press.

Louis, K. S., Toole, J., & Hargreaves, A. (1999). Rethinking school improvement. In J. Murphy & K. S. Louis (Eds.), *Handbook of research on educational administration* (2nd ed., pp. 251–276). San Francisco: Jossey-Bass.

McGregor, D. (1960). *The human side of enterprise.* New York: McGraw-Hill.

McNeil, L. M. (1988). *Contradictions of control: School structure and school knowledge.* New York: Routledge.

Murphy, J. (1999). *The quest for a center: Notes on the profession of educational leadership.* Columbus, MO: University Council on Educational Administration.

Oakes, J., Quantz, K. A., Ryan, S., & Lipton, M. (2000). *Becoming good American schools: The struggle for civic virtue in educational reform.* San Francisco: Jossey-Bass.

Patterson, J., Purkey, S., & Parker, J. (1986). *Productive school systems for a nanrational world.* Alexandria, VA: Association for Supervision and Curriculum Development.

Rowan, B. (1990). Commitment and control: Alternative strategies for the organizational design of schools. In C. B. Cazden (Ed.), *Review of research in education* (pp. 353–389). Washington, DC: American Educational Research Association.

Senge, P. (1990). *The fifth discipline.* New York: Doubleday/Currency.

Senge, P., Cambron-McCabe, N., Lucas, T., Smith, B., Dutton, J., & Kleiner, A. (2000). *Schools that learn.* New York: Doubleday/Currency.

Sergiovanni, T. J., & Starratt, R. J. (2002). *Supervision: A redefinition* (7th ed.). New York: McGraw-Hill.

Shepard, L. A. (1989). Why we need better assessments. *Educational Leadership, 46*(7), 4–9.

Stoldowsky, S. (1984). Teacher evaluation: The limits of looking. *Educational Researcher, 13*, 11–19.

Wise, A. (1988). Two conflicting trends in school reform: Legislated learning revisited. *Phi Delta Kappan, 69*, 328–333.

Wood, G. (2001, October). *First principle: A tone of decency.* Paper presented at the annual conference of the Center for the Study of Leadership and Ethics, Charlottesville, VA.

# Chapter 12

# Leading by Design:
# The Medium Is the Message

The clue that something is made by humans is that they add to the material elements and natural forms of wood and stone, fabric and food, a fingerprint of human intelligence, imagination, playfulness, and inventiveness. A branch may have a natural bend and curve as it leaves the tree trunk that would make it suitable for use as a ladle or scoop. The human sees the design of the ladle already in the bend and scoop, so he takes the branch and fashions it into a human instrument. Yet he often adds to the natural curve and scoop design by carving the image of a serpent, flower, or face on the handle. Animals build nests and burrows out of natural materials, and many add distinctive designs to these materials as they build. One species weaves the straw with mud, another with small pieces of wood. When humans build homes, they use natural materials, but they design and decorate the spaces so that they are both functional and pleasing. More often than not, the design carries symbolic value as well: One room is clearly a woman's room, one a man's; a family coat of arms decorates the parlor; a religious shrine sets off an interior room.

The way humans design their living environment communicates the values they attach to those environments. The austere, uniform, and simple design of a boot-camp barracks communicates the value of the spartan single-mindedness of the soldier/warrior preparing for mortal combat, the value of everyone doing exactly as ordered, the value of thinking only in terms of the group, platoon, regiment, and company. Prisons are designed to communicate other values. The design of factories, cathedrals, banks, and other kinds of social institutions reveals core values that those who commissioned the design wanted to communicate. Think of the design of a present-day bank. Ordinary customers stand in line and wait their turn to approach a high counter, where their business is transacted expeditiously. Normally the teller does not even call the customer by name. More valued customers—the prospective homeowner seeking a mortgage on which the bank stands to realize a substantial profit, or the executive who represents a company whose business with the bank can generate sizable profits—sit in another part of the bank, with walls hung with works of art, with fine drapery, carpeting, and upholstered furniture. The medium carries the message.


## THE DESIGN OF SCHOOLS

The layout of a school often reveals the educational philosophy of those who commissioned its construction. I usually look for the central space of the school because that usually tells me what activity is considered most important. If the principal's office sits at the center of the school, then I get a sense that the designers assumed the principal's office would be the control center of the school, providing roughly equal access to the office from all directions. However, if I find the library at the center of the school or at least in a more prominent location than the principal's office, then I assume that the designers of the schools value learning and storytelling more than administrative control. Sometimes I find the cafeteria at the center, or an auditorium, gymnasium, or even the boiler room. What is at the center and periphery of buildings often conveys the symbolic order of importance of the activities conducted in those spaces. I also like to visit the teachers' room, staff lounge, or whatever it is called. Where it is located and how it is fitted out often tells me a lot about how the administration thinks of its teachers and how they think of themselves.

I also look for what is displayed in the corridors, especially in those closest to the front door. In many schools, there are cabinets containing athletic trophies; in some, there are bulletin boards covered with student art work; in others, there are displays of photographs of student groups involved in a variety of projects and special events; and in others, there is nothing but walls.

Look at the way classrooms are arranged. Are they clustered by grade levels, with common rooms designated for that cluster's use, or are they all the same size? Do they all manifest the same configuration of desks in rows or are the seating arrangements in a variety of configurations? Is the building an egg crate of classrooms, or are there various sizes and shapes to the work spaces, some curved, some two-tiered, some triangular, some simply re-arrangeable into a variety of shapes?

All of these spatial design features reveal values and perspectives about the work of educating youngsters. The aesthetics of school designs reveal the educational philosophy of those in charge of the school. In a uniformly arranged series of identical classrooms with identical seating arrangements, it is difficult to introduce variety into the instructional methods of teaching and the performance of the learning tasks. Not impossible, but difficult. Access to books, computers, and audiovisual resources is also a measure of the difficulty of varying the learning tasks. If these resources are half a school away, then it becomes more difficult to use them—not impossible, but difficult. The way a room is equipped—the number and position of electrical outlets, sinks, closets, bookshelves, display boards, sizes and shapes of tables, variety of lighting possibilities—likewise add to or subtract from the possibility of variety in the teaching and learning activities. Clearly, the way a school is designed communicates the kind of work that is expected to go on in the various spaces of the school.

## A LARGER VIEW OF DESIGN

We often think of design as being involved exclusively with the design of space. Yet design includes much more. Choreography can be seen as the design of bodily movements to the flow of the music. Composing a musical score is designing sound into melodies, harmonies, and patterns. Clothes are designed to communicate a feeling or impression. Jewelry is designed to highlight form, texture, and color. Graphic design communicates feelings of energy and excitement or contemplative harmony or delicate fragility. In choosing the kind of lettering for a business card, an executive wants to communicate a sense of who he or she is. Packagers of commercial goods attempt, through the attractiveness of color and printing design, to draw prospective buyers' attention. Gardens, landscapes, neighborhood street patterns, computer software and hardware, book covers, cell phones, restaurant menus, pretty faces, record album covers—these and so many other things in our lives are products of design.

When we think of a learning community, therefore, we should think of how that community wants to design its work, the aesthetics of its work spaces, its concern for harmony and proportionality in its sequencing of the work, its use of sound and silence, its use of color and light, its communication processes, its disciplinary processes, its weekly and monthly schedules, its assessment processes, and its personnel procedures. The design of all of these aspects of the community's life reveals, or should reveal, the essential values espoused by that community. In other words, the values revealed by all of these aspects of the community's life, taken collectively, should be clearly expressive of the community's values and purposes.

## EXAMPLES OF DESIGN FEATURES IN SCHOOL

Consider something as prosaic as a report card. Most often they reveal a rather simple design: name and identification number; date; marking period; subjects listed down the left side; grades for achievement and effort in the middle columns; and terse, judgmental comments on the right. Why not add the school motto at the top and intersperse quotations from various sages about the value of effort, the joy of learning, and the significance of education for the building up of civil society? Perhaps a humorous short poem or ditty could lighten up the doomsday heaviness of report cards. Perhaps a cartoon of a Charley Brown-like character talking to his teacher about his homework could be placed in the bottom corner. At the bottom of the card, some information about upcoming school events could be added as a way to encourage parents to participate more in the life of the school. In other words, report cards can be designed as a more personal communication between the school and the home. Of course, performance assessments should also affect the design of report cards, with prose analyses of the student's work replacing or at least supplementing the perfunctory numbers and letters.

Memos from the principal or some other administrator is a weekly occurrence in most teachers' lives. Normally, these memos are not joyously and eagerly received by the teachers. Usually the memo brings news of added work on an upcoming event, warnings about the need to attend to something or other in the school rule book, complaints about teachers not doing something they are supposed to do, communication of parents' concerns (or complaints), news about some new regulation by the state department of education, family services, or whatever. Granted that sometimes these announcements are necessary, often the whole faculty appears to be accused of something one or two teachers have done, or even that one or two students have done. Besides the substance of the message, there is the style of the message, the impersonal, bureaucratic language, the officiousness of the format. Administrative memos could begin with a humorous limerick, cartoon, joke, or thought for the day. Every memo should carry some good news, some congratulations, or gratitude for something a student, teacher, or parent has done. Then the bad news can be received in a way that balances the burdens of the job of an educator with its satisfactions. Perhaps the format of memos could have some decorative (but unpretentious) edge to them, something that communicates a care for the aesthetic and human sensibilities of the recipients. Sometimes even such a small gesture communicates that the administrator cares enough about his or her teachers to go to the trouble of designing memos to be personal communications.

Much the same can be said about administrators' letters to parents. A touch of humor, an encouraging word, a thank-you for their trust in the

school, an invitation to participate on a school committee, a funny story—
these can go a long way toward establishing connections between the home
and school. The esthetics of the format, a touch of color, a symbol of parent–child relationships, a saying about the significance of parenting—all
these can create a tone of respect and caring.

As one approaches the main entrance to the school, one gets a sense of
the school. Are there flowers and shrubs around the entrance, or is it barren, even dirty? Is there attention to landscaping and to creating a natural
space where things grow, where squirrels and birds are visible? Schools
communicate how they feel about nature by the way they ignore or feature
it. If everything is covered over with asphalt and surrounded by high fences,
the school makes a statement by how it designs its exterior spaces.

Within the building, the walls can make a statement about art, about the
natural and social environments, about the school's pride in student
achievements, or they can be barren and functional. Are there plants and
fish tanks in classrooms? Lack of color and light contribute to the drab
impersonality that some schools communicate; other schools communicate
a vibrant sense of energy and excitement with bright colors, mobiles, student art work, and differentiated lighting that highlights different spaces
and contours of the rooms or hallways. The design of color and light can
make some buildings decidedly friendly and others decidedly unfriendly.

Getting closer to the bone, we have to look at the design of time and
space. Is the daily schedule broken up into uniform time blocks or is it flexible, more under the control of teachers and students? Is the weekly schedule always the same, or does it vary from week to week, allowing for intensive learning units here and for more steady, uniform learning units there?
Are learning spaces all the same, or are some more congenial to group
work, some more to individual work, some more to whole-class activities,
and indeed some outside the school building?

In the design of learning activities, do we find variety, creativity, and flexibility? Do we find teachers' lesson plans fairly uniform, conforming to one
model? A uniform design of learning activities communicates an assumption that all learning is the same, that all subject matter requires the same
approach, and that every hour of the school day should be filled with the
same student energy and interest. The design of the learning activities influences what is learned as well as how it is learned. A learning activity that
requires exact measurement of the weight and mass of a rock cannot teach
the same thing as a learning activity that considers the geological conditions that formed the rock, a learning activity that explores the shapes a
sculptor might chisel out of the rock, or a learning activity that requires the
student to demonstrate six different uses of a rock. Each of these learning
activities requires a design of sequential steps to approach the learning.
Each learning requires a different performance assessment design. The de-

sign comes from the teacher's understanding of the connections of this learning activity to the larger conceptual frameworks in which the learning is nested, as well as the teacher's understanding of the developmental readiness of the student to deal with more or less abstract thinking, and the student's past learning experiences that would support the drawing out of relationships. Perhaps the most essential talent of teachers is involved with the way they design learning activities because it reveals their own understanding of the subject matter, their understanding of the child, and their understanding of the complexities of the learning process (Wiggins & McTighe, 1998).

The design of learning activities by teachers also reflects their sense of the larger design of the curriculum. Teachers' involvement in the design and continuous redesign of the curriculum reveals the depth and breadth of their own scholarly grasp of the disciplines of knowledge (Wiske, 1998). Administrators who encourage teachers working continually on the larger design of the curriculum promote the sharpening of the teachers' intelligence, the deepening of their understanding of the conceptual material embedded in the disciplines. In other words, administrators' support and encouragement of teachers at this level, through staff development and program development activities, nurture the lifeblood of teachers' growth.

Another design issue has to do with the system of teacher evaluation and supervision. All too often school policy regarding teacher evaluation is framed in highly legalistic language, reflecting an exclusively contractual design of the process or even suggesting an adversarial relationship between teachers and administrators. A one-size-fits-all design of classroom observations suggests a simplistic view of teaching as well as a bureaucratic approach to supervision. The work of designing a system of teacher evaluation should include distinguishing between administrative summative evaluation and the more formative evaluation of teaching, which allows for many options and cycles of options that respond to the differing experience and needs of teachers (Sergiovanni & Starratt, 2002).

Parental involvement in the education of their children has been shown to be highly correlated with student achievement in school (Scott-Jones, 1995). An effective parental involvement program requires considerable planning and organization by school leaders. A teacher–parent advisory committee should be formed to look into the many details of initiating a workable system of continuous communication between the school and the home. Special care needs to be taken with the initial year of such an effort because first impressions have a lot to do with the success or failure of the effort. The system of communication should include print media, electronic media, TV and telephone media, and many opportunities for face-to-face communication. The design of the various messages and forms from the school to the parents requires careful attention because again the medium communicates much of the message. If the communications are impersonal, bureaucratic, condescending, sporadic, disconnected, and confusing, parental involvement suffers. Using parents to help with the design and implementation of a vibrant system of back-and-forth communication makes such a system more personal and effective. When the parents are recent immigrants with English as a second language, the tone of school communications must be especially sensitive. Some schools provide a dedicated room in the school for parents, equipped and run by parent volunteers, so that parents can come to the school for a variety of consultations, as well as for volunteer work at the school. The overall organization and design of parental partnership programs at the school go a long way toward bringing influential social capital to bear on children's learning.

## DESIGNS IN CONFLICT

Sometimes the designs of various aspects of the community's life work at cross-purposes to each other. For example, it may be expected that students in class engage in debate and heated discussion over the questions posed by the learning assignment. Students are encouraged to question the teacher. The design of the give and take of the classroom has established an accepted pattern of interaction. However, the assistant principal in charge of school discipline may have in mind a different design of the interaction between students and her or himself. The design of the disciplinary system may be quite authoritarian; no debates are allowed about the school rules and their uniform application. Furthermore, sanctions for misbehavior are applied without any therapeutic orientation. Students do not have a chance to consider other behavioral options to situations that occasioned the breaking of a rule. Students pick up two different messages. When it comes to exploring academic issues, they enjoy a certain freedom of speech and inquiry. Furthermore, academic mistakes are discussed with teachers in an effort to find the source of the mistake and the means to correct it. When it comes to questions of school discipline, such freedoms are suspended. But no reason for the difference in design of the relationships is given. We may say that in the design of academic learning, certain aesthetics were observed. When it comes to student discipline, questions of aesthetics are cast aside.

As another example, the school may try to promote individualized learning packages as well as group learning projects. Yet the design of the grading system may be a holdover from an earlier time, with allowance only for individual achievement. The design of the grading system, with its concentration on ranking of students, grading on a curve, and so on, may communicate negative judgments about collaborative learning outcomes. The design of the learning activities may be in conflict with the design of the grading system. Sometimes collaboration is called team learning; sometimes it is called cheating.

The more the designs of aspects of school life are disjointed or even contradictory, the more fuzzy becomes the messages the school communicates. Lesko's (1988) portrait of a Catholic girls' school provides a good example. The school stressed two primary values throughout the life of the school. The value of community was related directly to the religious purposes of the school, and the value of competition was tied to the larger American culture. The way the school designed its religious ceremonies, assemblies, and after-school activities communicated a valuing of community. The way the school leaders designed their grading system, exams, college guidance system, and pedagogy all communicated the value of competition. No one realized, however, that these two values were in conflict with each other. The designs of various aspects of school life were sending contradictory messages.

In contrast, the more the designs of the various aspects of school life are in sync with each other, the more powerful and lasting is the message the school communicates. Lightfoot (1983) hinted at this harmony of design in her portraits of good schools. We find even more explicit attention to design in the stories of "schools that work" in Smith's (1993) book on that topic. Similarly, Newmann's (1992) account of schools that redesigned themselves to promote student engagement in the learning task underscores this lesson.

## DESIGNS FOR COMMUNITY

Design is a subtle carrier of value and a shaper of culture. When we speak of cultivating community, we must attend to the ways we design the life and work of the school. The point is to bring the *way* we communicate, the *way* we learn, the *way* we celebrate, the *way* we govern ourselves, and the *way* we evaluate our progress into greater harmony and consistency so that we promote the value of community and the value of individual and collective empowerment in all these aspects of the school's life. The aesthetics of our community processes of communicating, deliberating, resolving conflicts, and organizing space and time involve us necessarily in design issues. Attention to the aesthetics of our designs or our disregard for these aesthetics communicate what we value or disvalue, what we honor or ignore. If we are committed to cultivating a community, then the design of the many ways we live and work as a community has to promote that value—not simply as a pleasant add-on to the more serious work of academic achievement, but as an essential characteristic and purpose of the school. We want, in short, to become a community that intentionally arranges and rearranges its work and life to honor a variety of excellences—excellences that require their own aesthetics.

## ACTIVITIES

1. Let us construct a hypothetical school and play out the design issues a little to make our point. Suppose that, after a year of discussions among the faculty, students, and parents, it was decided that they wanted to promote three central values: academic learning, community, and enrichment of diversity. Let us assume that this school is housed in a traditional school building in a multicultural neighborhood. The promotion of community amidst diversity and the enrichment of diversity within a bonded community are seen as two mutually intertwined values. Let us assume that this community also wants to move the teaching/learning work of the school toward a much greater sense of the student as the producer and performer of knowledge.

Now imagine how the school would work if, having agreed to these three values, the principal simply left it up to each teacher to incorporate those values into his or her work with the children. Imagine that the design of space, the class day and week, and the report cards and grading system remained the same. Imagine yourself as a teacher in that school. What would be some of the difficulties you would encounter as you tried to incorporate in your own classroom the central values decided on by the school community? The textbooks are the same, the curriculum guidelines are the same, the class periods are the same, and the technology available is the same. Write your reflections in your journal.

Next, imagine yourself in the same school during the year following the decision to promote the three core values. Assume that the school had received a sizable gift from a wealthy alumnus that would easily accommodate extensive remodeling of the school. Assume that you had been invited to join a faculty committee to propose the redesign of many aspects of your school to bring them more consistently in line with the core values. Sketch out five or six features of the school that you would redesign. Share these with the members of your working group. Have the group come up with a comprehensive redesign of the school.

2. Identify design features in your school that seem to be in conflict with each other. What are the consequences? How would you redesign to gain greater consistency with the mission of your school?

## REFERENCES

Lesko, N. (1988). *Symbolizing society.* London: Falmer.
Lightfoot, S. L. (1983). *The good school: Portraits of character and culture.* New York: Basic Books.

Newmann, F. M. (Ed.). (1992). *Student engagement and achievement in American secondary schools.* New York: Teachers College Press.

Scott-Jones, D. (1995). Parent–child interactions and school achievement. In B. Ryan, G. Adams, T. Gullota, R. Weissberg, & R. Hampton (Eds.), *The family-school connection: Theory, research, and practice* (pp. 75–107). Thousand Oaks, CA: Sage.

Smith, G. A. (Ed.). (1993). *Public schools that work.* New York: Routledge.

Sergiovanni, T. J., & Starratt, R. J. (2002). *Supervision: A redefinition* (7th ed.). New York: McGraw-Hill.

Wiggins, G., & McTighe, J. (1998). *Understanding by design.* Alexandria, VA: Association for Supervision and Curriculum Development.

Wiske, M. S. (Ed.). (1998). *Teaching for Understanding.* San Francisco: Jossey-Bass.

# Chapter 13

# Leading a Learning Community

The traditional mission of the school is to teach students to understand the natural, human, and social worlds to know who they are; how they can participate in public life; what their responsibilities are to the natural, human, and social worlds; and thereby to find fulfillment by participating in these worlds. In this time of transition, a fundamental task of educational administrators is to infuse that traditional mission of the school with a new meaning that melds the emerging perspectives from the sciences and humanities with the truths behind the old certainties.

Earlier we focused on the analysis of core meanings in early modernity and how they have been shifting. We saw how recent scientific understandings have revised our understanding of the dynamic relationships between human life and the evolving natural environment. Critical sociology and the sociology of knowledge illuminated the political, economic, and cultural forms we create and the way these forms can be used to dominate, control, and guide our sense of moral striving. Cognitive science points to the constructive and performative nature of learning and therefore students' necessarily active involvement in mastering the curriculum. These new understandings constitute the ground for a new vision of education.

By their work of building that collective vision, educational administrators engage in the initial stages of cultivating meaning, community, and responsibility. In this work, they initiate a conversation among teachers about the basic meaning behind what and how they teach, and the meanings that are implied and assumed in the curriculum.

In chapter 9, we saw that the central work of the school is the students' work, the work of learning and the performance of learning. The idea of a learning community thus implies a community of teachers and students who are actively engaged in producing knowledge and understanding—not simply as individual productions, but as productions of diverse groups within the community. In chapter 2, we proposed that four perspectives on meaning making guide the learning agenda:

- School meanings must be continuously related to students' experience of everyday life. Thus, the work of making meaning involves self-understanding as well as personal engagement with the social and natural worlds.
- The learning agenda of the school must be related to the large cultural projects of our current era as well as to the cultural projects of our history. Thus, school learnings are connected to a significant discourse about the making of history.
- The learning agenda of the school must be continually related to something intrinsically human—to the exploration of questions important to personal and social life.
- Learning must be situated in a critical community of inquirers who accept that knowledge is always partial and fallible and who support the enrichment of knowledge through sharing of meanings, interpretations, and learnings among all members of the community.

The conversations within a learning community are meant to take place within an empowering environment in which both teachers and students can own and express who they are and are becoming in the work of making meaning together. Such work is seen not only as academic work, but also as a moral work of communal concern for their world. The communal work of meaning-making, furthermore, must be supported in the management, organization, and design of the work; thus, the school bureaucracy serves, rather than dominates, the mission of the school. In this chapter, we pull these threads together to see how they might compose a learning community. In this sense, this chapter attempts a synthesis of the thinking explored in all of the preceding chapters.

A learning community implies a significant role for students, as well as teachers and administrators who are involved in continuous learning about the lives of their students and their ways of learning. Teachers and administrators, then, are accountable as learners, are accountable to learn. They are also accountable to see that students learn. The school as a learning community, therefore, is not a voluntary association of individuals who freely agree to associate for purposes of self-improvement, such as a reading club or a quilting circle. The school does not exist in a social and political vacuum. As a social institution, it is accountable to various stakeholders.

The issue of accountability has a lot to do with the nature of the school as a learning community. In an era of state-mandated efforts to improve the learning of all students, accountability is especially crucial to the character of the school as a learning community. As we have seen before, however, nothing is simple about life in schools. Unless we take apart the meaning of accountability, we cannot understand how to lead a learning community that can cultivate meaning, community, and responsibility.

## THE QUESTION OF ACCOUNTABILITY

To whom is the learning community responsible? Who is in charge? Schools are not independent corporations; they are agencies of the state. Even private schools must have some kind of legal charter granted by the state.

One would like to assume, as well, that schools belong to their local communities, and are therefore answerable to their local communities. This is true at least in the United States and, I understand, increasingly so in England, Canada, and Australia. Local educational authorities (LEAs) such as school boards can be sued by local parents for not providing customary educational services to their children or for neglect of their legal responsibilities. The state, however, is considered the primary authority in education and may step in to mandate new services, curricula, tests, sanctions, and funding arrangements. To be sure, the state is governed by officials elected by the electorate, so these officials must ultimately be answerable to those who elect them, as well as to the courts who monitor the protection of civil and human rights.

Two other voices also exercise influence over school policies: the voice of the scholarly community and the voice of the business community. The scholarly community produces and legitimates the disciplines of knowledge. These disciplines of knowledge ground the production of textbooks, learning materials, and technologies, which, for better or worse, operationalize the formal curriculum of schools. Textbooks are necessarily updated to take account of developments in the scholarly disciplines. They are also updated to take account of political and cultural developments in the fields of scholarship—for example, the inclusion of feminist views of historical events or literature by minority authors. Local communities do not have the right by commission or omission to promote racism and sexism in their schools' curriculum, just as they do not have the right to insist that their astronomy courses teach that the sun revolves around the earth. The scholarly community can require, by virtue of the authority of its scholarship, that the school's curriculum represent the best knowledge and understanding of the natural, human, and social worlds that the scholarly disciplines have produced.

This is not to say that local controversies over the curriculum can be settled simply by referral to scholarly sources. Religious and ethical beliefs held by various groups in the community may lead them to object, for example, to theories of evolution as taught in biology classes or to the curricula of health and sex education classes. Educators embroiled in such controversies need to turn to scholarly research in the sciences, theology, and ethics, as well as to constitutional authorities to work out some response to these objections. The weight of the scholarly community should be a strong influence in the conversation, even when it may not be the decisive voice.

Another influential voice in this whole question of the schools' accountability is the business community, including trade unions and associations of craftspeople. Schools are accountable to the whole civic community insofar as they are to prepare youngsters for participation in the public life of that community. Work and employment are central concerns in the public life of the community, and hence basic preparation for the world of work is necessary. In general, the business community is concerned with the preparation of youth for employment, including the development of a good work ethic in youth and their grounding in the basic skills required in the world of work. At the start of the 21st century, these basic skills now include computer literacy, collaboration, inventiveness, and flexibility, as well as language and computation skills, problem-solving skills, and higher order thinking skills. In the light of the many scandals and crimes committed by members of the business and finance community, publicized weekly in the media, additional basic skills must be added to the list: honesty, integrity, and responsibility.

Schools need to take these different voices into account, whether they choose to retain the centralized bureaucratic format or restructure in the direction of a learning community, because these groups make up the matrix of major influences over the substance of the curriculum and how it is learned. In other words, schools are accountable to multiple communities and must respond to the concerns and challenges, restrictions and opportunities they pose.

## ACCOUNTABILITY TO STUDENTS

Schools can passively allow these various voices to define their agenda or they can actively shape their own agenda while taking these voices into account. I want to argue that schools are made up primarily of students and should take their reality into account first and foremost. Students are not owned by the state, local community, scholarly community, or business community. They are not owned by the school either. They are human beings in their own right who are beginning a life journey that for all of us is altogether too short. They are in school to help find out who they are, what their potential is, to whom they belong, and to whom they are responsible. They are in school to learn something about human freedom, heroism, and its opposite; to explore the comedy and tragedy in human life; to explore the various examples of human fulfillment; and to explore, learn to understand, and respect their natural environment.

At the heart of all education is the belief that the truth we seek through the process of learning will set us free: free to be the best selves we can be; free to love the truth about ourselves, our fellows, and our natural world, and free to turn away from the destructive elements those same truths reveal; free to bend our backs and minds to the work society needs from us; and free to express and celebrate the truths we discover. This belief does not deny the struggle such a learning process involves. Rather it sustains it.

The self-definition of a learning community should be grounded on this belief. The learning community then enters into conversation with the local and state concerns, and into conversation with the scholarly and business communities. However, the conversation is not between a lackey and an owner; it is a conversation between partners—between colleagues who have the same human stakes in the learning process.

## ACCOUNTABILITY IN A DEEPER SENSE

There is another level of accountability that may be in conflict with the accountability to the four communities mentioned previously (local, state, scholarly, and business communities). This is an accountability to the historical moment and its tensions. We have already alluded to the school's responsibility to be aware of the transition from the early modern to the late modern redefinition of our civic and cultural agenda, and to the emerging perspectives on the natural, social, and human worlds being developed in the sciences and humanities. I believe schools have to be accountable for this awareness because it signifies an accountability to the historical moment.

Someone has said that we either make history or history makes us. I would opt for a middle ground—namely, that although we are shaped by our history, we are called to engage our history, to actively participate in the challenges and opportunities that our historical moment offers. Rather than the role of passive spectators of history, we are called to assume the roles of citizens taking responsibility to work together to make our world a better place: more human, more just, more civil, and more in harmony with the natural environment. In other words, we are accountable to both our ancestors who struggled to create the world we live in and to our progeny who must live with the public choices we collectively make. Thus, our accountability is not simply a legal concern, not simply an academic concern, nor, indeed, simply a social concern to protect children. Our accountability is also a moral concern to bring the work of learning to bear on our collective public responsibilities.

In still a deeper sense, we may speak of an existential accountability. The universe took quite a long time to produce us—you and me. So here we are, inserted in both cosmic and human history. It is our moment on the stage. That moment asks of us: "Well, what are you going to do with yourself? Who and what do you want to be?" The cosmic and human ancestors are sitting out there in the audience waiting expectantly. In our work together in school, we are exploring our possibilities, trying on various costumes, and rehearsing various scripts. We can squander our learning opportunities in superficial dalliance, distracted from distraction by distraction, touring on our intellectual cruise ship that touches briefly at various ports of call where we can observe with disengaged amusement the curious customs of the natives. Or we can embrace our learning opportunities as irreplaceable chances to become someone, a wide-awake actor engaged in the historical drama that we co-create with other autonomous actors in the moments where we *find ourselves*. In other words, we are responsible to ourselves, to the gift that is our life—both personally and socially.

## TWO VIEWS OF ACCOUNTABILITY

Adams and Kirst (1999) provided a helpful overview of educational accountability as it has emerged in the policy field of education. They distinguished between external and internal accountability: the external accountability imposed on schools through state policies and the internal accountability to which schools hold themselves. Adams and Kirst described six different kinds of accountability systems: bureaucratic, legal, professional, political, moral, and market. The *bureaucratic accountability* system involves a superior within the bureaucracy holding subordinates accountable for compliance with organizational rules, the superior having the power to reward or punish subordinates' behavior. *Legal accountability* involves policymakers requiring those responsible for implementing policy to comply with the legal mandates of the policies. Again, policymakers have the power to impose legal sanctions for noncompliance. *Professional accountability* refers to the expectation a lay person has that a professional has the special knowledge and training to provide the services the lay person is paying for. *Political accountability* involves the expectation constituents have that their representative will respond to their expressed interests if the representative wants their continued political support. *Moral accountability* is the expectation groups/communities have that the individual members will abide by their obligations to the group; the group has the power to censure or affirm the member's behavior. *Market accountability* refers to the expectation of customers/consumers that a provider/company will provide an acceptable service/product. The customer can continue or withhold patronage depending on the satisfaction with the service/product.

In the present policy environment of school reform/improvement, states have imposed accountability not only on school districts, but also on individual schools. The assumption behind the imposition of accountability is that the school can *cause* the results for which they are being held accountable. States, however, do not seem to be aware that agents cannot be expected to cause results when the resources necessary to bring about the results (curriculum resources, professional development of teachers, released time for such professional development, time available for *all* students to learn the more rigorous curriculum, the money to purchase the resources needed to improve student learning—to mention a few) are not provided. Adams and Kirst (1999) respond to the issue of causality with the broad term of *capacity*. That is, an agent of the state cannot be accountable to cause results unless that agent has the capacity to cause those results. They cited other scholars who define capacity in regards to school accountability as encompassing profession knowledge and skills required to bring about mandated results, technical and financial resources, organizational autonomy to act, and the capacity and know-how to integrate all the resources needed to carry out the causative work. Beyond these capacities, the authors suggested that schools traditionally have not used the results of student performance to improve student learning. Now, however, they have to learn how to do that. Citing the research of Newman, King, and Rigdon (1997), the authors emphasized that the internal accountability system of the school must somehow be aligned to and support the external accountability system.

The internal accountability system of most schools is not designed around teachers holding themselves accountable for quality learning of *all* students. There has been no practice of schoolwide attention to student underperformance as providing evidence for needed changes in teacher classroom instruction. Given the relative isolation of teachers behind their classroom doors, there was no motivation to accept a *collective* responsibility for having all students succeed at learning. Furthermore, the results of student test scores were not used to identify student learning difficulties that could be targeted for remediation—not by the student's teachers, nor by any other educator in the school.

By calling attention to the need for schools to create an internal accountability system, the absence of which defeats the intended effects of the external accountability system, Adam and Kirst (1999) identified the major challenge to both local administrators and those who legislate accountability. Accountability has to be linked to internal capacity building. The internal capacity building, however, must emerge from the cultivation of an internal accountability system. This is something new; schools have never been asked to do this before. It will take time to learn.

It is here that we recall the theme of empowerment. We saw that empowerment has a bureaucratic, professional, moral, and existential form. These forms of empowerment can now be seen as creating a dynamic relationship between the work of empowerment and the capacity building for internal accountability. Figures 13.1, 13.2, and 13.3 attempt to map the conceptual links of this accountability scheme.

In Fig. 13.1, we see the logic behind the linking of external and internal accountability. When state and local authorities mandate both kinds of accountability—accountability for student performance and accountability to develop internal capacity to improve student performance—then schools may more reasonably be expected to cause improved student achievement. That logic assumes that state and local authorities hold themselves responsible to provide the resources for internal capacity building and recognize the needed time it will take for most schools to develop the internal structures, processes, and cultural landscape of this set of capacities. Notice that a key to focusing on improved learning for all students as well as building

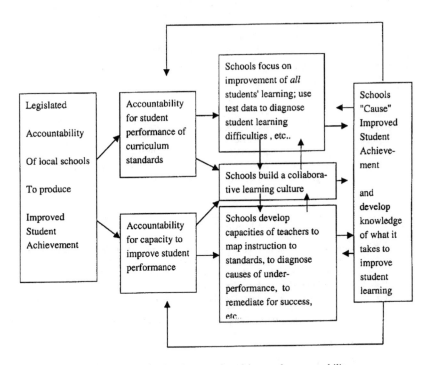

FIG. 13.1.   The logic of external and internal accountability.

teacher capacities to effect improvement for all students is the development of a school culture committed to collaborative learning.

As schools develop their internal capacities to improve student learning and close the student achievement gap, their accounts (reports to the state and local authorities) can provide necessary feedback about what works and what does not work in the capacity-building efforts of local schools. This feedback makes it possible for policymakers to modify school improvement policies and implementation guidelines.

In Fig. 13.2, we can see how the external accountability demands and internal supports for empowerment both contribute to the capacity-building efforts of the school. Again, we can see the enormously powerful *motivating force* behind the internal shared accountability system that is rooted not only in bureaucratic and professional accountability, but also in moral and existential accountability. When teachers feel empowered at the moral and existential levels, that fuels the expression of their shared professional and

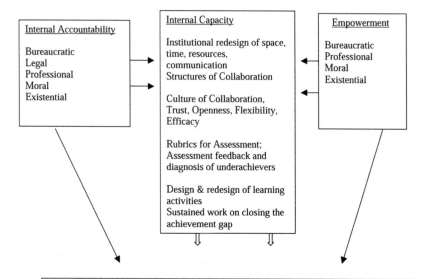

FIG. 13.2.  Accountability and empowerment: Ingredients of a learning community.

---

**Elements of Internal Accountability**

<u>For What</u>: High-quality learning for all students in the academic curriculum, the community curriculum, and the responsibility curriculum.
<u>Who</u>: All of us are collectively responsible (including students and parents) for quality learning.
<u>Why</u>: The State requires it: the profession requires it; we require it of ourselves; history requires it.
<u>How</u>: We will find the ways: through action research, dialogue, invention, trial and error, continuous collegial feedback on what works and what does not, reflection, honesty, and perseverance.
<u>Cultural Supports</u>: Trust, caring, mutual support, time to learn, concentrated and sustained professional development, dialogue with students and parents, distributed leadership, communal ownership of responsibility.

---

FIG. 13.3.   Elements of internal accountability.

bureaucratic empowerment, which plays right into the levels of shared accountability within the school.

Coming at capacity building from a clearly defined internal accountability for the success of all children enables the learning community to explore what it will take. Stimulating and resourcing empowerment at all levels will energize those capacity-building efforts. These sources of energy and focus provide the primary elements of the contemporary school as a learning community. Rather than focusing exclusively on the state curriculum guidelines, however, the learning community, accountable to itself as a human community, integrates the learning of the academic curriculum with the curriculum of community and the curriculum of responsibility.

Figure 13.3 attempts to highlight the elements of internal accountability of this learning community. Although this figure provides a general map of key ingredients to internal accountability, it can only suggest in a general way how this system of internal accountability is developed and sustained. So much more design work remains to be done through local initiative.

## THE SITUATED NATURE OF A LEARNING COMMUNITY

Although the preceding treatment of a learning community's sense of accountability tried to emphasize the temporal location of schools as learning communities within the current emphasis on school renewal and development, we need to recognize that each learning community is unique, nested in a cultural and geographic locale. School communities do not exist in isolation from their surrounding communities. What and how they learn needs to be in dialogue with their surroundings. Therefore, a learning community, tries to learn together in a defined space, with specific local challenges, problems, and opportunities with given specific resources. Sustained social interchanges among familiar people in a familiar terrain with recognizable landmarks nurtures the sense of connectedness, much the way village life does. Even in large cities, the local neighborhood serves the same purpose. Some communities build themselves around a religious center or place of worship. Some build themselves around a university and share in the intellectual and cultural life it supports. Some build around ethnic origins and traditional culture, such as the Chinatowns, the Little Italys, the Germantowns. Some build around a common race, such as The Harlems, The Watts, the South Sides.

Schools are nested in neighborhoods or include youngsters who come from many different neighborhoods. For 6 or 7 hours a day, schools that are learning communities become extensions of these neighborhoods; they become a place with defined spaces, with familiar people, and with friends and enemies. Students in learning communities develop a sense of being connected to their learning community. That connectedness implies trust, loyalty, and responsibility for relationships; it becomes a micro life world— an extension of the feeling of family and kin.

Learning communities can become extensions of neighborhood and family when they recognize and honor the life world of children in these neighborhoods and families. Children come to school brimming over with interesting experiences, funny stories, and frightful exposures to human spitefulness; they come with unformulated questions, curiosity about things in their life world they do not understand. Learning communities take the time to listen to youngsters' stories and questions. They find ways to relate the curriculum to the life world.

If schools are to teach the larger connections—connections to our ancestors, the biosphere, the cultural heroes of the past, the agenda of the future—they must begin with the connections of everyday experience, the connections to our peers, our extended families, the cultural dynamics of our neighborhoods, and the politics, economics, and technology in the homes and on the streets of the neighborhood. In other words, they have to learn to understand the life world of their immediate environment, how people relate to authority, beauty, nature, and conflict. They should be led to appreciate all the connections in their immediate environment because that environment is a metaphor for the field physics of the human, social, and natural worlds.

Youngsters who begin to understand these connections also begin to recognize, at least tacitly, the interdependence of everything in that place. This helps overcome the alienation from place bred by the individualism of naive modernity (the assumption that one is free to choose one's place— that one is not accountable to or for one's place). The learning community teaches again and again that you have to be responsible for your place. That means knowing the history of the place as well as the present life-sustaining resources of the place. It means situating yourself in a place and understanding yourself in relationship to the natural and social ecology of that place. It also means taking account of the future of that place, joining with others to discuss the possibilities and dreams they might share. Hence, a learning community seeks to strengthen the bonding and participatory processes necessary for membership in both school and civic communities.

## CORE PROCESS OF THE LEARNING COMMUNITY

Every school that restructures itself as a learning community is unique. Each school has a particular chemistry of subcommunities from which its students come, a specific mix of talents and interests among the teaching staff, a variety of local limitations and resources in the neighborhoods surrounding the school, and so forth. Nevertheless, learning communities manifest some common core processes. The following are at least a beginning listing of them.

### Learning Takes Place in a Caring Environment

This means that every child feels that he or she is cared for as a valuable member of the school community, that others believe he or she has something to offer the work of the community. The kind of feeling of being cared for takes time to build. Youngsters learn to listen to one another, how to disagree without hurting, and how to cooperate and collaborate on learning projects. The same goes for teachers, both in their dealings with students and with one another.

The caring environment should also encourage caring for what is being studied and the knowledge being produced and performed, as we saw in earlier chapters. This core process involves intentionally and programmatically teaching youngsters how to cooperate on projects, how to resolve conflicts, how to take charge of and organize their work together, and how to set up ground rules to guide their work together. Furthermore, because more and more schools experience cultural diversity in their members, youngsters need to spend time becoming acquainted with the cultural traditions and perspectives of their classmates, and appreciating the unities that bridge the cultural differences among them. They need to be encouraged to value diversity of backgrounds and perspectives as *constituting the learning medium* for so much of their learning agenda (Martinez Aleman, & Salkever, 2001).

## Learning Takes Place Through Storytelling

Telling stories is a natural way for humans to communicate. Learning the art of storytelling provides continuous practice of the grammar and rhetoric not only of one's language, but also of the construction of one's life. Listening to the stories of others allows bridges to be built across the existential and cultural distances between the other. Their stories reveal the common human journey and also facilitate the cultivation of affection and friendship. Stories also nurture the development of imagination and the use of images and metaphors for understanding in the human and natural worlds. Most of all, storytelling provides a foundation for conveying and exploring meaning (Bruner, 1990). Often it provides the link between the lesson of the curriculum and the life world of the student.

## Learning in School Is Related to Home and Neighborhood Experiences

The home and neighborhood represent the life world where students relate and apply their science and history lessons, where they discover reflections in their art classes, where they mine the stories of their families and neighbors, and where they test their understanding of their school learning with adults (Brown, Collins, & Duguid, 1989). Homework assignments should include projects to (a) discover all the uses of electricity in the home, including the wattage and voltage used by the various appliances; (b) gather family history from family elders; (c) map their neighborhood, with attention to scale and identification of key locations; (d) identify neighborhood heroes and characters, including discussions of the values they exemplify; (e) study the commercial businesses in the neighborhood, with an attempt to describe how they manage their finances; (f) interview local politicians and probe their positions on various issues in the community; (g) meet with local artists, musicians, and writers to learn about their work and the meanings they are exploring; (h) explore the weather patterns of their region and how these affect the growth of vegetation in their area; (i) explore the various careers in their communities, with perhaps a statistical breakdown of the types of work that people in their neighborhood do; (j) study how local banks interact with their neighborhood, giving attention to how loans are secured, how much money the bank makes on various types of loans, who benefits most from using the local banks; (k) study local newspapers and the types of editorial positions those newspapers take on a variety of positions; (l) study the various utilities in the neighborhood and how they function; and (m) study various tax-supported pub-lic services in the neighborhood. The list is limited only by our imagination.

In all of these projects related to family and neighborhood, students ex-ercise the academic skills of careful observation, storytelling, organizing, and summarizing, as well as various mathematical skills. They also deepen their learning of much of the content of the school curriculum in science, history, and humanities, and make a connection between the academic learnings and their life world. They also learn much about the complica-tions of a mass-administered society and the mass-produced services and commodities that saturate their homes and neighborhood. Along the way, they encounter human beings engaged in the daily work of making a living, making do, getting by, and striving for some kind of moral consistency and legitimated meaning in their lives. This kind of exposure to human realities should become food for reflection and discussion with teachers and peers in the school, discussions of values, lifestyles, and human qualities that they find appealing and not so appealing.

Much of this doing of science, history, and art in the home and neigh-borhood can be done with relative dispatch. Some of the projects require more extended time, perhaps released time during school hours. The de-tails of scheduling a curriculum that required this grounding of learning in the life world of the community and the exploration of the way a mass-administered and mass-produced world works differ from school to school. Obviously, setting up these kinds of learning projects requires prior conver-sations with parents and community leaders. Also assessment of this kind of learning requires some changes from current forms of assessment. Teachers who design such projects know the kind of learning they expect from such projects and should be able to build in various criteria for assessment.

### Learning Should Lead to Some Product or Performance

This can be an individual or group product or performance. In either case, it should be a product or performance that should be shared with others. Whenever possible and appropriate, the product or performance should be useful to the community of the school and to the community at large (Newman & Associates, 1996). In this respect, I mean *useful* in the broad meaning of the term: A project might involve and attempt to pro-pose, for example, a more environmentally appropriate way to dispose of a community's waste; an entertainment that enriches the cultural life of the community (such as a musical production, poem, film); a design for a different kind of shopping mall; a report of an evaluation of some com-munity service that could be improved; or simply a story about an unsung hero of the community.

The performances and products of the younger members of the learning community might not seem to have significant usefulness. Nonetheless, young children are creative in coming up with ideas that engage their peers in helpful ways. Youngsters can create one-act plays that portray in story some human value or, even through imaginary characters, demonstrate a scientific principle. Again, what constitutes a learning product or performance is limited only by our imaginations. The point is to have youngsters make connections between the learnings of the formal curriculum and then make something with those learnings. It is the making that brings the ideas, skills, and understandings into a visible reality that will be much more real than the producing of the right answer on a multiple-choice exam.

This connection of learning to production and performance personalizes the learning. It allows students to own the learning. It also shows students that learning can be useful, that it does have consequences beyond getting grades. In the process, students produce selves with much more clarity because they, the learners, put their fingerprints on something tangible as a result of the struggle to learn something. Other people will see this product or performance and thank them for it. Students realize they can actually do something that makes a difference or a contribution—something that other people appreciate.

### There Should Be Periodic and Continuous Reference to an Exploration of Meta-Narratives

By meta-narratives I mean the larger stories we tell one another about the central ideological and mythical elements of the culture. Geertz's (1973) definition of *culture* can help set our focus here. Culture, said Geertz, is

> . . . an historically transmitted pattern of meanings embodied in symbols, a system of inherited conceptions expressed in symbolic forms by means of which men communicate, perpetuate and develop their knowledge about and attitudes toward life. (p. 89)

Against the backdrop of these larger stories of the culture, all our smaller stories make sense or nonsense. In this core process of periodically exploring the meaning of our meta-narratives, teachers and students can look at what they are coming to understand by the following core terms in our culture. (They are presented in no particular order.)

| | | |
|---|---|---|
| a) *E pluribus unum* | b) Science | c) Wealth |
| d) Community | e) Responsibility | f) Work |
| g) Human rights | h) Friendship | i) Justice |
| j) Freedom | k) Democracy | l) Competition |

| | | |
|---|---|---|
| m) Truth | n) Beauty | o) Goodness |
| p) Death | q) Time | r) Self-worth |
| s) Nature | t) Love | u) Heroism |
| v) Patriotism | w) Power | x) Parenting |
| y) Law | z) Authority | |

That is my list; others would cross out some terms and add others. Every learning community should come up with some kind of list of core terms that they all agree to explore from time to time with their classes.

Such discussions would not be the kind of abstract discussions of Socrates and his friends. Rather, teachers would raise a theme as it emerged from the material the students were engaged in at the time. Students and teacher would attempt to uncover deeper meanings underneath the narratives being offered at the time, either by the students or the curriculum. Students might be encouraged to compose a poem or musical piece to express their thoughts and feelings about a particular meta-narrative. Teachers might pause to refer to a story from Greek mythology, from Cervantes, Shakespeare, or Faulkner, or from one of the great storytellers of another culture that illustrates or problemitizes an aspect of the meta-narrative theme. Students might be encouraged to ask an older member of the family to talk about that theme or to recount a story they heard within their extended family that illustrates the theme.

The point of these periodic reviews of meta-narratives is not to come up with one, absolutely perfect definition of the concept. Rather, it is to bring home the lesson that these themes are interwoven with the great questions about life with every community must wrestle. These themes circulate within the practical, everyday way a community and the individuals in it define and perform themselves. If the members of the learning community are to learn how to be human beings, they too have to wrestle with the meanings and practical consequences embedded in these meta-narrative themes.

### The Learning Community Should Periodically Explore the Really Big Questions

What does it mean to be human? What does it mean to be a community? What is the meaning of life, of suffering, of death? What does it mean to be a global society? In what do I find my ultimate fulfillment? What is my relationship to the universe? Again, the purpose is not to answer these questions definitively. Rather, students at various points in their development should be brought up against these questions and asked to respond from within their own experience and understanding. Of course, assessment of these responses should be handled with great sensitivity and tact.

Every other year or so, administrators and teachers should oblige themselves to respond to these big questions. They should be encouraged to share and discuss their responses as ways to authenticate their own search for meanings as members of a learning community. They also need to explore appropriate ways to raise these questions with their students. Such discussions help them recognize that from time to time the material under study in their classes may lend itself to a diversion into one of these larger questions.

## ORGANIZATIONAL CONCERNS

Learning communities can be organized in any number of ways. Many large schools are now restructuring themselves into a tapestry of small schools within schools, structured around grade clusters or age clusters, or around large unifying themes. Size seems to be an important consideration. The unit in question should be small enough to promote quality interactions between teachers and students. Some of these units also look to duration as an important feature; they build in continuity over 2 or 3 years so that teachers come to know their students well and can facilitate their development more responsively. Some schools use the city or region as their classroom; others focus on in-depth concentration on a profession or career (say in music, science, or design); others focus on replicating features of village life in the school by constructing their own money, their own cottage industries, their own governance and judicial structures, and their own cultural events. Again the organization of learning communities is limited only by our imaginations.

There is no one way to build a learning community. Much depends on what the local circumstances are, the chemistry among the faculty and students, and the willingness of parents and community leaders to investigate other possibilities in the shape and process of the school. There is no magical formula that guarantees success. We are still in the process of inventing genuine learning communities, so there are various examples in most regions that we can turn to, although no one model transfers exactly to another school. Ultimately, each school has to invent itself as a learning community.

## ACTIVITIES

1. Design your school as a learning community. Share that design with some of your colleagues at work and record their reactions and suggestions.

2. In your study group, share your individual designs of a learning community. Compare similarities and contrast differences. What common elements can you agree on?

3. What are the major obstacles to turning your school into a learning community? As an administrator, what are some strategies you can employ to overcome these obstacles?

## REFERENCES

Adams, J. E., & Kirst, M. W. (1999). New demands and concepts for educational accountability: Striving for results in an era of excellence. In J. Murphy & K. S. Louis (Eds.), *Handbook of research on educational administration* (2nd ed., pp. 463–489). San Francisco: Jossey-Bass.

Brown, J. S., Collins, S., & Duguid, P. (1989). Situated cognition and the culture of learning. *Educational Researcher, 18*(1), 32–42.

Bruner, J. (1990). *Acts of meaning.* Cambridge, MA: Harvard University Press.

Geertz, C. (1973). *The interpretation of cultures.* New York: Basic Books.

Martinez Aleman, A. M., & Salkever, K. (2001). Multiculturalism and the mission of liberal education. *The Journal of General Education, 50*(2), 102–139.

Newman, F. M., & Associates (1996). *Authentic achievement: Restructuring schools for intellectual quality.* San Francisco: Jossey-Bass.

Newman, F. M., King, M. B., & Rigdon, M. (1977). Accountability and school performance: Implications from restructuring schools. *Harvard Educational Review, 67,* 41–74.

# Chapter 14

# School Administration
# as Autobiography

I have said or implied throughout this book that educational administration is not a work for the faint-hearted. It requires both brains and heart: brains because the problems of schooling in late modernity present "wicked problems" (Louis, Toole, & Hargreaves, 1999) of enormous complexity requiring levels of understanding and analysis honed both by years of study and years of experience; heart because the key to responding to the challenges of the work is all about caring relationships—caring for the welfare of all the youngsters in your school and caring for the teachers who carry such demanding burdens and such sacred trust in their daily work (Beck, 1994; Noddings, 1992). The work also requires courage and a tough skin because school leaders are attacked on all sides by people with single-issue views of schooling for not paying adequate attention to *their* issue and too much attention *other* issues. Those attacks are often quite personal, sometimes vicious, and sometimes bitingly sarcastic. Certainly the views proposed in this book about the substance of educational leadership will strike many as hopelessly unrealistic. Nevertheless, if we are to educate for a hopeful future, we have to think beyond the failed and failing systems of education that serve a minority of students at the expense of the majority of students. Even those who succeed in this system, moreover, are served poorly because their *achievements* in school are so narrowly bounded, superficial, and one dimensional.

I want to return at this point to the theme of internal accountability again, but this time to a different sense of *internal*. Here I refer not to the sense of accountability internal to the school community, but to accountability to oneself as an individual educator and an individual human being—to that interior self that Palmer (1998) spoke of in his book, *The Courage to Teach*. I suggest that the only way one can begin the challenging work of educational leadership is to take account of oneself. Furthermore, to continue in the work, one must continuously take account of oneself throughout the years of service in that role. That taking account—being accountable on the inside to oneself—is something that, although needing to be shared with significant companions, ultimately is done alone. It involves asking oneself questions such as the following: Is this what I want to do with my life? Am I being true to my deepest convictions, truest values, and ideals? Is this work the best way I can contribute something worthwhile to my community? Am I getting anywhere in sharing and advancing my dreams of what learning can become even within the limitations we face at present? Am I helping others in my work to find some reasonable human fulfillment in their work? Am I continuing to learn in this work—learning how to do things better and how to work with people better; learning how to be more patient, understanding, and encouraging; learning how and when to let go, as well as how and when to take a stand?

## CHARTING OUR LIVES

That taking stock of what is happening to our insides is a necessary way to acknowledge the unfolding of our biography—our charting, so to speak, of our bios, our life. For better or worse, our work is a way of writing our autobiography, our way of making history. That making of history is, to be sure, a social activity. It is also deeply personal. Writing one's autobiography in one's work can be relatively mindless or it can (and should) be quite intentional. The ongoing reflection on how we "compose our life" (Bateson, 1990) enables us to be morally responsible for the choices we make, engendering a greater autonomy and ownership of the selves we are creating. Given the pressures of the job, however, reflection often seems a luxury. These pressures often lead us into pathological behavior patterns. As we consider how we are composing our lives as educators, we might pause to review some of the pathologies of administration to clarify whether we occasionally engage in them.

It is not surprising that educational administrators get a little crazy from time to time. The daily pressures of the job can drive anyone to distraction. The routine of many school administrators involves reacting to one crisis after another—now a drug bust outside the school, announced by three squad cars with flashing lights and wailing sirens; next an angry teacher complaining that someone parked in her parking space; then a parent on the phone complaining about racial prejudice toward her child; and, of course, the superintendent on the phone wanting test results that have not arrived as scheduled. Administrators career through the day, responding to demands, complaints, injuries, deadlines, and meetings that somehow never resolve the problems they were called to address. It is the stuff of a Charlie Chaplin movie.

The daily cascade of crises distracts everyone from the larger questions of purpose and accountability. Schools are supposed to serve multiple purposes, from teaching the basics of language, science, and math to bringing about racial harmony, controlling childish impulses, solving the drug crisis, teaching good manners, preparing workers to keep America competitive in world markets, responding to the multicultural needs of their constituents, preventing violence within the school, keeping youngsters in school, communicating care and respect for children while giving failing marks and forcing them to repeat a grade, and, most of all, ensuring that all the children can get into the top colleges. When one of these purposes is seen as not being achieved, it is the principal's fault.

Although there may be 20, 40, and even 80 professional staff members in the school, with an additional 6 to 12 support staff—any of whom can make a mess of things at any given moment of the day—the expectation is that if the principal were really doing his or her job, messes would not happen. Despite that perhaps half the student body does not particularly want to be in school on any given day, the principal is held to blame for student truancy and misbehavior: "If the principal were in charge, these things wouldn't happen here." When anything goes wrong at the school, the public, teachers, and superintendent all assume that the principal is to blame. Rather early on in their career, principals start to believe all this.

Moreover, the principal is blamed no matter which set of purposes he or she supports. If there is a high academic press in the school, the principal is criticized for overemphasizing academics to the detriment of other developmental social goals of the school. If the principal pursues greater involvement of the school in the socialization of youngsters (and a winning football or soccer program), the principal is faulted for neglecting academic achievement. If the principal strictly enforces the rules, he is a dictator; if he allows mitigating circumstances to soften the punishment for breaking a rule, he is a lax disciplinarian. The same principal is criticized by some for efforts to be sensitive to various ethnic and racial communities and by others for not being sensitive enough. Principals simultaneously receive praise and condemnation for encouraging a whole-language approach to reading and writing. Maintaining ability grouping and tracking is interpreted as serving the goals of equal educational opportunity or opposing the very same goal.

Principals are always subjected to criticisms, many of them contradictory. It is the nature of the job. When principals attempt to respond to every criticism they receive, they end up being caught in a frenzy of reactionary activity: The principal's job is steeped in ambiguity and unrealistic expectations. Many principals feel uncertain and defensive in the face of this ambiguity and pressure. No one wants to be seen as a bungler, incompetent, stupid either by superiors or subordinates. We all try to create, as the Italians would say, a *bella figura*—to exude a sense of confidence in our physical carriage and offer a vague response with the appropriate furrowing of the eyebrows and confident touch on the shoulder. We put on a performance for those around us—a performance whose underlying message is: "I know what I'm doing; things are really under control; this is no big problem; not to worry, help is on the way." Even when we can focus on the essentials of the job, we are often faced with a small but messy problem that has no immediate solution. So we fudge our response and hope it disappears by tomorrow; we carry on with what we think is the important work in front of us. Most conscientious principals admit at the end of a busy day that there are still a dozen or more problems needing immediate attention, but that there simply is not enough time right now to deal with them. These problems are added to the next day's list, although the principal knows he or she will be lucky to deal with two of them by the end of the next day.

## ADMINISTRATIVE PATHOLOGIES

What happens to some administrators, unfortunately, is that they develop unhealthy ways to cope with the pressure and ambiguity. I exaggerate somewhat by labeling these unhealthy ways a *syndrome.* Thus, one can point to a power-wielding syndrome in some administrators. These persons, unsure of themselves and afraid to let others see their weaknesses, try to dominate and control others by asserting power over them. They use the authority of their position, subtly or explicitly, to threaten sanctions and public criticism of those who work with them to get them to do what they want. In an effort to cover up their own feelings of inferiority, they adopt an attitude of superiority, giving the impression that others are inferior in intelligence, judgment, or drive. Having people do their bidding feeds their need for power, makes them feel in control, and validates their sense of superiority.

Such power-wielding administrators are sick. They sometimes appeal to the sickness in their subordinates—a sickness that prefers an authority figure to make decisions for them. In contrast, healthy, adult professionals want to have the discretion to make decisions on the job. That is what being a professional means: You possess the expertise to respond to the client in this particular circumstance in ways that are helpful. The professional's response is based on some diagnosis of need as contextualized by the present circumstances. Administrators removed from the immediacy of the circumstances cannot decide for the professional on the line what should be done. The power-wielding principal creates alienation and frustration among healthy, professional teachers on the staff. If they accept his demands, they may end up doing the wrong thing for the students. Students will resist and thus frustrate the compulsion to control that drives the power wielder. If teachers do not accede to his demands, but pretend that they do (which is often the case), then again the need to dominate and control is frustrated.

Other principals exude what I call the *superfather* or *supermother* syndrome. This is a controlling compulsion covered over with smiles and warm fuzzies. These principals act like loving parents toward their children, making sure that the children are given clear instructions about what they are to do, making sure that they stay out of harm's way, stepping in to fix something when a child makes a mistake, and protecting the child from outside criticism. These principals need to be needed. They do not know what to do when teachers go about their business with efficiency and dispatch without first checking with the principal to see if they are doing it right. Such principals try to keep teachers dependent on them for their feelings of self-worth. They often arrange parties where they hand out awards to good teachers, especially to those who have listened to their advice, who check out their ideas with the principal first. Such *parenting* may be helpful to a first-year teacher, but the longer it keeps the teacher dependent, the longer it takes the teacher to grow into a mature professional.

Some principals exhibit a hyperrational complex. These principals have constructed the school in their own minds as a perfectly rational system. The goals of the school are clearly spelled out. Student outcomes are defined in measurable terms. Appropriate teacher interventions, described in the research literature as effecting these outcomes, are mandated. Teacher evaluation schemes are tied to evidence of the use of these teacher protocols. Staff development programs are designed around these protocols. Thus, the school is a rational system of ends and means tied to rational ways of evaluating how well the means produce the ends, and to schemes for increasing the production of the desired ends. Such a system is supposed to guarantee maximum predictability and control. It is tidy, neat, and efficient. Memos from the principal carry the logic of this rational system. The expectation is that teachers and students cooperate by functioning rationally within the system.

The problem is that teachers, students, and parents have other goals besides the achievement of the preordained learning outcomes the system establishes. They have affiliative needs, recreational needs, economic needs, and personal interests different from the prescribed focus of the school. Furthermore, the prescribed teacher protocols are too limited to apply to every child's learning style and interests in each classroom. Not every child is ready to learn the prescribed curriculum on every day or in every week.

Teachers may need to attend to the emotional upset of a child who is experiencing difficulty at home. The hyperrational principal has no sympathy for these deviations from the preordained schedule. These variations do not fit into the teacher evaluation criteria. Students whose interests do not coincide with the curriculum must be judged as failures.

Granted that the previous descriptions are exaggerated, the stereotypes help us realize that various forms of psychopathology may be present in the behavior of school administrators. As a professor in a graduate school of education, I never cease to be amazed by the stories my students tell me about administrators in their school systems. I find it hard to believe that school boards and superintendents tolerate such behavior, but often the pathology has been there for many years. Most veteran teachers can point to more than one administrator in their experience whose actions were immature, childish, or even pathological.

The moral is that administrators should know themselves well. With even a little candid self-reflection, most of us can recognize how we engage in small subterfuges, rationalizations, denials, and distortions to make ourselves appear in the right and other people in the wrong. One part of us is always at the back of our heads editing the tape of our present experience as it unfolds, offering a self-congratulatory and self-serving commentary on what is happening. We cover over a careless comment, a stupid mistake, perhaps even a really mean wisecrack with rationalizations such as, "He provoked me," "She had it coming," or "Had I known that, I never would have done it." We protect ourselves from seeing our faults by these defenses; we make excuses for ourselves; we do not want to admit that there are times when we are not nice, when we are stupid, when we are boring or unlovely, or unconcerned for the feelings of others. We would be ashamed if people really saw us that way. We are afraid, in short, of not measuring up to our own and other people's expectations. We all need to feel good about ourselves; to feel good about ourselves, we distort our experience to make ourselves look good. It is important to realize that everyone does this. This is healthy behavior, although of course the definition of health may be quite elastic in this context (Becker, 1971). More mature persons come to admit their shortcomings more freely, especially if they have experienced unconditional love from someone else—someone who knows their faults and loves them nevertheless. The problem is not that we have these faults or that we cover them up. The problem arises with the intensity and absoluteness of the cover-up. In other words, as long as self-deception is relatively mild, it does not prevent us from experiencing reality in any major way. It is still perceivable by us, especially when we see ourselves as a character in a comedy.

I used to love Jackie Gleason's portrayal of the character Ralph Kramden because I could see myself and others I knew doing the same foolish things Ralph did. The television show *All in the Family* also helped us to appreciate the outrageous ways we treat one another. A relative of mine whom I knew to be a racist told me that his friends at work had started calling him "Archie Bunker." This led him to start watching *All in the Family*, where he recognized himself in the words and actions of Archie Bunker. He confided, however, that, "Hey, I'm bad, but not *that* bad."

The problem with the power wielder or hyperrationalist is that his or her distortion of reality is so absolute that it causes real harm to others. Such people cause others to adopt defensive strategies to protect themselves. Often these protective strategies detract severely from the work at hand. Sometimes a sick administrator can force both teachers and students to leave the school.

## MAINTAINING PERSPECTIVE/MAINTAINING HEALTH

Every school administrator needs to adopt measures for maintaining perspective, which is necessary for maintaining mental and emotional health. Space and time are key resources for maintaining perspective. Simply getting away for a few days provides the spatial distance to disentangle the small annoyances from the major issues. Taking time to reflect on our behavior and people's reactions to us may enable clarity about motives to surface. Feedback from others is also helpful. A trusted confidant can help us evaluate our behavior on the job. Another way is to ask for an outside evaluation of our performance by a neutral party. Some principals ask their teachers to fill out anonymous evaluation surveys every year to get a reading on the teachers' perceptions of the principal's performance.

Spending some time every month or two in self-reflection enables us to get in touch with what we are afraid of, what drives us, and what fulfills us. We need to be able to read ourselves especially in situations of crisis or stress. We need to take soundings of our feelings and uncover what is making us feel stressed, uneasy, or afraid. Often an unattended intuition is lying right below the surface of our awareness and is causing some feeling of discomfort; sometimes a pause, a 1-minute break from the matter before us, allows the intuition to surface.

## THE SELF AS TOOL

Blumberg (1989) suggested that we are our primary tool in our craft of administration. Our sensitivity to issues, our ability to carry around the whole school in our head, our ability to remember events from last week and see their connection to present events, our ability to be patient with the shortcomings of others, our ability to read the unspoken messages of parents and teachers, and our ability to see the connection of the present decision to the long-range plan all enable us to become this primary tool of our craft. If we keep that tool fine tuned, we can serve the school well. If we know that tool well—its blind spots, sore points, biases, and dreams—we can deal with the matter in front of us with a minimum of unintended distortion.

## THE SELF AS FILTER

Administrators need to understand that in every person's apprehension of reality there is always distortion. The self is inescapably involved in interpretation. Our experiences are always being interpreted through language, custom, worldview, personal beliefs, pressures of present circumstances, and so on. We are historical persons. How we perceive the world, the categories we use to name things, are given to us by our culture and traditions (Shils, 1981). Were we born in Tahiti in the 12th century, we would interpret experience quite differently than we do as contemporary Americans. Terms such as *cold war, planetary village,* and *terrorism* carry different connotations for us now than they did 20 years ago. Our history has changed; hence, our view of the world has changed.

The self is always a filter; we gain a feel for the moment, a hunch about what the problem really is, an intuition about a course of action. We look at a piece of the reality in front of us and see it according to certain categories, metaphors, and perspectives; we see the details or we see the whole *gestalt.* What we apprehend in front of us puts us in touch with that reality, but what we apprehend simultaneously prevents us from apprehending another aspect of that reality at the same time. Every reality is multidimensional, but we usually perceive it only under one dimension. If perception is always and necessarily partial for healthy people, then for those whose distortion of reality is deeper and more intense the apprehension of reality is even more limited. Defensive, fearful, and compulsive people filter and interpret their experience in ever more distorted ways. If we know our fears, biases, and compulsions, we can check the impulse to go with the first interpretation.

School administrators need to practice using both a filter of trust and a filter of suspicion. A filter of trust assumes that we can find out what really happened. We trust that we can find the facts if we keep asking the right questions and following the rules of evidence. For example, a student with a discipline problem may be expressing anger over a poor self-image, parental abuse at home, or simply problems with impulse control. The filter of trust assumes that the principal, student, and parent(s) can come to some meaningful interpretation of the problem, which points in the direction of an appropriate solution or response to the problem.

A filter of suspicion assumes that sometimes the problem is much deeper—that the language we use to frame the problem may be inappropriate or even self-serving. Freud used a filter of suspicion. He believed that people's actions often conceal a much deeper problem with their sexuality. Marx developed an economic filter of suspicion. He believed that all of social life was a reflection of people's relations to the means of production, and that Western politics was a cloak for maintaining the economic status quo. Much of what can be called *postmodern sensibility* is based on a filter of skepticism—namely, that modernity's claims to rational progress through science and history as the charting of the development of the human race have all proved bankrupt (Delanty, 2000).

A more general use of the filter of suspicion or skepticism assumes that every interpretation is probably distorted—that self-interest unwittingly enters into *my own* as well as the other's interpretation of events. By *suspicion* I do not mean that I suspect the other person of malicious intent. Rather, I may have to look more deeply into the cultural assumptions behind my definition of the event because my interpretation may be driven by a distorting ideology, and these assumptions may prevent a genuine interpretation of the event.

Consider the distorted interpretations in the following comments overheard in some schools. "Why do all the African-American kids have to sit together in the cafeteria? Why can't they mix with the other kids?" "Parents aren't as committed to their children's education as they used to be. Just look at how attendance at parent–teacher nights has fallen off!" "Kids from the Projects are the most disadvantaged students in the school. Their home environments clearly place them at risk." Using a filter of suspicion enables us to look behind these biased statements at racial, cultural, and class assumptions that generate these distorted judgments.

These considerations of administrative pathologies and everyday distortions of perceptions pose a critical challenge to administrators—namely, that we seek to probe the values and philosophical assumptions we bring to the job of running a school. We all are victimized by our ideologies, whether they be of the left, right, or middle. We need to know what we stand for and to ask whether we are ready to take responsibility for all the assumptions we make about schooling. This challenge calls us to an intellectual depth and a critical moral stance with ourselves. To avoid this challenge puts us in danger of growing comfortable using the distorted interpretations we bring to events as an excuse for intellectual and moral indifference.

## ADMINISTRATION AS AUTOBIOGRAPHY

Calling attention to the work of administration as autobiography announces both good and bad news. The bad news is that we tend to impose our neuroses on others, either through projecting or acting out our distorted interpretation of events. The good news is that, at our best, we live as authentic human beings in our work. We write our history—although not all of it to be sure—in our work. We take our place on the public stage of history in our work. We make our special contribution to the lives of others through our work. One way or another, we achieve our destiny through our work. Even with all our limitations, we achieve much of our human fulfillment in our work. This fulfillment comes as we give our best selves to the work in service to others.

In the previous chapter, we looked at the deeper dimensions of empowerment as feeding the deeper sense of accountability. That is to say, beyond the bureaucratic accountability of shared decision making, beyond the professional accountability to incorporate best practice into the classroom work with youngsters, we find the moral accountability to the lives of the youngsters we serve being fed by the moral empowerment to own our responsibilities. We likewise find the existential accountability to ourselves being fed by the existential empowerment to be our own best and fullest selves.

Somehow even accepting the vulnerability of admitting that we do not quite know how to do it, our leadership involves us engaging teachers at all of these within-school levels of accountability. In a general sense, understanding the forms of empowerment provides some guidance for approaching teachers about developing this collective sense of accountability for enriched learning for all children. The ideal is to work together to build a genuine learning community—a community that is continually building its capacity to effect learning within the large curriculum of meaning making, community making, and performing responsibility.

When we accept this as a life-long commitment, we recognize that what we are engaged in is a human journey—one with high ideals and aspirations. Working together as a learning community, we strive every year to deepen and enrich the learning of all of us, with particular attention to closing the learning gap between segments of the community that high-stakes tests reveal. We work with parents to help all students meet standards expected of everyone while calling attention to the limited view of knowledge tied to systems of mass administration and mass consumption that those standards tend to reflect. In other words, as a learning community, we accept the challenge of meeting state standards, but we add value to the learning of these standards by situating the knowledge they require in a larger agenda of making meaning, building community, and performing multiple responsibilities.

In their review of the research on school improvement, Louis, Toole, and Hargreaves (1999) suggested that administrators need a long-range view on the agenda of school improvement. They suggested that the term *school development* might suggest a larger perspective on the change process.

Their research on school change shows that strategic, planned efforts to bring about change (as suggested in the literature on school improvement) come up against realities of organizational life cycles that include the aging and replacement of staff, replacement of leadership at both the school and district levels, changes in technology and in the cultural mix of students. Planned efforts at change also encounter major and minor unanticipated events, such as changes in local and regional policies and funding sources; violent events such as bombings, shootings, and gang wars; and environmental disasters such as hurricanes, floods, tornadoes, and earthquakes. "School development is a process that occurs as a result of interacting influences of three sources of change—that which is deliberately planned, that which is naturally occurring in the life cycle of organizations and that which is unforeseen or unknowable in advance" (Louis, Toole, & Hargreaves, 1999, p. 258). Their perspective and other research that documents the slow pace of organizational change suggest that school improvement involves a generation's worth of work. It is a work that can involve the span of a whole career. Leaders with that perspective work more patiently and compassionately with their colleagues.

I suggest that involvement in educating work like this within a learning community committed to a life's work of learning provides a rich script for enacting the drama of human life. It provides the plot for our narrative. It defines the way we make history. Such a vision of our life and work together is capable of elevating our spirits for the detailed, ambiguous, and messy work of our daily lives in a learning community. This view of the profound and sacred work of education centers and ennobles the work of educational administration.

## ACTIVITIES

1. Review your behavior on the job for the past 3 working days. Were there times when you reacted to people angrily or derisively? Were there times when you cut corners on your own standards for quality work? Were there simply some aspects of your workdays of which you are not proud? How did you rationalize your behavior when you did not act up to your own high standards? Is there a pattern of this?

2. Ask a colleague with whom you have a good relationship to point out one area where you could improve. How do you feel about your colleague's response?

3. Identify three examples of administrative pathology in your workplace. How do people in the workplace deal with each of these pathologies? Is there anything that can be done to improve the situation?

4. Identify three examples of healthy administrative behavior. How do people respond to being treated this way? Is there anything that can be done to improve these already healthy practices?

5. Devise a reasonable, simple plan to maintain your perspective as an administrator, including strategies for increasing self-knowledge. Compare notes with your classmates.

6. Do you empower yourself to pour your best self into your work and thereby make a special contribution to the lives around you? Do you ever talk about this within the faculty?

## REFERENCES

Bateson, M. C. (1990). *Composing a life.* New York: Plume.

Beck, L. G. (1994). *Reclaiming educational administration as a caring profession.* New York: Teachers College Press.

Becker, E. (1971). *The birth and death of meaning* (2nd ed.). New York: The Free Press.

Blumberg, A. (1989). *Administration as craft.* New York: Longmans.

Delanty, G. (2000). *Modernity and postmodernity.* London: Sage.

Hargreaves, A., & Fullan, M. (1998). *What's worth fighting for out there?* New York: Teachers College Press.

Louis, K. S., Toole, J., & Hargreaves, A. (1999). Rethinking school improvement. In J. Murphy & K. S. Louis (Eds.), *Handbook of research on educational administration* (2nd ed., pp. 251–276). San Francisco: Jossey-Bass.

Noddings, N. (1992). *The challenge to care in schools.* New York: Teachers College Press.

Palmer, P. (1998). *The courage to teach: Exploring the inner landscape of a teacher's life.* San Francisco: Jossey-Bass.

Shils, E. A. (1981). *Tradition.* Chicago: University of Chicago Press.

# Author Index

# Subject Index

## O–P

Onion Model, 17–19
Power
  to be, 186
  to be oneself, 186–187
  of connected activity, 191–192
  to do, 186
  of ideas, 192
  over, 185–187
  with, 187
Principalship
  new understandings of, xi–xii

## R

Rationality
  substantive, 192–193
  technical, 192–193
Responsibility, 110–114
  and communication, 117–118
  contested interpretations of, 114
  cultivating, 109, 114–115
  curriculum of, 118,148
  for, 111–113
  learning of, 115–118,
  as a pedagogical policy, 110–111
  and reciprocity, 116–118
  responsible community, 146–154
  social, 103–104
  social construction of, 115–118
  to, 111–113, 115
Rights,
  individual, 143, 144

## S

Scaffolding, 166, 172
School improvement, 9–10
  states narrow definition of, 10–11
Schooling
  colonization of, 76
  democratic purposes of, 67
  moral purposes of, 67
  unjust, 101
Self
  as filter, 249–250
    filter of trust, 239
    filter of suspicion, 249–250
  as tool, 248–249
Self-construction, 161–163
Self-governance, 115, 203
  collective, 115, 203
Social contract, 47, 143
Student
  accountability to, 227–228
  personal experience, 160
  as worker, 160
Subsidiarity
  four elements of, 202–208
  principle of, 201

## T

Teaching
  a model of, 171–174
  for understanding, 163, 166–167, 172–174
Teacher Capacity, 207–208
Transcendence, 138–139
Trust, 189–190, 202–204

## V

Vision
  of an educated person, 13–22
  empowering, 193
  institutionalization of, 20
  of leader, 15–19, 21–23
  of schooling, 36–41
  statement, 17
  of teachers, 193
  two senses of, 15